WORKING
WITH
IMMIGRANT
FAMILIES

The Family Therapy and Counseling Series
Series Editor
Jon Carlson, Psy.D., Ed.D.

WORKING WITH IMMIGRANT FAMILIES

A PRACTICAL GUIDE FOR COUNSELORS

EDITED BY
Adam Zagelbaum and Jon Carlson

Routledge
Taylor & Francis Group
New York   London

This book is part of the Family Therapy and Counseling Series, edited by Jon Carlson.

Routledge
Taylor & Francis Group
270 Madison Avenue
New York, NY 10016

Routledge
Taylor & Francis Group
27 Church Road
Hove, East Sussex BN3 2FA

© 2011 by Taylor and Francis Group, LLC
Routledge is an imprint of Taylor & Francis Group, an Informa business

Printed in the United States of America on acid-free paper
10 9 8 7 6 5 4 3 2 1

International Standard Book Number: 978-0-415-80061-7 (Hardback)

Library of Congress Cataloging-in-Publication Data

Working with immigrant families : a practical guide for counselors / edited by
Adam Zagelbaum and Jon Carlson.
        p. cm. -- (The family therapy and counseling series)
    Includes bibliographical references and index.
    ISBN 978-0-415-80061-7 (hardcover : alk. paper)
    1. Cross-cultural counseling--United States. 2. Immigrant
families--Counseling of--United States. I. Zagelbaum, Adam. II. Carlson, Jon.

    BF636.7.C76W67 2011
    158'.3086912--dc22   2010018617

**Visit the Taylor & Francis Web site at
http://www.taylorandfrancis.com**

**and the Routledge Web site at
http://www.routledgementalhealth.com**

Contents

Series Editor's Foreword

> There isn't a country in the world today that doesn't need to ponder how to get different populations, local and immigrant, to live together. Everywhere there are tensions more or less skillfully contained; usually they show signs of getting worse.
>
> **—Amin Maaloaf (2000)**

My paternal grandparents migrated from Sweden, and my maternal great-grandparents migrated from Scotland via Canada. I, however, grew up in a home that was assimilated to American life. I do not remember hearing any ethnic stories or family traditions that were present in my upbringing. Although I had immigrant classmates in the public schools, it never occurred to me that their lives were any different from my own. As an exchange student to Sweden, I developed my first understanding of cultural difference and complexity. However, it was a several-year process that involved living in Detroit, Chicago, south Florida, and Hawaii before I developed any level of meaningful understanding and appreciation. Exchange students, our adopted children from Korea, and extensive world travel have helped to shape my appreciation of the magnitude and challenge of immigrating to a new nation.

All families have migrated somewhere in their history. Each, however, has a different, personal story. Adam (the book's coeditor), for example, had a different immigrant story. He grew up in a second-generation immigrant home and was very connected to his cultural roots. His immigrant Polish grandparents spoke Yiddish and shared many stories of being relocated and having to deal with life-threatening anti-Semitism.

The impact of immigrating takes two or more generations to recover. Language, social status, dress, appearance, diet, hobbies, occupation, and so on are often significantly changed. Having your world turned upside down is an apt description of the immigration process. With these changes come challenges creating mental health issues. How well prepared are clinicians to work with this population? What is the required knowledge needed to understand and help this population? What are the special skills and strategies needed? How we understand and value each unique situation is the challenge for today's culturally sensitive therapist. The contributors to this volume address these and many other issues that provide insight into how to work effectively with this population.

—Jon Carlson, PsyD, EdD
Series Editor

Reference

Maaloaf, A. (2000). *On identity*. London: Harvill.

Preface

The White/Caucasian majority that has traditionally dominated the American landscape has been significantly reduced in size while other demographic groups such as Hispanic/Latino(a) and African American citizens have increased. Many of these individuals are immigrants who have come to America for opportunities to live, work, and contribute to society in ways that are designed to help their families as well as themselves. Being in a new country with new demands creates unique stresses and strains associated with mental health, family problems, and emotional needs that counseling professionals are ill prepared to treat. The need for counseling professionals, therefore, to develop skills and open dialogues that consciously focus their attention on how to serve these immigrant clients and their families is practically a requirement.

Family counseling services and supporting research associated with helping families have focused more on multicultural and cross-cultural data with little emphasis on the needs of immigrant clients. However, there are many theories of acculturation and identity models that have come into prominence within the fields of counseling and psychology. Also, it is clear that many systems-based theories have been rooted in collectivistic perspectives largely associated with many of the countries that some of these immigrants claim as their native lands.

Considering the largely individualistic emphasis of American society, immigrant families face issues when they join the host culture. Therapists trained in America may not necessarily understand the dynamics of immigrant families. For example, a child who acts out within a family system serves as the identified patient under many traditional family systems approaches; however, some immigrant families would not take this position. Some families from a collectivist culture would share the concern and place equal identification of all members as identified clients. A child who acts out is an extension of issues contained within the parental relationship(s) and partner relationship(s) within the family, and all have equal identity as those who are to work within the therapeutic alliance. Other families extend their system to include neighbors and other citizens, such as those who live in a kibbutz or integrated village. Therapists who are largely unfamiliar with these norms and dynamics often struggle with these differences and may actually contribute more to family conflict rather than to family therapy. Some immigrant families can experience significant frustration and resistance when they feel their collectivist values are being challenged or devalued by even the most well-intentioned therapists. This point is made not to oversimplify the dynamics and differences that exist between host and native countries or the cultural variables that impact the counseling and acculturation process but rather to consciously prepare a foundation for mental health practitioners to think about what practical ideas and discussions they need to have about serving immigrant families. The purpose of this book is to create a foundation that respects theory, culture, and the mental health professions and to initiate the practical and needed discussions about how to work with immigrant families.

Our goal was to unite various individuals who have professionally worked with immigrant clients and their families and to share research and theoretical approaches that appear to be effective as seen from the perspectives of both the clients and the therapists. Instead of repeating the message of how more research is needed to effectively address the needs of immigrant populations, the book starts a dialogue that showcases what therapists have done and intend to bear in mind as immigration and societal trends continue. Though certainly there is no universal technique or model that can be applied to all immigrant populations, the presentation of each chapter will provide opportunity for debate and discussion about how to develop more ideas and techniques about how to reach out to immigrant families and how therapists can professionally refine and further develop their skills and interests in working with such clientele.

This book will also provide definitions of mental health services from the native countries of immigrant clients. This integration of material allows for cultural values and customs of immigrant clients to be retained as much as possible and respectfully allows for material to synthesize. Regardless of whether the dialogue created by this book is fully agreed on by its audience, it represents an important first step toward giving a voice to immigrant populations throughout the world who seek professional help while adjusting to new cultures and societies to which they have emigrated.

This book is an important first step for therapists to take when it comes to identifying and practically addressing the needs of immigrant families. Certainly, the journey to be taken when it comes to completely understanding these needs will be a lengthy one filled with many twists and turns that will occur as more immigrant families come to America, and make no mistake, more immigrant families will be coming to America in years and generations to come. This text is designed not only to rely on theoretical concepts presented in literature that may or may not have direct application to working with immigrant families but also to describe and apply specific tools, techniques, and approaches that thera-pists have actually conducted with immigrant families so that concrete points can be established, points that we hope will help professionals actively approach and address immigrant families who seek counseling services. We are happy to present this text for professionals who are set to embark on this journey, and we hope that the lives of people encountered along the way are greatly benefited by this practical guide for working with immigrant families. May it be the first of many steps taken to serve this clientele!

Contributors

Editors

Adam P. Zagelbaum, PhD, NCC, is an assistant professor in the Department of Counseling within the Pupil Personnel Services Program at Sonoma State University in Rohnert Park, California. Adam has written several book chapters and articles regarding the counseling of new citizens, at-risk children and adolescents, school counseling literature and research, and group counseling apporaches. He has produced a training video about his technique for conducting career counseling for middle school students (*The Creative Career Constellation*). He has school counseling certification and worked and
trained within various settings such as child and family centers, community counseling centers, correctional facilities, university counseling centers, and public and private K-12 schools. He has also been the recipient of Faculty Excellence awards for teaching, community, and university service.

Jon Carlson, PsyD, EdD, ABPP, is a distinguished professor, psychology and counseling, at Governors State University and a psychologist at the Wellness Clinic in Lake Geneva, Wisconsin. Jon has served as editor of several periodicals including the *Journal of Individual Psychology* and *The Family Journal*. He has authored 150 journal articles and 50 books, including *Time for a Better Marriage, Adlerian Therapy, Inclusive Cultural Empathy, The Mummy at the Dining Room Table, Bad Therapy, The Client Who Changed Me, Their Finest Hour, Creative Breakthroughs in Therapy*, and *Moved by*
the Spirit. He has created over 250 professional trade video and DVDs with

leading professional therapists and educators. In 2004, the American Counseling Association named him a "Living Legend." Jon and Laura have been married for 43 years and are the parents of five children.

Contributors

Naji Abi-Hashem, PhD, is a Lebanese American clinical and cultural psychologist who has worked in various therapeutic settings for many years and has published numerous journal articles, encyclopedia entries, and book chapters. He is a regular presenter at national and international conventions on topics related to cross-cultural psychology, religion and spirituality, globalization, counseling, geopolitics, East–West relations, fundamentalism and extremism, grief and trauma, and coping and adaptation. He is currently involved in teaching, writing, training, networking, caregiving, reflecting, and international service. Among his recent projects was a professional DVD produced by the APA Psychotherapy Series on *Working With Arab-Americans.*

Robyn Brammer, PhD, LMHC, is an associate professor, director of the School and Mental Health Counseling Programs, and codirector of the Community Counseling and Psychological Assessment Center at Central Washington University. She graduated from the University of Southern California with a doctorate in counseling psychology. She has published a variety of articles on multiculturalism as well as a textbook.

Ernesto R. Escoto, PhD, is a licensed psychologist in the state of Ohio and currently serves as the Associate Director of Clinical Services at Counseling and Consultation Services at The Ohio State University and as an Advisory Board Member at Encuentro Latino-National Institute on Family Violence. Dr. Escoto is a consultant and presenter in the areas of multicultural counseling competencies and diverse workforce management.

Omar Fattal, MD, MPH, is a staff psychiatrist at Lutheran Hospital (Cleveland Clinic) and is an assistant clinical professor at the Cleveland Clinic Lerner College of Medicine at Case Western Reserve University. He is also the assistant training director for the psychiatry residency program at the Cleveland Clinic. He started an outpatient psychiatry clinic where he sees Spanish-speaking patients in collaboration with local community mental health agencies that specialize in counseling and case management of Spanish-speaking patients.

Joy K. Harden, PhD, is a licensed psychologist at the University of Georgia Counseling and Psychiatric Services (CAPS) and also a private practitioner. In her work at CAPS, she serves as the liaison to the Office of International Student Life and works with many international students on issues including adjustment to life in the United States and familial concerns. She has also given several presentations in the areas of cultural competency and ethical concerns when working with underserved populations to counseling professionals.

Sally Hunter, PhD, senior lecturer at the University of New England (UNE), Australia, is the coordinator of the counseling and mental health program of studies. Dr. Hunter has a research interest in immigration and has extensive clinical experience working with immigrant families in Australia. She is a published author and was recently awarded a commonwealth government grant designed to meet the mental health needs of rural and remote Australians, including immigrants.

Gregg Kuehl, PhD, NCC, currently works in private practice in Muncie, Indiana. He also teaches as a contract faculty member at Ball State University where he has both counseled and educated culturally diverse students.

Garima Lamba, PhD, is a staff psychologist at Johns Hopkins University Counseling Center. She coordinates counseling center services for international students and students from Asian American origin. Formerly an international student, she has experience in working with international students along with other areas of interest such as relationship issues, depression, anxiety, couples counseling, and training/supervision of new psychologists.

Irene Lopez, PhD, Assistant Professor, Kenyon College (Gambier, OH), is a cross-cultural and clinical psychologist with interests in the impact of acculturation on Latino mental health, and cross cross-cultural psychopathology. She has received a number of teaching awards for her work and teaching. Currently, she is a Task Force member of the American Psychological Association Committee on Socioeconomic Status.

Eréndira López-García, PsyD, is the associate director of clinical training at the Office of Disability Services at Wright State University in Dayton, Ohio. She is a bilingual licensed psychologist (Spanish and English) and provides clinical services mostly to Latino immigrants and seasonal migrant workers through the Salud Community Clinic located in Tipp City, Ohio. She has been an active participant in the Latino community and currently serves as vice president of Del Pueblo, Inc., a nonprofit organization that serves the local Latino community.

Mala Madathil, PhD, is an assistant professor in the Department of Counseling at Sonoma State University. She has presented at several national and regional conferences and written several articles on providing mental health services to Asian immigrants. Her research interests are in the areas of multicultural counseling, and she is particularly interested in studying arranged marriages.

Marsha Mitchell-Blanks, MSW, LSW, is President/Owner of Blanks Training and Consulting Service, an adjunct professor at Cleveland State University School of Social Work, and the Multicultural Outreach Coordinator for the National Alliance on Mental Illness—Greater Cleveland chapter. She has spent more than 30 years in community based practice working first as a direct service mental health worker. Marsha has provided services to and worked closely with Eastern European, Latino and African American communities in the Greater Cleveland, Ohio area.

A. Zaidy MohdZain, PhD, LPC, NCC, ACS, is dean and professor in the College of Education at Southern Arkansas University, Magnolia, Arkansas. An immigrant himself, he was born and raised in Malaysia and earned his degrees and has all clinical counseling experiences in the United States. He has presented at many international, national, regional, and state conferences; written several articles; and serves on the editorial board of *The Family Journal: Counseling and Therapy for Couples and Families.*

Tyffani Monford-Dent, PsyD, is the clinical coordinator of residential services at the Cleveland Christian Home. Dr. Dent also works in private practice completing psychological evaluations on children and adolescents. She serves on local and state committees addressing the mental health needs of children, adolescents, and their families.

Marina Prado-Steiman is an English and Psychology double major at Kenyon College (Gambier, OH). Her interests lie in cross-cultural and abnormal psychology, as well as the interplay of reality and magical realism in Latino literature.

Evelyn Rivera-Mosquera, PhD, is a clinical psychologist who serves as the Latino(a) coordinator at the National Alliance for the Mentally Ill Greater Cleveland (NAMI GC) Chapter. Her expertise is in developing and implementing culturally and linguistically competent mental health prevention education programs for Latino families. She has developed community- and church-based interventions targeting immigrant Latino youth such as Latinos on the Path to Higher Education and Proyecto RAICES (Recognizing and Integrating Culture, Education, and Service).

Julie Shulman, PhD, is an assistant professor in the Counseling Department at Sonoma State University and a licensed psychologist in the state of California. She has focused much of her clinical work, teaching, and research on the provision of culturally competent, feminist-informed therapy to diverse clients. In addition, she has conducted cross-disciplinary research on the ordinary conception of race in the United States.

Dolores D. Tarver, PhD, licensed psychologist, Counseling and Psychiatric Services, University of Georgia, had an emphasis in graduate school of multicultural counseling with diverse racial/ethnic adolescents and young adults. She has provided therapy to voluntary and involuntary immigrants including persons of African descent, as well as Asian, Hispanic/Latino, and Middle Eastern populations. She has presented research at conferences on multicultural counseling competency.

Chapter 1

Orientation to Working With Immigrant Families

Adam Zagelbaum and Jon Carlson

Contents

Mr. A, a 45-year-old businessman from Africa, immigrated to the United States with his wife, Ms. A, and their three children, X (16), Y (14), and Z (13), four years ago. Mr. A wanted to establish himself in America, in the hopes that he could achieve the "wealth of the American dream." There were severe gaps between rich and poor, as well as great tensions, within his native country's caste system. He viewed America as an opportunity to "escape" the slow growth and progress made within his community and to provide his children with "greater opportunities to learn and achieve success." Visitors from church groups and universities had shown him how the American dream could be possible for him and his family. Ms. A stood by her husband's decision to move, even though the children were less than enthusiastic about leaving close friends behind. Mr. A believed that the church and university he was admitted to would help everyone with this transitioning process.

When he began his initial work at the university's accounting program, Mr. A found himself putting significant amounts of time and energy into his studies, which kept him away from his family during many hours of the day. He remained at the university from what appeared to be sunrise to "pitch black" for nearly every weekday. Though he was respected for his knowledge and determination back home, Mr. A found some of the people within the university to be somewhat "controlling" and "demanding," whereas he had been accustomed to making most of his decisions without questions. His children had not adjusted well to the move, as his eldest son, X, was placed into a juvenile detention center for participation in a theft from a neighbor's home. His youngest son, Z, was also getting into trouble at the local middle school for not listening to the teachers and not following the orders of administrators. The daughter, Y, was close to her mother and seemed to be diligently following the wishes of both parents to behave properly and do well in school. Mr. A believed that it was the community's responsibility to work with him and his family, especially because the communal approach was commonplace for everyone in his home country. Many of the interactions that he would have with schoolteachers, administrators, and university staff would be perceived as confrontational because of the fact that Mr. A was identified as "unwilling to take responsibility" for his children's actions. Some of his younger university classmates would also perceive Mr. A as "bossy" and "condescending" because he would often speak in class from what they perceived to be an "expert" view. The communal viewpoint and collectivistic worldview became a problem for the individualistic people Mr. A would encounter in America. Though members of the local church and some neighborhood friends would assist Ms. A with matters from time to time, the boys were largely unsupervised on a consistent daily basis. Frustrated and stressed from the pressures of his academic responsibilities, Mr. A would have a difficult time during parent–teacher conferences where negative behaviors of his youngest son would be discussed. He believed his intelligence and abilities as a father and student were constantly being doubted, and he saw the school staff as "insulting" people who were calling his child "mean and delinquent." It seemed that they were viewing Z as someone likely to follow the path of his oldest brother, and Mr. A was angered and hurt that he appeared to be viewed as the main cause.

Ms. A appeared to be in a difficult position herself, often becoming teary during these school encounters and upset that her husband would be upset. She appeared hurt that she could not "keep order" among her sons like her husband could but also knew that her husband had to do his best to succeed in school. She was often too upset to speak.

Mr. A would continue to call Z's school counselor as a way of trying to monitor the situation brewing with his son at school. He also agreed to have his eldest son placed into an alternative school, in hopes that this would remedy the situation. Mr. and Ms. A believed that these actions would be able to "get them through" these situations, so that Mr. A could complete his schooling and be able to work at a "regular job" that would allow for more time to be spent with his family. Ms. A was eventually able to find some temporary work as well, to become more active in the community and befriend more people.

Unique Influences on the Client. Mr. A, though clearly a talented and gifted individual, had both significantly high academic expectations within the university to perform well and high interpersonal expectations among staff and faculty of his sons' public schools to properly "adjust" his children's behaviors. These were pressures not placed on Mr. A in his country of origin. Mr. A became highly defensive and agitated when most school officials would strongly recommend that his children be placed in alternative settings, because it indicated a lack of concern or interest in aiding Mr. A with his personal and family issues. He believed people were not able to see his strengths and abilities and were looking for faults within his children to corroborate these negative beliefs.

I (Adam) first encountered Mr. A while I was an intern, and his son, Z, was referred to me for his school-based disciplinary issues. Up until this point in my professional life, I mostly gathered information from teen clients to assess interpersonal issues, as well as ways in which their academic goals could be better reached in accordance with school guidance concerns. I worked with Z for about eight sessions. Of which, about four included interactions with Mr. A and another two included Mr. and Mrs. A.

Working with Mr. A demonstrated to me the fact that certain aspects of the American educational system, as well as acculturating to American communities, were difficult for immigrants to work with. Though Mr. A and his family were capable of learning English as a second language and were respected for their hard work in terms of individual successes such as gaining admittance into graduate school, and being able to find individual work, they were not viewed by their children's schools as a well-functioning family unit. This individualistic way of thinking leads highly educated and experienced immigrants like Mr. A to believe that people are looking for faults within the family. Many of the issues regarding his sons that Mr. A was being challenged on appeared to be beyond his sole responsibility. Immigrants like Mr. A are not always informed of how deep the individualistic mode extends when dealing with assessment and treatment of behavioral and psychological concerns.

Working in the school counseling intern and school counselor roles, I encountered other immigrant clients like Mr. A even when I was working in different regions of the United States. There were many people who achieved well educationally and socially within their countries of origin but were not viewed as talented and capable individuals when their children were having difficulty following directions or maintaining on-task behaviors in classrooms.

The experience underscored the frustrations that communalistic clients often experience with individualistic values, which create a circle of finger-pointing and defensiveness when disciplinary issues arise. One important lesson I learned from working with Mr. A and his family was that men can experience extreme disadvantages within their family and social interactions when faced with this clash of individualistic and communalistic values. Being targeted as an ineffective parent, along with the stresses and strains of needing to perform well in graduate school, creates a sense of global failure for the individual who was previously viewed as an effective contributor to the village. The A family found financial assistance for family therapy, which they were able to receive at a nominal fee as a result of Mr. A's status as a graduate student. It would later uncover some key issues for Mr. A and his family. Mr. A had reduced contact with his family because of his academic pursuits in the first place. When he was spending time with his family, he was focused on how to deal with the failures of his sons, which further reinforced how Mr. A had been struggling within his roles as a worker and a father. His wife was also challenged to become more involved with the issues of X and Z, suggesting that she was not working hard as well to make things more manageable. The loss of communal perspective and spotlighting of individual shortcomings that Mr. A had been experiencing forced him to reach out to others, which was a different circumstance of obtaining community resources than he would normally have done in his native country. Nevertheless, it did allow him and his family to better cope with his son's issues that arose during the resettlement process.

Issues That May Be of Common Consideration for Working With This Population

The importance of recognizing the "person as community" as well as the communal worldview cannot be understated in this case. Cohen (2009) implored psychologists to consider many forms of culture that include variables such as religion, socioeconomic status, and region within a country to better address how similarities and differences can allow for clients and mental health professionals to most effectively work together. The American mind-set of individualism does not allow for many to understand that sometimes it actually does "take a village to raise a child." Although many have heard this saying, just hearing the saying does not always translate into fundamental action and/or understanding of what it means to have a shared responsibility for the development and adjustment of a child. Many theoretical assertions have often placed primary responsibility on the parents when a child misbehaves and can devalue the strengths of the family system when doing so.

Ogbonnaya's (1994) concept of the person as community takes into account that individuals are the product of past relationships with family, groups, and institutions. When this concept is coupled with Amir's (1992) notion of the contact hypothesis, counselors are encouraged to start their work with positive expectations of a group or family to recognize the strengths and effective aspects they possess. In doing so, resistance among participating clients is likely to be minimized, and a better working alliance can be formed.

For example, another family that I encountered was the B family, which was from Asia. The family was composed of a husband, wife, eldest son in high school, and younger daughter in middle school, almost identical to the A family. The family members also followed a collectivistic norm in that they focused on each other's needs more than any one of their own. If the mother was sick, it was the son's and daughter's duty to care for her while the father would be at work. It is not an uncommon practice for children to miss school for such a reason. Many Americans do not understand this concept and often view this as a poor practice that hinders the educational rights of the children. This is yet another issue that immigrant families encounter when they demonstrate values that go against the lifestyle norms of the United States. Fortunately, as a result of learning this concept and seeing the collectivistic strengths of this family system, many teachers and administrators at the B children's schools were able to make alternative arrangements for homework assignments and missed days of academic work, which would eventually allow for the children to catch up on assignments and lessons, which allowed them to remain on pace with their peers. The social stressors of fitting in at school and within the community were also that much more easy for the B family members to process during the course of family therapy because of the positive contact that they had with the therapist, who understood their system in a way that was not "weak" or "anti-American."

The members of the C family, who were devout to their Islamic heritage, would have a more difficult time while adjusting to the United States. This husband, wife, and teenage son followed specific practices that many of their American neighbors and peers did not fully understand. The wife kept herself covered when out in public and would not make eye contact with other men. Though the son was a good academic student, following the requests of some of his female teachers was often difficult because of the gender roles and customs he was familiar with in his native county. They also faced some tension from Americans who reacted to the way they physically looked. Though no direct threats or acts of violence were ever reported, they could sense some feelings of tension within their neighborhood by the way that people would often not include them in conversations or community functions. Fortunately, an Islamic center was located within their county, and some opportunity existed for them to be with others who worshipped Islam. However, bridging the gap between the Islamic community and the C family's neighborhood remained a difficult pursuit. Cases like these show that it is essential to consider what therapists need to know and what they need to do when working with immigrant families. It was because of these various cases, coupled with a paucity of literature regarding the practices of how to therapeutically work with immigrant families, that the authors composed this text.

Immigrants come to America for numerous reasons, which will be explored later and throughout this text, but as psychotherapists, we must be available and prepared to assist these individuals and their families with a variety of services. Several of these people endure language barriers, financial concerns, emotional strains associated with being away from their community of origin, and social stigmas that can often take a toll on the ways in which immigrants and their families adjust to a host culture. Although not all immigrants fit this description, therapists should be aware of the fact that there appears to be an increasing number of immigrants who do. From a social justice perspective, it is not only a justifiable act but also one that is imperative to the nature and duties of the profession. What is also apparent is that there are many places in America where immigrants and immigrant families come to live. The notion that such individuals are more apt to settle in major metropolitan areas because of the sheer size of the area and diverse composition of people does not always hold true. There are immigrant and immigrant family populations within rural, urban, suburban, coastal, and noncoastal areas that showcase the fact that such a notion is not well founded. In other words, it appears to be a fair statement that all therapists throughout America would be wise to become familiar with information and theoretical knowledge of how to work with immigrants and immigrant families because there is always a possibility of encountering such clientele.

Immigration Defined

The definition of *immigration* simply refers to the fact that one has entered into a new environment that is different from that of the one from which he or she originated. The complex issues associated with immigration, however, are vast and plentiful. From war-torn refugees who are physically unable to remain in their country of origin to those people who value socioeconomic opportunities that may not readily exist within their birthplace, there are varied and diverse reasons why people immigrate that are as varied and diverse as the people themselves. There are also immigrants who relocate as families, and it is for this reason that this textbook exists.

In the United States, a person who has gained lawful permanent residence through the process of immigration and has the right to own property; attend public schools, colleges, and universities; join certain branches of the armed forces; and apply for citizenship is termed a *legal permanent resident* (LPR). The more common term used among laypeople for these individuals is *green card recipient*. When compiling data on the immigrant population defined as legal residents of the United States, the Department of Homeland Security and Office of Immigration Statistics included all persons who were granted lawful permanent residence, granted asylee status, admitted as refugees, or admitted as nonimmigrants for a temporary stay in the United States and not required to leave by the first of January (Jeffreys & Monger, 2007). In 2007, the Office of Immigration Statistics reported a total of 1,052,415 people who became LPRs. The leading regions of birth of people who became LPRs in 2007 were Asia (36%) and North America (32%). The leading countries of birth of new LPRs were, in order from greater to lesser, Mexico (14%), China (7.3%), the Philippines (6.9%), India (6.2%), Colombia (3.2%), Haiti (2.9%), Cuba (2.8%), Vietnam (2.7%), and Korea (2.1%). These countries accounted for more than 50% of new LPRs. Females often compose the larger portion of new LPRs, and in 2007, they accounted for 55% of this group. The majority of LPRs fell in the age range of 25 to 44 years. Fifty-eight percent of the LPRs in 2007 were classified as married, and 37% were classified as single (Jeffreys & Monger, 2007).

The Office of Immigration Statistics also estimated 11.8 million unauthorized immigrants were living in the United States in January 2007. The majority of these individuals were reported as males (57%), and the median age for these unauthorized residents is identified as 30 years (Hoefer, Rytina, & Baker, 2007). Unauthorized immigrants are defined as foreign-born persons who entered the United States without inspection or were admitted temporarily and stayed past the date they were required to leave. Although this status can change once they have been granted LPR status, the condition does not change if unauthorized immigrants apply for asylum or temporary protected status (TPS). This is also why the statistics reflecting unauthorized immigrants within the United States may be at a higher level than what is currently reported (Hoefer et al., 2007).

Refugees and Asylees

Refugees and asylees also compose a large portion of the immigrant population of the United States. The main distinction between these two categories is that a refugee is a person who is unable or unwilling to return to his or her country of origin and/or country of nationality because of persecution and is located out-side of the United States at the time of application; an asylum seeker is typically a person who is located in the United States or at a port of entry but tends to seek immigration for similar reasons as that of a refugee (Jeffreys & Martin, 2007). Numerous laws and acts have been created and instated within the United States and through the work of the United Nations to protect refugees and those seek-ing asylum from having to return to countries and nations whereby their lives would be threatened upon their return. Under current laws and restrictions, case-by-case decisions are typically made to determine in what cases an indi-vidual and his or her family may attain refugee status (Jeffreys & Martin, 2007). Currently, spouses and unmarried children under the age of 21 can obtain deriv-ative refugee status from a family member who is a principal refugee applicant. Should the spouse or child enter the United States with the applicant or within four months after the principal applicant's admission, he or she is referred to as an *accompanying derivative*. A spouse or child who enters after this four-month period of time is referred to as a *following-to-join derivative*.

The Office of Immigration Statistics reported that in 2007, there were 48,217 refugees admitted to the United States. Of these refugees, 19,911 were principal applicants whereas their children composed 15% and their spouses composed 43% of this total count. The leading countries of nationality for refugee admis-sions were Burma (29%), Somalia (14%), Iran (11%), Burundi (9%), Cuba (6%), Russia (4%), Iraq (3%), Liberia (3%), Ukraine (3%), and Vietnam (3%). The majority of refugees admitted to the United States in 2007 were under 25 years of age (57%), and 38% were under the age of 18. Fifty-two percent of these individuals were males, 60% were reported as single, and 36% were reported as married (Jeffreys & Martin, 2007).

Naturalization

Another important category for classifying immigrant populations within the United States comprises those individuals who become naturalized citizens (Rytina & Caldera, 2007). These are individuals who receive U.S. citizenship by fulfilling criteria established by Congress according to the Immigration and Nationality Act. With this status, individuals are afforded the same benefits, rights, and responsibilities as natural-born U.S. citizens, which includes the right to vote and travel oversees with governmental protection once abroad. In 2007, 660,477 immigrant individuals became naturalized U.S. citizens. The leading countries of birth and origin for these individuals were Mexico (19%), India (7%), the Philippines (6%), China (5%), and Vietnam (4%). Females com-posed the majority of this group (55%) in terms of gender, and the majority age range was between 25 and 44 years. Sixty-six percent of this group was identified as married, and 21% of this group was identified as single (Rytina & Caldera, 2007).

As we hope can be discerned from the aforementioned statistics, immigrant families have long been a part of the American tapestry. Though there are fluctuations in terms of the data, the fact remains that immigrants are a constant part of American society. Immigrant families may not necessarily arrive in the United States in one fell swoop, though there are many that do. There are numerous family members who come to the United States after the primary applicant has established some stability, relatively speaking, and this process of transitioning and acculturation takes on a different meaning than for families that simply relocate from one American state to another.

Immigrant Family Needs

Immigrant families have unique and important needs that psychotherapists must not only be cognizant of but also be able to put into their practices when working with these clients. To say that working with immigrant families is no different from working with nonimmigrant families is an understatement that denies many psychological processes and issues that these groups experience as a result of acculturation, acclamation, and communication. *Acculturation*, which is more specifically discussed in subsequent chapters, refers to how individuals or groups that have different cultural backgrounds act, react, adapt, do not adapt, adjust, and readjust to one another and the environment in which this contact occurs (Berry, 1997). Though this process also refers to how society changes as a result of making contact with immigrants, it has largely been studied as a process under which immigrants adapt to society (Schwartz & Zamboanga, 2008). It is currently being argued that all individuals are multicultural because all individuals each have a national origin, ethnic origin, regional origin, religious value (which includes a lack of religious value), and level of socioeconomic status and/or social class (Cohen, 2009). The question, therefore, is not "What information do I lack about immigrant families?" but rather "What needs do these families have?"; the latter appears to be the more appropriate one to ask to help these families adjust to the society to which they immigrate. *Acclamation*, which can also be referred to as *adjustment*, is a term that is used to reflect the process by which immigrants deal with the shock of living in a society composed of a culture different from that of their homeland (Milstein, 2005). The need for belongingness and acceptance while remaining true to one's cultural roots creates a dynamic that affects individuals and families in such a way that therapeutic intervention is often necessary and can aid immigrants with their acclamation. *Communication* is the process by which language and expression is conveyed and, within this text, will refer to both verbal and nonverbal methods. Language barriers often exist when immigrants first settle in their new surroundings, and certain features of personal space and nonverbal cues that exist within their countries of origin may not effectively match with the customs and practices of their new surroundings. Therapists must be aware of how to effectively approach immigrant clients and families in a way that allows for effective communication to be both heard and understood. Establishing a good rapport means not only choosing the best words to establish effective communication but also reading the cues and signals that clients present. It is through these proper readings that therapeutic alliances form and common ground can be provided as a foundation on which further intervention can occur. Certainly, the family system is a unit that has many parallel processes that showcase many commonalities between and among clients throughout the world. However, when one considers the way in which some cultures value individualism over collectivism, matriarchal systems over patriarchal systems, and independence over communalism, as well as a host of other values that can impact the presence or absence of certain family dynamics, the common ground becomes harder to find.

It is our hope that this text provides psychotherapists a way of landscaping this common ground. Before we present the chapter overviews, readers should bear in mind that this text is not meant to serve as a one-size-fits-all approach to defining immigrants, countries, regions, cultures, ethnicities, or psychotherapeutic approaches. Common threads determined by research, literature, experience, theory, and practice of psychotherapy are delineated throughout each chapter as a way of informing readers about what practical pieces of information are deemed to be most critical when working with immigrant families. Ultimately, people are reminded of the fact that between and within group differences will always exist, and such differences are what make the field of psychotherapy, along with its clientele, necessarily complex and valuable. To construct a text that comprehensively addresses every possible immigrant family, every context within which immigration occurs, and all processes that unfold as therapy and interventions are provided to these families is nearly impossible. It is for this reason that therapists use this practical guide as a way of becoming more aware of immigrant families and using this information not only to better inform their practices but also to stimulate discussion and seek consultation whenever possible about how to better serve these clients.

Roles of the Therapist

Because awareness, knowledge, and skills are deemed by the American Counseling Association's *Code of Ethics* (ACA, 2005) to be the cornerstones on which competent professionals are to serve diverse clients and client needs, this text is designed to whet the reader's appetite regarding how to approach immigrant families and develop a hunger to do more work to serve this clientele. More specifically stated,

> Counselor educators actively infuse multicultural/diversity competency in their training and supervision practices. They actively train students to gain awareness, knowledge, and skills in the competencies of multicultural practice. (ACA, 2005, p. 17)

The American Association for Marriage and Family Therapy (AAMFT, 2001) has a *Code of Ethics* that, although it does not specifically address diversity and culture in an explicit section of the document, contains several principles that articulate the therapist's duty to serve culturally diverse populations. Such principles include the following:

1.1 Marriage and family therapists provide professional assistance to persons without discrimination on the basis of race, age, ethnicity, socioeconomic status, disability, gender, health status, religion, national origin, or sexual orientation.

1.11 Marriage and family therapists do not abandon or neglect clients in treatment without making reasonable arrangements for the continuation of such treatment.

3.1 Marriage and family therapists pursue knowledge of new developments and maintain competence in marriage and family therapy through education, training, or supervised experience.

6.7 Marriage and family therapists are concerned with developing laws and regulations pertaining to marriage and family therapy that serve the public interest, and with altering such laws and regulations that are not in the public interest.

The International Association of Marriage and Family Counselors (IAMFC, 2005) also has particular principles that recognize the importance of culturally diverse clients' welfare. These principles include the following:

4. Marriage and family counselors respect cultural diversity. They do not discriminate on the basis of race, gender, disability, religion, age, sexual orientation, cultural background, national origin, marital status, or political affiliation.

12. Marriage and family counselors establish fees that are reasonable and customary depending upon the scope and location of their practices. Couple and family counselors in community agencies, schools, and other public settings do not solicit gifts or charge fees for services that are available in

the counselor's employing agency or institution. Culturally sensitive counselors recognize that gifts are tokens of respect and gratitude in some cultures. Marriage and family counselors may receive gifts or participate in family rituals that promote healthy interaction and do not exploit clients.

13. Marriage and family counselors maintain ethical and effective practices as they address the benefits and limitations of technological innovations and cultural changes. Psychotherapy may be conducted or assisted by telephones, computer hardware and software, and other communication technologies. Technology-assisted distance therapy services may expand the scope and influence of marriage and family therapy. However, counselors are responsible for developing competencies in the use of new technologies and safeguarding private and confidential information.

The American School Counselor Association (ASCA, 2005) stated in an even more explicit fashion the ways in which awareness, knowledge, and skills are to inform the practices of counselors. The ASCA specifically stated that the professional school counselor

1. Affirms the diversity of students, staff, and families;
2. Expands on and develops awareness of his/her own attitudes and beliefs affecting cultural values and biases and strives to attain cultural competence;
3. Possesses knowledge and understanding about how oppression, racism, discrimination, and stereotyping affects her/him personally and professionally; and
4. Acquires educational, consultation and training experiences to improve awareness, knowledge and skills and effectiveness in working with diverse populations: ethnic/racial status, age, economic status, special needs, ESL or ELL, immigration status, sexual orientation, gender, gender identity/expression, family type, religious/spiritual identity and appearance.

Thus, therapists need to be prepared to work with immigrant families, not only because it is part of the *Code of Ethics* but also because the work requires self-awareness and understanding, which may not come as easy to those who have never even lived outside of the United States. There is also notable concern that much of the research published in journals of the American Psychological Association (APA) focuses too narrowly on Americans only, who compose about less than 5% of the world's population (Arnett, 2008). There are specific issues and perspectives that immigrant families face that cannot come from a review of literature alone. It is expected that this text will stimulate self-development as much as it will academic understanding when it comes to working with immigrant families. Clearly, a publication that encompasses research and experiential data about immigrant families is long overdue, and this book is meant to be an important stepping-stone that can lead therapists down an important path of enlightenment that will greatly improve their awareness of this clientele and how to best provide them with effective services.

Therapists must also be aware of the fact that many of their services can, and probably should, involve doing more than individual and family therapy. Immigrant families may need services of advocates, educators, consultants, community volunteers or liaisons, and other forms of service that therapists are trained to provide and/or assist with. Although this text primarily emphasizes the approaches and strategies that therapists can use when providing therapy and related family work, professionals must bear in mind that the needs of immigrant families often extend beyond the scope of a mere session. The ACA and ASCA provide these pieces of information in their ethical guidelines and standards of practice, but psychotherapists are reminded of the concrete ways in which these concepts translate into practice.

Race, Ethnicity, and Culture

There are essential definitions that are to be presented at this time as a way of providing a basis for understanding some of the common threads involved with understanding issues of diversity. The concepts behind these terms are often more complex than the definitions, but as a way of making sense out of each subsequent chapter, readers are encouraged to bear in mind the following information.

Race is often thought of as a biological concept that is often constructed on the basis of physical characteristics (Paludi, 2002). However, psychotherapeutic and psychological applications of the term strongly suggest that this concept is more than genetic or physical. Helms (1994), for example, extended the definition to include sociopolitical factors, economic considerations, values and belief systems, and psychological characteristics. This text intends to incorporate more of the latter than the former, though readers are advised that biological correlations certainly exist when it comes to defining and exploring racial topics.

Ethnicity is a concept specifically thought to include one's nationality, religion or spirituality, language, and cultural background (Paludi, 2002). However, psychotherapeutic and psychological applications of this term strongly suggest that the notions of ancestry and family also contribute valuable constructions. Ben-Yoseph (2005), for example, noted that one may not even be fully aware of one's ethnicity especially when negotiating the memories one has of the place where he or she was born and the place where he or she is growing up because of displacement. Ethnicity can be communicated and transmitted to people through their families and communities, and it is for this reason that work with immigrant families can present a unique opportunity for therapists and clients to become more consciously aware of their identities through further exploration and transmission of this concept.

Culture is a concept that has the most variability in terms of definition and approach. Taken one way, culture is defined as common ways of viewing the world through interactions with others who are members of society and its various social groups (Kramsch, 2005). It is a structure that provides insights and explanations to events and occurrences and, at the same time, a method by which values and beliefs are exchanged and solidified. However, there is also a historical component to culture. Specifically, Kramsch (2005) stated, "People identify themselves as members of a society to the extent that they can have a place in that society's history and that they can identify with the way that it remembers its past, turns its attention to the present, and anticipates its future" (p. 7). It is this dimension of culture that showcases a need for belongingness that immigrant families can often struggle with as they leave one area for another.

The Concept of Family

The concept of family is also mentioned throughout this text, and it should be noted that this text was written primarily from the perspective of genetically related individuals to construct the definition. This is not to say that close friends and relatives who are not part of the nuclear family unit do not compose a family; certainly there are many cultures and societies that exemplify this concept. However, primary reviews of literature and research tend to primarily focus on this biological notion of what composes a family in terms of providing data about intervening with immigrant families. Readers are encouraged to recognize that the composition of family can vary among clients, and this can certainly impact who attends family therapy sessions and the techniques that can be employed during said sessions. It is also recommended that therapists gather relevant family information from the perspective of the clients they are working with and not to assume that all clients define the concept of family from a biological/nuclear unit perspective. Bearing all of this information in mind, the text aims to provide practical approaches to working with immigrant families in an inclusive manner that helps to establish effective therapeutic alliances along the way.

Text Overview

As we hope can be noted from the construction of this chapter, the composition of this text is intended to be focused on practicality. The overall text is meant to develop an initial rubric on which therapists can further enhance and apply strategies that will aid immigrant families in ways that are more specific to the area and community in which they exist. The issues discussed in each chapter are carefully reviewed topics that are considered to be of major significance for therapists to know as they engage in their work with immigrant families. The initial chapters (1–3) are designed to define essential concepts that apply to the psychological and interpersonal development of culturally different individuals. The scope of these chapters is meant to be relatively broad and expanded approaches whereby therapists can gain a fundamental understanding of terminology and theoretical concepts that link the more specific chapters of the book (4–13) together. Chapters 4 through 13 of this text are designed to provide specific information about particular immigrant families along with available research and experiences that encompass what therapists believe to be the most effective strategies involved with assisting immigrant families from particular parts of the world. The entire text has been constructed to provide a truly global perspective about immigrant families. Finally, Chapter 13 is included to provide future directions and goals for therapists to consider as the ever-changing conditions of the world impact the issues that affect immigrant families and the services they will need from therapists. Thus, this text is a practical guide that takes into consideration the past, present, and future characteristics of immigrant families and the issues with which they most need assistance.

The specifics of each remaining chapter are as follows.

Chapter 2: "Theories of Acculturation and Cultural Identity." This chapter provides overviews of the major theories that help to explain some of the common issues associated with individuals who immigrate to other countries and the psychological, socioeconomic, and social factors incurred along the way. These theories are presented to give the reader an important sense of what makes working with immigrant families different from working with domestic clients. Furthermore, the chapter demonstrates the importance of working with families as a result of acculturative stressors that provide significant impacts to family dynamics, which can invariably affect the psychotherapeutic relationship if not addressed by the therapist.

Chapter 3: "Theories of Family Therapy." This chapter provides overviews of the major theories that are often applied to working with families who seek therapy. These theories are presented to give the reader an important sense of what makes working with immigrant families different from working with domestic clients. This chapter also provides an important backdrop on which the subsequent chapters of the book are designed to showcase each theory with respect to particular immigrant clients.

One important theoretical difference in working with immigrant families is the notion that in cases where immigration is more of a conscious choice, as opposed to a political threat, adult family members are less likely to accept responsibility for the problems that the family system is incurring. In other words, the adult immigrant family members are more likely to view themselves as hardworking and well-intentioned individuals who have made significant sacrifices for the good of the entire family. Thus, the therapist must be prepared to deal with the fact that immigrant families are likely to benefit from reframing techniques that engage the entire system in exploring and engaging the strengths of the family to overcome issues. Challenging the adult members to accept full responsibility for their actions, which some therapists may traditionally choose to do based on many mainstream psychological theories, is not likely to benefit such clients.

Another important theoretical difference the therapist must be aware of when providing services to immigrant families is the notion of asking specific questions of particular family members to effectively engage the system in a positive asset search. Many traditional approaches would stress the importance of treating all family members as equals when conducting family therapy sessions. However, immigrant parents often come to a host country with particular hopes they envisioned for their family, whereas immigrant children often do not have this position. Therefore, children are often asked to speak about the people they left behind to immigrate being that their experience is often not one of choice. This questioning is important not only for delineating the roles and responsibilities that exist within the immigrant family system but also for allowing the therapist to maintain appropriate boundaries among family members. There are many specific examples like this notion that therapists must be aware of when working with this clientele and therefore what makes this chapter a critical emphasis point with respect to the overall theme of the book.

Chapter 4: "Working With Hispanic/Latino(a) Immigrant Families." This chapter outlines specific issues and approaches that are significant for working with immigrant families from Hispanic/Latino(a) origin. Central America, South America, and other areas of the world where individuals of Hispanic/Latino(a) origin exist are included to showcase both similarities and differences among these immigrant families.

Chapter 5: "Working With European Immigrant Families." This chapter outlines specific issues and approaches that are significant for working with immigrant families of European origin. Numerous regions of Eastern and Western Europe are included as a way of displaying the variety and common threads that link these immigrant families together, along with specific techniques and approaches that appear to benefit the therapeutic work performed with this clientele.

Chapter 6: "Working With African Immigrant Families." This chapter outlines specific issues and approaches that are significant for working with immigrant families from African origin. Historical context along with contemporary issues facing a variety of African countries provides significant background information when it comes to understanding the needs of these immigrant families. This chapter not only surveys the various cultures that exist within the African continent but also shows how the historical impact of sociopolitical issues have influenced the needs of the immigrant families that come from this part of the world.

Chapter 7: "Working With Asian Immigrant Families, Part I: Far East, Southeast Asia, and Pacific Islands" and *Chapter 8: "Working With Asian Immigrant Families, Part II: South Asia."* These chapters outline specific issues and approaches that are significant for working with immigrant families from Asian origin. Important differentiations between Southeast Asian and other Asian cultures are noted throughout the chapters. Being that this part of the world is one of the most diverse and largest in terms of landmass, readers are exposed to numerous immigrant families that exist within each region of Asia as well.

Chapter 9: "Working With Middle Eastern Immigrant Families." This chapter outlines specific issues and approaches that are significant for working with immigrant families from Middle Eastern origin. Within America, significant negative biases and stereotypes are often associated with this population of immigrant families. Recent wars and political pressures have cast a tremendous spotlight on the Middle East that has impacted the knowledge that many Americans have of this part of the world and the people who live within it. This chapter intends to inform therapists of what the needs of immigrants from the Middle East are, along with important ways in which the acculturation process can be affected by the negative biases that uninformed Americans may hold about Middle Eastern culture.

Chapter 10: "Working With Australian Families: Invisible Immigrants." This chapter outlines specific issues and approaches that are significant for working with immigrant families from Australia. Historical data as well as notable contemporary issues are provided as a way of understanding what reasons are associated with Australians desiring to immigrate to America, as well as what specific needs they have once they become naturalized citizens.

Chapter 11: "Immigrant Families From Regions With Emerging Research." This chapter outlines specific issues and approaches that are significant for working with immigrant families from regions of the world that research studies have recently uncovered or areas that are not as widely researched as the countries mentioned in previous chapters. This chapter is an extension of the "Counseling With New Citizens" chapter (Zagelbaum, 2009) in Ellis and Carlson's text. Specific regions to be mentioned in this chapter include Turkey, Cyprus, Barbados, Jamaica/West Indies, and the Northern Mariana Islands. Available research and theoretical writings provide the major emphasis points by which recommendations and suggestions are made to the reader. Discussion questions at the end of the chapter allow for important dialogue to occur between professionals who may have particular opinions and insights about these clients.

Chapter 12: "Working With Intercultural Immigrant Families." This chapter outlines specific issues and approaches that are significant for working with immigrant families within blended, bicultural, or multicultural backgrounds. Specific attention is given to transnational immigrants, as well as the dynamics that unfold as extended family members become involved with the immigrant family system. The need for therapists to address issues that blended immigrant families often experience as a result of settling in a host culture and forming family bonds along the way has long been underemphasized in research. This chapter is meant not only to introduce this topic to many readers but also to further suggest ways that psychotherapists can continually aid this population of immigrant families.

Chapter 13: "The Future of Counseling Immigrants and Their Families." This closing chapter provides suggestions and guidelines for professionals to consider as the amount of immigrants within the United States increases and the need for professional mental health services must adjust accordingly. Further directions and specific research needs are highlighted in an attempt to have professionals develop and engage more strategies and methods by which these services can be expanded and improved to serve this clientele. Specific informational resources and consultation-based materials are also provided as follow-up materials for readers to use.

Readers are presented at the end of each chapter with discussion questions designed to create open dialogues about concepts and presented strategies. Some of these questions require self-reflection on the part of the reader, whereas others specifically instruct readers to evaluate the techniques and therapeutic approaches identified in each chapter. The point of these questions is not simply to fill space but to challenge the reader to develop a working understanding of one's self and the way in which one sees the opportunities and challenges associated with providing services to immigrant families.

Conclusion

Statistically, it is becoming more likely that American psychotherapists will be working with immigrant families on a more consistent basis than is currently the case. Global economic and political concerns are placing many people into positions where they have to relocate and seek opportunities that may be available only in countries other than their place of birth. The competent therapist not only is aware of these concerns but also acts and applies this awareness to the work and clientele that he or she encounters. This text is designed to present to many professionals their first encounter with issues associated with working with immigrant families. Some individuals may not be using this book as an initial point of their professional development, and for that we expect the content will further stimu-late and challenge these readers to confront contemporary issues that impact the work they will continue to do with immigrant families. In any case, the point of these chapters is to define the areas and regions that immigrant families come from, discuss what the concept of therapy is defined as within their countries of birth, analyze therapeutic approaches and techniques that have been identified by research literature as well as professional experiences as effective, and stimulate debate and discussion about how to practically apply these approaches to the clients who need them. Readers are reminded that there are always between- and within-group differences that exist when exploring issues of cultural and ethnic diversity. The information presented in this text is attempting to take this matter into account whenever possible. Readers will make the ultimate determination as to how the information will best serve the clients with whom they are to work. With this in mind, we hope that the content of this text plants important seeds on which the decision trees associated with making these determinations will grow.

Discussion Questions

1. What is a home or homeland? Does it relate to your parents? Does it relate to your household? Consider what this means for an immigrant family. How would this impact a displaced immigrant family? How would this impact a nondisplaced immigrant family?
2. What does longing for home mean? How does this indicate optimal or less than optimal adjustment?
3. What do you believe are the main reasons that people immigrate? How does this impact adjustment?
4. What are the major concerns clients would have if their family came with them as part of the immigration process? What are the major concerns clients would have if their family did not come with them as part of the immigration process?
5. How effective and efficient do you believe the process of becoming a natu-ralized U.S. citizen is at this time? How do you believe this impacts the work of the mental health and family counselor?

References

American Association for Marriage and Family Therapy. (2001). *Code of ethics.* Alexandria, VA: Author.
American Counseling Association. (2005). *Code of ethics.* Alexandria, VA: Author.

American School Counselor Association. (2005). *Code of ethics.* Alexandria, VA: Author.

Amir, Y. (1992). Social assimilation or cultural mosaic. In J. Lynch, C. Modgil, & S. Modgil (Eds.), *Cultural diversity and the schools* (Vol. I). Washington, DC: Falmer.

Arnett, J. (2008). The neglected 95%: Why American psychology needs to become less American. *American Psychologist, 63,* 602–614.

Ben-Yoseph, M. (2005). Longing for home: Displacement, memory and identity. *Journal of Prevention and Intervention in the Community, 30,* 117–125.

Berry, J. (1997). Immigration, acculturation, and adaptation. *Applied Psychology: An International Review, 46,* 5–34.

Cohen, A. (2009). Many forms of culture. *American Psychologist, 64,* 194–204.

Helms, J. (1994). The conceptualization of racial identity and other racial constructs. In E. J. Trickett, R. J. Watts, & D. Birman (Eds.), *Human diversity: Perspectives on people in context* (pp. 285–311). San Francisco: Jossey-Bass.

Hoefer, M., Rytina, N., & Baker, B. (2007). *Estimates of the unauthorized immigrant population residing in the United States: January 2007.* Washington, DC: Office of Immigration Statistics.

International Association of Marriage and Family Counselors. (2005). *Ethical code of the International Association of Marriage and Family Counselors (IAMFC).* Alexandria, VA: Author.

Jeffreys, K. & Martin, D. (2007). *Refugees and asylees: 2007.* Washington, DC: Office of Immigration Statistics.

Jeffreys, K. & Monger, R. (2007). *U.S. legal permanent residents: 2007.* Washington, DC: Office of Immigration Statistics.

Kramsch, C. (2005). *Language and culture.* Oxford, UK: Oxford University Press.

Milstein, T. (2005). Transformation abroad: Sojourning and the perceived enhancement of self-efficacy. *International Journal of Intercultural Relations, 29,* 217–238.

Ogbonnaya, O. (1994). Person as community: An African understanding of the person as an intrapsychic community. *Journal of Black Psychology, 20,* 75–87.

Paludi, M. (2002). *Human development in multicultural contexts: A book of readings.* Upper Saddle River, NJ: Prentice Hall.

Rytina, N. & Caldera, S. (2007). *Naturalizations in the United States: 2007.* Washington, DC: Office of Immigration Statistics.

Schwartz, S. & Zamboanga, B. (2008). Testing Berry's Model of Acculturation: A confirmatory latent class approach. *Cultural Diversity and Ethnic Minority Psychology, 14,* 275–285.

Zagelbaum, A. (2009). Counseling with new citizens. In C. M. Ellis & J. Carlson (Eds.), *Cross cultural awareness and social justice in counseling* (pp. 243–282). Alexandria, VA: American Counseling Association.

Chapter 2

Theories of Acculturation and Cultural Identity

Irene López, Ernesto R. Escoto, Tyffani
Monford-Dent, and Marina Prado-Steiman

Contents

Key to understanding the life experiences of immigrants is obtaining an appropriate understanding of what the term *immigrant* means. Immigrants may be legal or undocumented residents, permanent residents or short-term guest workers, refugees, asylum seekers, naturalized citizens, or, in the case of Puerto Ricans, American citizens who migrate to the continental United States (L. A. Miller, 2007). In short, the term *immigrant* encapsulates a variety of experiences and historical legacies that may often mask important distinctions between subgroups. However, despite these varied definitions and experiences, there are a host of commonalities that immigrants may share as they migrate to the United States and acculturate to their new environment. In this chapter, we will review the research and various models associated with acculturation and immigrants to demonstrate how working with immigrant families may be different from working with domestic clients.

Definition of Acculturation

Historically, *acculturation* has been defined a variety of ways (Chun, Organista, & Marín, 2003). In 1936, anthropologists Redfield, Linton, and Herskovits offered one of the first formal definitions of acculturation as "those phenomena which results when groups of individuals having different cultures come into continuous first-hand contact, with subsequent changes in the original cultural patterns of either or both groups" (p. 149). This definition, with its focus on bidirectional change and sustained group contact, was then further expanded by Graves (1967) to include specific behavioral changes that individuals may incur as a result of culture contact.

Since then, acculturation has been understood to include group and individual changes resulting from sustained intercultural contact. From a psychological perspective, this would entail changes in the behavior, values, and identity that individuals undergo when they are in continuous contact with others who may hold different values, norms, beliefs, and customs (Negy & Woods, 1992; Padilla, 1980). However, recent research has noted these definitions do not fully acknowledge the role of human agency in interpersonal relationships (see Chirkov, 2009, for further review). Thus, acculturation is not a process that occurs to an individual. Instead, an individual may affect how acculturation can occur.

To this effect, one recently proposed definition of individual acculturation, or second-culture acquisition, defines it as "a process that is executed by an agentic individual … after meeting and entering a cultural community that is different from the cultural community where he or she was initially socialized" (Chirkoc, 2009, p. 178). Furthermore, within this revised definition, acculturation "involves a deliberate, reflective, and, for the most part, comparative cognitive activity" and is "an open-ended, continuous process that includes progresses, relapses, and turns which make it practically impossible to predict and control" (Chirkoc, 2009, p. 178).

Models of Acculturation

Unidimensional and Linear Models

Just as there has been controversy regarding the definition of acculturation, there has been equal difficulty in devising models and methods that best capture the experience of cultural acquisition. Despite earlier definitions that understood acculturation as an ongoing bidirectional process, many models of acculturation focused exclusively on the life experiences of immigrants and conceived of this experience as a unidimensional process (Cuéllar, Harris, & Jaso, 1980; Gordon, 1964). Within this framework, immigrants moved linearly from one polar extreme (i.e., low acculturation) to another (i.e., complete assimilation). The assumption of these models was that assimilation would be related to better psychological functioning. However, further elaborations of this model, subsequently conceived of the notion biculturalism, or dual cultural involvement, as an alternative to complete assimilation. Expanding on these models' biculturality was conceived as occurring at the midpoint of these two extremes.

However, despite these changes in measurement and conceptualization, the association between acculturation and psychological outcome remained unclear. According to Rogler, Cortés, and Malgady (1991), acculturation was associated with psychological functioning in three contradictory ways: (a) a positive association, indicating that as acculturation increased, adjustment increased; (b) a negative association, indicating that as acculturation increased, adjustment decreased; and (c) a curvilinear association, in which acculturation could be correlated with either optimal or worse adjustment at the extreme ends of the acculturation spectrum. In addition, there was, of course, an unstated fourth outcome in which acculturation was not at all related to adjustment.

Bidimensional and Multidimensional Models

Many have argued that such contradictory findings were in part due to the variety of ways that acculturation was conceptualized and measured, as well as the use of research designs and samples used (Cabassa, 2003; Rogler et al., 1991; Ryder, Alden, & Paulhus, 2000). For example, assessing acculturation has been difficult because many measures have relied on proxy measures, such as generational status (e.g., first or second generation), frequency of language use (e.g., English vis-à-vis language of origin), length of U.S. residency, socioeconomic status, and even food use. Yet, because many of these variables are often correlated, it can be difficult to assess the unique predictive value of each variable (Cabassa, 2003; Negy & Woods, 1992).

However, one of the most prominent criticisms of the unidimensional models was that acculturation did not occur in such a zero-sum manner. Instead, immigrants could hold and adapt to various aspects of their heritage and host cultures without relinquishing either culture. Therefore, acculturation to these different cultures needed to be assessed on separate dimensions (or orthogonally), rather than assumed to occur on a single bipolar continuum.

The most prominent bidimensional model has been Berry's Acculturation Model (Berry, 1990). Briefly, according to this model, individuals had a variety of strategies for dealing with the process of acculturation. In particular, involvement in the host and immigrant culture was assessed separately with regard to whether individuals believed (a) it was of value to maintain their immigrant identity and (b) it was of value to maintain contact with other groups. On the basis of responses to these questions, individuals were categorized into one of the four strategies: assimilation, separation, marginalization, and integration (or biculturality). Although this model has been subsequently critiqued (Rudmin, 2003), at least recent research is indicating that newer measures of bidimensional acculturation scores are quite robust (see Huynh, Howell, & Benet-Martínez, 2009 for meta-analytic review).

Of all of these strategies, much emphasis has been placed on understanding the experiences of biculturality. In contrast to earlier definitions, within this model biculturality is conceived no longer as occurring at the midpoint of two polar opposites but rather as an experience that needs to be assessed along two separate dimensions (Cortés, Rogler, & Malgady, 1994; Szapocznik, Kurtines, & Fernandez, 1980; Szapocznik, Santisteban, Kurtines, Perez-Vidal, & Hervis, 1984). Currently, the latest research indicates that there are multiple types of biculturals and that individuals can acculturate to multiple domains (Benet-Martínez & Haritatos, 2005; Guo, Suarez-Morales, Schwartz, & Szapocznik, 2009; Schwartz & Zamboanga, 2008; Zea, Asner-Self, Birman, & Buki, 2003). Furthermore, individuals can acculturate at different rates, to different domains, during the process of acculturation (Kang, 2006). Bicultural individuals thus represent the possibility of an infinite host of value sets, making a portrayal of the typical "bicultural individual" almost impossible.

Models of Ethnic and Racial identity

In addition to the difficulties of assessing acculturation and biculturality, there has been growing concern that variables assessed in these models do not fully capture the values associated with acculturating to another environment, such as changes that might occur in cultural or group awareness and affiliation (Padilla, 1980). Thus, researchers have expanded their studies to include this mode of identity development (Atkinson, Morten, & Sue, 1993; Bernal, Saenz, & Knight, 1991; Cross, 1971; Helms, 1984; Phinney, 1992). Many of these models have drawn from identity development models developed by Marcia (1980) as well as social identity models (Tajfel, 1981). Among the most influential of these theories have been Phinney's conceptualization of ethnic identity (Phinney, 1992; Phinney & Ong, 2007) and Cross's (1971) model of psychological nigrescence.

Ethnic Identity Models

Briefly defined, ethnic identity reflects the attitudes or emotional significance people attach to their social group (Phinney, 1990; Phinney & Ong, 2007), such as a group with a common nationality or culture (Betancourt & López, 1993). For many it is an integral part of their sense of self and their interactions with the world. Although various ethnic-specific models have been proposed to understand the experience of ethnic identity, most theorists have assumed that this process typically occurs in stages. For example, according to Phinney's (non-ethnic-specific) model of ethnic identity, minority adolescents may go through periods of having an unexamined identity, then go through a period of searching or moratorium, and proceed to achievement (Phinney & Ong, 2007).

Within this framework, there has also been attention paid to the multidimensional components of ethnic identity. For example, one definition of ethnic identity offered by Bernal and Knight (1993) integrates the variables of self-concept and group membership, including related constructs such as knowledge, understanding, values, behaviors, and feelings, and defines ethnic identity as "a construct or set of self-ideas about one's own ethnic group membership" (p. 33).

Racial Identity Models

Concurrent with the development of ethnic identity models was the development of racial identity theories. In contrast to ethnic identity, racial identity refers to the significance and meaning that individuals ascribe to being a member of their racial group (Sellers, Smith, Shelton, Rowley, & Chavous, 1998). Cross (1971) developed the first model of racial identity development, the nigrescence model, which offered a framework in which to understand Black identity development. Like early acculturation models, Cross's model offered a series of sequential developmental stages of Black identity, beginning with preencounter, moving to encounter and immersion, and ending with internalization and commitment.

Subsequently, other models of racial identity development have expanded on Cross's model, moving toward a more fluid view of the process of identity formation and adding elements reflecting the ethnic minority individual interaction with an oppressive environment (Atkinson et al., 1993; Helms, 1984). The Racial/Cultural Identity Development Model (Atkinson et al., 1993) further elaborates on the work of Helms (1984) and Helms and Carter (1990).

The strengths of these models are that, unlike previous acculturation models, they have focused more directly on issues of identity development. In addition, unlike acculturation, there appears to be a more consistent relation between higher levels of ethnic and racial identity and greater adjustment. In fact, a growing body of research indicates that, in particular, ethnic identity can suffer as a buffer against psychological distress (López, 2008). Furthermore, with regard to racial identity, exploratory research indicates that among some immigrant groups, preencounter racial attitudes are related to more depressive symptomatology (Kibour, 2001).

However, in general, the applicability of these ethnic and racial models to various immigrant groups has been lacking. This is unfortunate because immigrant groups can identify in a variety of ways. For example, although some Latinos(as) can racially self-identify in a multitude of ways, for a variety of reasons, some may still find it important to ethnically identify as Latinos/Latinas (López, 2008; Itzigsohn, Giorguli, & Vazquez, 2005). In contrast, African immigrants migrating to the United States may sometimes feel forced to choose between identifying as Black and holding on to their native identity. In short, although many of the models presented have discussed the role of cultural contact, they have not explicitly discussed how these processes specifically affect the lived experiences of immigrants who may come to therapy.

Application of the Acculturation and Identify Models to Immigrants

For clinicians working with immigrants, it is important not only to understand the various models of acculturation, ethnic identity, and racial identity but also to understand how these processes can differ for various family members. Although the formation of the family can differ according to how preexisting immigration laws are executed, a review of the research indicates a number of clinical issues that appear to be similar across groups.

Acculturation and the Immigrant Man

In the United States, roughly 58% of the unauthorized immigrant population is male compared to only 42% of the immigrant population being female. In contrast to immigration patterns around the globe, most of the immigration to the United States occurs in some unauthorized form (Fry, 2006). Within this group, men are most likely to be the first to migrate and arrive in the host country, leaving behind important extended support networks. In addition, recently arrived immigrant men, who mostly arrive from Latin America and Asia, generally moved into established communities of like individuals, often largely composed of males.

This encapsulation thus engenders some of the first barriers to seeking mental health care, low acculturation, and self-reliant attitudes (Cabassa, Zayas, & Hansen, 2006). These patterns often translate into multiple barriers for male immigrants. Men who have immigrated to the United States using an unauthorized form face barriers such as lacking health insurance, having limited to no English-language skills, and not having a network that can point them to available local mental health resources (Cabassa et al., 2006).

Another particular difficulty that has been noted in the clinical research on immigrant men is substance abuse (Gil, Wagner, & Vega, 2000; Karriker-Jaffe & Zemore, 2009; Zamboanga, Raffaelli, & Horton, 2006). For example, Karriker-Jaffe and Zemore (2009) examined drinking patterns among Latino males with both high and low levels of acculturation and with a sample of U.S.-born English speakers and foreign-born Spanish speakers and found that Latino males with a high level of acculturation were significantly more likely to be drinkers than Latino males with low levels of acculturation. However, this was true only for high-level income (i.e., above average) Latino men and not for Latino men with high levels of acculturation who have below-average incomes. Thus, although the general research on acculturation and mental health is still debated, at least for men there appears to be a relation between migration and substance abuse.

Acculturation and Immigrant Women

For immigrant women, current profiles indicate that those who arrive are typically older, are better educated, have a tendency to have never been married, and are less likely to have children than earlier streams (Fry, 2006). However, although there are differences between earlier and later cohorts, on the whole, these differences are not dramatically different. For example, in 2004, only 30%, as opposed to 27% in 1980, of female migrants were never married. Furthermore, there was only a slight drop in the percentage of women who reported that they had children of their own, from 51% in 1980 to 47% in 1994 (Fry, 2006).

Thus, large portions of immigrant women still come to the United States previously married and currently caring for their children. Therefore, it is not surprising that many of the therapeutic concerns of immigrant women concern their children. These concerns can range from postpartum issues to concerns over how to raise their adolescent children who, along with them, are undergoing the process of acculturation. In addition, although there is great heterogeneity in the life experiences of different immigrant groups, the growing feminization of poverty indicates that worldwide women are at much higher risk for poverty (Brady & Kall, 2008). These "push factors" can consequently affect whether a woman immigrates to the United States and what types of jobs she acquires or is forced into.

In conjunction, at least on the basis of clinical observations, immigrant women can also face a number of psychological issues. For example, past clinical studies have reported an increase in the relationship between past trauma, relocation, and post-traumatic stress disorder (PTSD) and depressive symptomatology, with one study finding that abused women had three times the odds of meeting PTSD criteria (Fedovskiy, Higgins, & Paranjape, 2008). In addition, some have debated whether immigrant women, when compared to nonimmigrant women, are at higher risk for abuse or if immigrant-specific factors, such as language difficulties, isolation, discrimination, restriction to resources, and issues related to their legal statuses, exacerbate an already elevated problem in a vulnerable population (Menjívar & Salcido, 2002). Still, recent studies, such as by Hass, Dutton, and Orloff (2000), have found lifetime prevalence rates of domestic violence to be as high as 49.8%, and more recent research with 78 Pakistani and Indian women found the prevalence rate to be as high as 77% (Adam & Schewe, 2007).

One factor that has been linked with increased abuse, and that is intimately tied to the process of acculturation, is the laws that were associated with the immigration of women. With the passage of the Immigration and Marriage Fraud Amendment in 1986, immigrant women who migrated were subject to a two-year conditional resident status before they could become citizens (Bhuyan, 2008). During this two-year period, the immigrant woman's U.S. husband, who could be either a U.S. citizen or a legal resident, was in effect a woman's legal guardian and responsible for her acculturation. The notion was that a woman could be introduced to American culture and, through a man's assistance, could learn all the appropriate skills to become a knowledgeable citizen.

However, although this arrangement was assumed to not cause any undue hardships for those marriages that had occurred in good faith, advocates for immigrant women have argued that this "legal dependence" in effect created situations of abuse and control (Bhuyan, 2008). As a result, fearing deportation, immigrant women sustained physical and psychological abuse at the hands of their spouses because they either were unaware or were too fearful to seek civil protection orders against their abusive partners (Conyers, 2007). This is on top of the fact that many times immigrants may not fully know the status of their immigration because of the changing and complex laws (L. A. Miller, 2007).

We can see how patriarchal notions, viewed from a feminist perspective, of how men should provide for the acculturation of women in effect led to the abuse of women. Thus, in recognition of the abuses that immigrant women, and their children, could be subject to, a series of Violence Against Women and Department of Justice Reauthorization Acts (e.g., VAWA, 2000, 2004, 2005) were passed. Each subsequent act enlarged the class of immigrant victims protected. Specifically, abused women could now formally identify as a "battered immigrant" and self-petition for their legal status, without the fear of deportation (Conyers, 2007).

Although these laws have increased the protection afforded to immigrant women, recent research based on community samples, with different immigrant groups, using a variety of methodologies, suggest abuse is still occurring (Lee, 2007; Rianon & Shelton, 2003; Salcido & Adelman, 2004). Clinical observations, as well as interviews with treatment providers, have also documented the difficulties of service delivery for this population (Keller & Brennan, 2007; Latta & Goodman, 2005; Liao, 2006; Nicolas et al., 2007). Still, although the stressors of acculturation are clearly linked to the life experiences of women, it is yet unclear if this relationship is linear or whether there are multiple feedback loops that can better explain the relationship between acculturation and the mental health of immigrants. This is especially of concern because there are only a limited number of epidemiological and longitudinal studies on the mental health of immigrants.

Finally, a dominant theory in the immigrant-acculturation literature concerns the differences in the rate of acculturation between men and women, as well as between women and their children, who are often assumed to acculturate faster than their parents. In fact, research has also documented conflicts between mothers and their adult children, namely, daughters (Usita & Du Bois, 2005).

Acculturation and Immigrant Youth

As such, differences in acculturation are not only gender based but also generational. Because of issues of faster acquisition of the new culture's language, developmental stages, and the adopted country's mainstream culture, the acculturation of children and adolescents must be viewed as its own phenomenon. With specific regard to acculturation, because of adolescents' ability to understand and speak various languages at a more rapid pace than their adult counterparts, children are more prepared to engage in social interactions within their adopted culture, resulting in a faster level of acculturation. In addition, children and adolescents are more likely to have the opportunity to acquire English, by way of participation in school-sponsored English as second language (ESL) classes or more informal means such as contact with classmates or teachers, for whom English is the primary language.

In examining retention of the adolescents' original language, immigrant children often do retain a tight hold on their ethnic roots for practical purposes, including communication with their parents and other adult family members (who perhaps struggle with learning English) or to assist their families in navigating North American society, for which English is the "unofficial" official language. Outside of this, retention of native languages also serves the purpose of maintaining a connection to one's ethnic identify and reinforcing acceptance of one's native culture (Lu, 2001). When one is working with immigrant children or adolescents, the role their native language serves for them must be taken into consideration, especially for how the provision of services occurs (whether in the native language or in English), as well as what role language holds in their lives. For instance, it is not uncommon for adolescents to feel a social pressure to speak English only (Shi & Lu, 2007). Such pressure must also be taken into consideration as it relates to the child's acculturative stress. Unable to insulate themselves from the requirement to speak English (because of societal constraints in and out of school), adolescents are required to learn English in greater proficiency than their original language and at an increased speed. Providers of services to children and adolescents and their families must be cautioned to not fall into the trap of contributing to the pressures of English-only mental health provision, as it has the potential to impact willingness to seek services and serves to further marginalize immigrant clients.

As children and adolescents are often quicker to speak the language of the new country (English in the United States), they are often relied on to serve as informal translators and guides for their parents in both language and cultural norms (Padilla, 2006; Weisskirch & Alva, 2002). This new role as the cultural brokers has been shown to cause a burden on children and adolescents because of the awkward role reversal of their parents relying on them for their English skills (Padilla, 2006). In addition, because of the need to serve as translators for their parents in areas of business and with other facets of the new culture, children and adolescents are often put in the uncomfortable situation of being privy to adult discussions, issues, and so on that their parents would otherwise keep from them (Weisskirch & Alva, 2002). Although these children simultaneously act as guides and mentors for their parents, these same adolescents will then be expected to maintain the role of being children within the household, even when they must mediate adult disputes.

Language is often tied to the level of assimilation of children and adolescents and their parents. Farver, Narang, and Bhadha (2002) noted that the acculturation gap is common within families based on generation. As many immigrant parents choose to come to the United States because of better opportunities for themselves and their families (perhaps enduring evading conditions such as wars, famines, and so on in their homeland), parents at times struggle to determine which culture deserves more emphasis: their ethnic background or the U.S. culture. In this acculturation process, it is often the family who plays a major role. The way in which this is undertaken can occur in actual verbal directives being given by parents, modeling of immigrant cultural norms, and parenting style.

Children and adolescents may feel torn between these two worlds, neither of which do they feel a part of. This isolation from both cultures contributes to problems in their relationships with parents and other adult family members. Parents with low-level acculturation may push their children to also maintain the native culture, including its values and ideas, which may not necessarily be in sync with those of the mainstream U.S. culture or what the children or adolescents want (Cote & Bornstein, 2005). Therefore, when the children or adolescents choose to acculturate more than their parents would like, it may be taken as sign of rebellion and may cause additional problems in the parent–child relationship. This conflict may be even greater within immigrant cultures where parents were separated or marginalized by the majority culture, as noted in a study of Asian American immigrants (Farver et al., 2002). The level of assimilation of caregivers, as well as the acculturation gap that may exist between children and adolescents and their parents or caregivers, may influence service delivery as well as issues presented in counseling sessions and how they may be viewed differently by the parents and children or adolescents.

The Provision of Culturally Appropriate Services

The multitude of concerns that some immigrant families face makes it especially important that we provide culturally competent and accessible resources for this population. However, the first issue to realize is that on the whole, immigrant groups, typically defined as those who are first generation, in fact overall have better mental health outcomes than those who are born in the United States (Alegria et al., 2008; Takeuchi et al., 2007). Thus, as clinicians we must understand that those patients who come to our clinical practice are not always fully representative of the population at large. In part, because of issues surrounding stigma (Abu-Ras, 2003; Nadeem et al., 2007), differences in self-perceived need (Nadeem et al., 2007), and difficulties in resource allocation, immigrants who come to therapy can vary substantially from those who do not and from immigrants in general. Providing culturally competent services would first recognize the overall resiliency among immigrant groups.

Furthermore, as clinicians we need to understand that the expression of distress and psychopathology can vary extensively by culture, and thus any intervention would need to be specifically tailored to the group (Bernstein, Lee, Park, & Jyoung, 2008; Cabassa, 2003; Sellers, Ward, & Pate, 2006). Unfortunately, there is still much more work that needs to be done in providing such services. In fact, a review of the research shows that there were a limited number of community-based studies that explicitly targeted immigrant populations in their treatment protocols. Furthermore, to our knowledge, there were no randomized clinical trials that specifically targeted the mental health problems of immigrants.

Clearly, the most effective types of treatment programs are the ones that targeted the family (Paris, 2008; Pearl, 2008; Seto & Woodford, 2007). In our view, the most effective types of treatment would also require that clinicians not only address current problems but also work with the community to improve and address its needs. The most effective programs understand that structural forces, such as the ever-changing laws that govern immigration, can encourage or discourage the settlement of immigrants into this country, and the consequences of these laws have affected the possibilities for acculturation. For example, depending on the immigrant group, some residential laws have been extremely restrictive and as a result have strongly impacted the establishment of ethnic enclave. Neighborhood characteristics, such as the density of its ethnic population, can lead to different trajectories of acculturation and subsequently can change mental health outcomes (A. M. Miller et al., 2009).

Thus, in discussing the life experiences of immigrants, it is important not only to understand the interpersonal factors that can influence these issues but also to have an appreciation of the laws that can influence the stratification of immigrant communities and to appreciate the context from whence immigrants emigrated and of where they resettled. In short, the acculturation of immigrants, and their subsequent mental health, is simultaneously constrained and buffered by interpersonal and structural forces.

Discussion Questions

1. How can changes in the definition and measurement of acculturation affect therapeutic practices?
2. How does gender or one's relationship in the family affect the acculturation process? What clinical issues are most salient in these groups?
3. What individual and social factors contribute to resiliency among the individuals, ethnic groups, or immigrants as a whole?

4. What are the individual or social factors that contribute to lower rates of mental health concerns among immigrants that could be translated to native-born populations in the United States?
5. In what ways can a mental health professional balance the native cultural values of parents with the bicultural values of their children when determining services goals and issues?
6. What are the different issues that may arise based on the age of immigrants at time of immigration?

References

Abu-Ras, W. M. (2003). Barriers to services for Arab immigrant battered women in a Detroit suburb. *Journal of Social Work Research and Evaluation*, *4*, 49–66. doi:10.1177/1077801207306019

Adam, N. M. & Schewe, P. A. (2007). A multilevel framework exploring domestic violence against immigrant Indian and Pakistani women in the United States. *Journal of Muslim Mental Health*, *2*(1), 5–20.

Alegria, M., Canino, G., Shrout, P., Woo, M., Duan, N., Vila, D., & et al. (2008). Prevelance of mental illness in immigrant and non-immigrant U.S. Latino groups. *American Journal of Psychiatry*, *165*, 359–369. doi:10.1176/appi.ajp.2007.07040704

Atkinson, D. R., Morten, G., & Sue, D. W. (1993). *Counseling American minorities* (4th ed.). Dubuque, IA: Brown and Benchmark.

Benet-Martínez, V. & Haritatos, J. (2005). Bicultural identity integration (BII): Components and psychosocial antecedents. *Journal of Personality*, *73*, 1015–1050.

Bernal, M.E. & Knight, G.P. (1993). *Ethnic Identity: Formation and Transmission among Hispanics and Other Minorities*. Albany: State University of New York Press.

Bernstein, K. S., Lee, J. S., Park, S. Y., & Jyoung, J.-P. (2008). Symptom manifestations and expressions among Korean immigrant women suffering with depression. *Journal of Advanced Nursing*, *61*, 393–402. doi:10.1111/j.1365–2648.2007.04533.x

Berry, J. W. (1990). Psychology of acculturation: Understanding individuals moving between cultures. In R. W. Brislin (Ed.), *Cross cultural psychology* (pp. 232–253). Newbury Park, CA: Sage.

Betancourt, H. & López, S. R. (1993). The study of culture, ethnicity, and race in American psychology. *American Psychologist*, *48*(6), 629–637.

Bhuyan, R. (2008). The production of the "battered immigrant" in public policy and domestic violence advocacy. *Journal of Interpersonal Violence*, *23*(2), 153–170.

Brady, D. & Kall, D. (2008). Nearly universal, but somewhat distinct: The feminization of poverty in affluent Western democracies, 1969–2000. *Social Science Research*, *37*, 976–1007. doi:10.1016/j.ssresearch.2007.07.001

Cabassa, L. J. (2003). Measuring acculturation: Where we are and where we need to go. *Hispanic Journal of Behavioral Sciences*, *25*(2), 127–146.

Cabassa, L. J., Zayas, L. H., & Hansen, M. C. (2006). Latino adults' access to mental health care: A review of epidemiological studies. *Administration and Policy in Mental Health and Mental Health Services Research, 33*(3), 316–330.

Chirkov, V. (2009). Summary of the criticism and of the potential ways to improve acculturation psychology. *International Journal of Intercultural Relations, 33,* 177–180. doi:10.1016/j.ijintrel.2009.03.005

Chun, K. M., Organista, P. M., & Marín, G. (2003). *Acculturation: Advances in theory, measurement, and applied research.* Washington, DC: American Psychological Association.

Conyers, J. (2007). The 2005 reauthorization of the Violence Against Women Act: Why Congress acted to expand protections to immigrant victims. *Violence Against Women, 13*(5), 457–468.

Cortés, D. E., Rogler, L. H., & Malgady, R. G. (1994). Biculturality among Puerto Rican adults in the United States. *American Journal of Community Psychology, 5,* 707–721.

Cote, L. R. & Bornstein, M. H. (2005). Child and mother play in cultures of origin, acculturating cultures, and cultures of destination. *International Journal of Behavioral Development, 29,* 479–488. doi:10.1080/01650250500147006

Cross, W. E., Jr. (1971). Stereotypic and non-stereotypic images associated with the Negro to Black conversion experience: An empirical analysis. *Black World, 20,* 13–27. doi:10.1177/009579847800500102

Cuéllar, I., Harris, L. C., & Jaso, R. (1980). An acculturation scale for Mexican Americans normal and clinical populations. *Hispanic Journal of Behavioral Sciences, 2,* 199–217.

Farver, J. A. M., Narang, S. K., & Bhadha, B. R. (2002). East meets West: Ethnic identity, acculturation, and conflict in Asian Indian families. *Journal of Family Psychology, 16,* 338–350. doi:10.1037/0893–3200.16.3.338

Fedovskiy, K., Higgins, S., & Paranjape, A. (2008). Intimate partner violence: How does it impact major depressive disorder and post-traumatic stress disorder among immigrant Latinas? *Journal of Immigrant and Minority Health, 10,* 45–51. doi:10.1007/s10903–007–9049–7

Fry, R. (2006). *Gender and migration* (pp. 1–42). Retrieved July 25, 2009, from http://pewhispanic.org/files/reports/64.pdf

Gil, A., Wagner, E., & Vega, W. (2000). Acculturation, familism and alcohol use among Latino adolescent males: Longitudinal relations. *Journal of Community Psychology, 28,* 443–458. doi:10.1002/1520–6629(200007)28:4<443::AID-JCOP6>3.0.CO;2-A

Gordon, M. M. (1964). *Assimilation in America life.* New York: Oxford University Press.

Graves, T. D. (1967). Psychological acculturation in a tri-ethnic community. *Southwestern Journal of Anthropology, 23,* 237–350.

Guo, X., Suarez-Morales, L., Schwartz, S., & Szapocznik, J. (2009). Some evidence for multidimensional biculturalism: Confirmatory factor analysis and measurement invariance analysis on the Bicultural Involvement Questionnaire–Short Version. *Psychological Assessment, 21*(1), 22–31.

Hass, G. A., Dutton, M. A., & Orloff, L. E. (2000). Lifetime prevalence of domestic violence against Latina immigrants: Legal and policy implications. *Domestic Violence: Global Responses*, *7*(1/2/3), 93–113.

Helms, J. E. (1984). Toward an explanation of the influence of race in the counseling process: A Black–White model. *The Counseling Psychologist*, *12*, 153–165. doi:10.1037/0022–0167.33.2.220

Helms, J. E. & Carter, R. T. (1990). Development of the White Racial Identity Inventory. In J. E. Helms (Ed.), *Black and White racial identity: Theory, research, and practice* (pp. 66–80). Westport, CT: Greenwood. doi:10.1037/0022–0167.41.2.149

Huynh, Q. L., Howell, R. T., & Benet-Martínez, V. (2009). Reliability of bidimensional acculturation scores: A meta-analysis. *Journal of Cross-Cultural Psychology*, *40*(2), 256–274. doi:0.1177/0022022108328919

Itzigsohn, J., Giorguli, S., & Vazquez, O. (2005). Immigrant incorporation and racial identity: Racial self-identification among Dominican immigrants. *Ethnic and Racial Studies*, *28*, 50–78. doi:10.1080/0141984042000280012

Kang, S. M. (2006). Measurement of acculturation, scale formats, and language competence: Their implications for adjustment. *Journal of Cross-Cultural Psychology*, *37*, 669–693.

Karriker-Jaffe, K. & Zemore, S. (2009). Associations between acculturation and alcohol consumption of Latino men in the United States. *Journal of Studies on Alcohol and Drugs*, *70*, 27–31. doi:10.1016/j.socscimed.2005.01.016

Keller, E. M., & Brennan, P. K. (2007). Cultural considerations and challenges to service delivery for Sudanese victims of domestic violence: Insights from service providers and actors in the criminal justice system. *International Review of Victimology*, *14*, 115–141.

Kibour, Y. (2001). Ethiopian immigrants' racial identity attitudes and depression symptomatology: An exploratory study. *Cultural Diversity and Ethnic Minority Psychology*, *7*, 47–58.

Latta, R. E. & Goodman, L. A. (2005). Considering the interplay of cultural context and service provision in intimate partner violence: The case of Haitian immigrant women. *Violence Against Women*, *11*(11), 1441–1464.

Lee, E. (2007). Domestic violence and risk factors among Korean immigrant women in the United States. *Journal of Family Violence*, *22*(3), 141–149.

Liao, M. S. (2006). Domestic violence among Asian Indian immigrant women: Risk factors, acculturation, and intervention. *Women and Therapy*, *29*(1–2), 23–39.

López, I. R. (2008). Puerto Rican phenotype: Understanding its historical underpinnings and psychological associations. *Hispanic Journal of Behavioral Sciences*, *30*, 161–180. doi:10.1177/0739986307313116

Lu, X. (2001). Bicultural identity development and Chinese community formation: An ethnographic study of Chinese schools in Chicago. *The Howard Journal of Communications*, *12*, 203–220. doi:10.1080/106461701753287723

Marcia, J. E. (1980). Identity in adolescence. In J. Adelson (Ed.), *Handbook of adolescent psychology* (pp. 159–187). New York: John Wiley & Sons.

Menjívar, C. & Salcido, O. (2002). Immigrant women and domestic violence: Common experiences in different countries. *Gender and Society*, *16*(6), 898–920.

Miller, A. M., Birman, D., Zenk, S., Wang, E., Sorokin, O., & Connor, J. (2009). Neighborhood immigrant concentration, acculturation, and cultural alienation in former Soviet immigrant women. *Journal of Community Psychology, 37*, 88–105. doi:10.1002/jcop.20272

Miller, L. A. (2007). The exploitation of acculturating immigrant populations. *International Review of Victimology, 14*(1), 11–28. doi:10.1093/jac/dki297

Nadeem, E., Lange, J., Edge, D., Fongwa, M., Belin, T., & Miranda, J. (2007). Does stigma keep poor young immigrant and U.S.-born Black and Latina women from seeking mental health care? *Psychiatric Services, 58*, 1547–1554. doi:10.1176/appi.ps.58.12.1547

Negy, C. & Woods, D. (1992). A note on the relationship between acculturation and socioeconomic status. *Hispanic Journal of Behavioral Sciences, 14*, 248–251.

Nicolas, G., Desilva, A. M., Subrebost, K. L., Breland-Noble, A., Gonzalez-Eastep, D., Manning, N., et al. (2007). Expression and treatment of depression among Haitian immigrant women in the United States: Clinical observations. *American Journal of Psychotherapy, 61*, 83–98. doi:10.1037/a0016307

Padilla, A. M. (1980). The role of cultural awareness and ethnic loyalty in acculturation. In A. M. Padilla (Ed.), *Acculturation: Theory, models and some new findings* (pp. 47–84). Boulder, CO: Westview.

Padilla, A. M. (2006). Bicultural social development. *Hispanic Journal of Behavioral Sciences, 28*, 467–497. doi:10.1177/0739986306294255

Paris, R. (2008). "For the dream of being here, one sacrifices…": Voices of immigrant mothers in a home visiting program. *American Journal of Orthopsychiatry, 78*, 141–151. doi:10.1037/0002–9432.78.2.141

Pearl, E. S. (2008). Parent–child interaction therapy with an immigrant family exposed to domestic violence. *Clinical Case Studies, 7*, 25–41. doi:10.1177/1534650107300939

Phinney, J. S. (1992). The multigroup ethnic identity measure: A new scale for use with diverse groups. *Journal of Adolescent Research, 7*(2), 156–176.

Phinney, J. S. & Ong, A. D. (2007). Conceptualization and measurement of ethnic identity: Current status and future directions. *Journal of Counseling Psychology, 54*(3), 271–281.

Redfield, R., Linton, R., & Herskovits, M. J. (1936). Memorandum for the study of acculturation. *American Anthropologist, 38*, 149–152. doi:10.1234/12345678

Rianon, N. J. & Shelton, A. J. (2003). Perception of spousal abuse expressed by married Bangladeshi immigrant women in Houston, Texas, U.S.A. *Journal of Immigrant Health, 5*(1), 37–44.

Rogler, L. H., Cortés, D. E., & Malgady, R. G. (1991). Acculturation and mental health status among Hispanics: Convergence and new directions for research. *American Psychologist, 46*, 585–597. doi:10.1037/0003–066X.46.6.585

Rudmin, F. W. (2003). Critical history of the acculturation psychology of assimilation, separation, integration, and marginalization. *Review of General Psychology, 7*, 3–37.

Ryder, A. G., Alden, L. E., & Paulhus, D. L. (2000). Is acculturation unidimensional or bidimensional? A head to head comparison in the prediction of personality, self-identity, and adjustment. *Journal of Personality and Social Psychology, 79*(1), 77–88.

Salcido, O. & Adelman, M. (2004). "He has me tied with the blessed and damned papers": Undocumented-immigrant battered women in Phoenix, Arizona. *Human Organization, 63*(2), 162–172.

Schwartz, S. J. & Zamboanga, B. L. (2008). Testing Berry's models of acculturation: A confirmatory latent class approach. *Cultural Diversity and Ethnic Minority Psychology, 14*, 275–285.

Sellers, R.M., Smith, M., Shelton, J.N., Rowley, S., & Chavous, T.M. (1998). The multidimensional model of racial identity: A reconceptualization of African American racial identity. *Personality and Social Psychology Review, 2*(1), 18–39.

Sellers, S. L., Ward, E. C., & Pate, D. (2006). Dimensions of depression: A qualitative study of wellbeing among Black African immigrant women. *Qualitative Social Work: Research and Practice, 5*, 45–66. doi:10.1177/1473325006061538

Seto, A. & Woodford, M. S. (2007). Helping a Japanese immigrant family cope with acculturation issues: A case study. *The Family Journal, 15*, 167–173. doi:10.1177/10664807062979587

Shi, X. & Lu, X. (2007). Bilingual and bicultural development of Chinese American adolescents and young adults: A comparative study. *The Howard Journal of Communications, 18*, 313–333. doi:10.1080/10646170701653677

Szapocznik, J., Kurtines, W., & Fernandez, T. (1980). Bicultural involvement and adjustment in Hispanic-American youths. *International Journal of Intercultural Relations, 4*, 353–365.

Szapocznik, J., Santisteban, D., Kurtines, W. M., Perez-Vidal, A., & Hervis, O. E. (1984). Bicultural Effectiveness Training (BET): A treatment intervention for enhancing intercultural adjustment. *Hispanic Journal of Behavioral Sciences, 6*, 317–344.

Tajfel, H. (1981). *Human groups and social categories*. Cambridge, UK: Cambridge University Press.

Takeuchi, D. T., Zane, N., Hong, S., Chae, D. H., Gong, F., Gee, G. C., Walton, E., et al. (2007). Immigration-related factors and mental disorders among Asian Americans. *American Journal of Public Health, 97*, 84–90. doi:10.2105/AJPH.2006.088401

Usita, P. M., & Du Bois, B. C. (2005). Conflict sources and responses in mother–daughter relationships: Perspectives of adult daughters of aging immigrant women. *Journal of Women and Aging, 17*, 151–165. doi:10.1300/J074v17n01_11

Weisskirch, R. S. & Alva, S. A. (2002). Language brokering and the acculturation of Latino children. *Hispanic Journal of Behavioral Sciences, 24*, 369–378. doi:10.1177/0739986302024003007

Zamboanga, B., Raffaelli, M., & Horton, N. (2006). Acculturation status and heavy alcohol use among Mexican American college students: Investigating the moderating role of gender. *Addictive Behaviors, 31*, 2188–2198. doi:10.1016/j.addbeh.2006.02.018

Zea, M. C., Asner-Self, K. K., Birman, D., & Buki, L. P. (2003). The abbreviated Multidimensional Acculturation Scale: Empirical validation with two Latino/Latina samples. *Cultural Diversity and Ethnic Minority Psychology, 9*, 107–126. doi:10.1037/10999809.9.2.107

Chapter 3

Theories of Family Therapy

Julie Shulman and Garima Lamba

Contents

Many have begun to draw attention to and critique the previous, dominant focus on acculturation in therapy with immigrant families (Strier, 1996; Turner, 1991), an approach that has often viewed the therapist's primary role as one of an agent of assimilation to the new culture. Research suggests, however, that immigrant families who maintain a balance between retaining pieces of their home culture while incorporating parts of the new (in other words, who find an *integration* of the different cultures) (Berry, Kim, & Boski, 1988) experience the best outcomes (Beckerman & Corbett, 2008; Berry et al., 1988; Berry, Kim, Power, Young, & Bujaki, 1989; Coatsworth, Maldonado-Molina, Pantin, & Szapocznik, 2005).

Maintaining some values and customs from the country of origin may be better for the mental health of the family members (Darvies & McKelvey, 1998; Hsu, Davies, & Zane, 2004; Le & Stockdale, 2005). Moreover, involvement in ethnic community networks in the new country is also critical in buffering against discrimination, creating some continuity, and coping with some of the inevitable social and cultural losses. Indeed, recreating ethnic community networks highly correlates with general health and mental health as well (Berry, 2001; Vega, Kolody, Valle, & Weir, 1991).

Twenty-First-Century Immigrants

New immigrants differ in some key ways from previous generations who moved to the United States with few ties maintained with or intentions of returning to the home country. One major difference is that among today's immigrants, there are often lengthier separations between immigrant family members (Falicov, 2007; Pottinger, Stair, & Brown, 2008; Turner, 1991). In the immigration patterns of families from the Caribbean to the United States, "migratory separation … is a fairly common practice" (Pottinger et al., 2008, p. 15), in which a family seasonally migrates (a parent migrates for several months at a time), serial migrates (a parent migrates first and later sends for the rest of the family), or parentally migrates (a parent or parents migrate, leaving children behind to be reared in the home country). Many maintain these transnational relationships indefinitely. In distinguishing between previous and today's immigrants, Falicov (2007) aptly described the former as living "with a broken heart" (p. 157) and the latter as dealing with "the ambiguities of living with two hearts" (p. 158). Family therapy with today's immigrant families needs to address these newer ambiguities that can accompany transnational relationships. Novel therapeutic approaches, such as those involving virtual (e.g., Internet) connections and unique rituals of relationship, need to be readily incorporated into our work. In many ways, the inherent challenges in letting go of some of the old and adapting to some of the new may be exacerbated for transnational families who have continued connections to their home culture. These connections can make attempts to adapt to the new culture seem particularly unappealing and perhaps even unnecessary for some family members. With the collaborative efforts of counselors to help families find helpful balances that work for each member, those families who straddle two worlds, with "two hearts," may in fact be uniquely positioned to adapt anew without giving up all that is old.

Another major shift is the significant feminization of migration patterns (Falicov, 2007; Pottinger et al., 2008). More often than ever before, women are migrating independently, sometimes without their children, who stay back in the home country with extended family members. Research has suggested that female immigrants from diverse places such as Latin America, China, and Iran tend to adapt to mainstream American values and customs, including those related to sex and marriage, faster than males from the same regions (Chia et al., 1985; Chung, 2001; Espin, 1987; Hojat et al., 2000). Called acculturative dissonance (Rumbaut & Portes, 2002) and more commonly a phenomenon that occurs cross-generationally (Farver, Narang, & Badha, 2002; Le & Stockdale, 2008; Rumbaut & Portes, 2002), these tensions involving familial differences in levels of assimilation to a new country are a common impetus among immigrant families for seeking therapy. This acculturative dissonance between men and women, along with the fact that women are often preceding male partners in the immigration process, may raise important, new issues related to acculturation for the family therapist to address.

The feminization of the immigration process may also require that counselors reconsider many assumptions the field of family therapy holds about the parent–child, typically mother–child, attachment. Historically and within a Western framework, attachment to a primary caregiver has been viewed as a universal task of infancy (Ainsworth, 1968; Main, Tomasini, & Tolan, 1979). However, recent cross-cultural research on infant attachment suggests that in many collectivist cultures, this crucial developmental task need not be associated with a single caregiver (van IJzendoorn & Sagi, 2008). Indeed, infants in many collectivist cultures form secure attachments to multiple caregivers, suggesting that the mental health of a child is not as dependent on the accessibility of the parent, most notably the mother, as has been typically assumed. In communities where several adults act as caregivers and are actively involved in the rearing of the child, separations from the parent may not necessarily be a critical concern. However, having these secure attachments to caregivers in the country of origin, children can experience relational difficulties when reunited with the parent(s) in the new country. For example, among Caribbean families, for whom this pattern (of the mother immigrating before her children and the family often living apart for several years) is quite common, some have posited that challenges related to the separation–reunion phenomenon are the most frequent presenting concerns in family therapy (Smith, Lalonde, & Johnson, 2004).

Multigenerational Family Therapy

Bowenian theory has been described as having the most comprehensive view of human behavior and human problems of any approach to family treatment (Nichols & Schwartz, 2006). Bowen was one of the early pioneers who paid attention to the larger network of family relationships. The primary emphasis in this model was to provide a theory of family functioning with the model of therapy and interventions as secondary concerns.

According to Bowen (1978), the core goal of therapy is differentiation of self, namely, the ability to remain oneself in the face of group influences, most importantly the intense influence of the family. Bowen addressed two kinds of differentiation: the highly differentiated individuals who display a solid sense of self with behaviors that are guided primarily by their intellect (rather than emotions), and the individuals with lower levels of differentiation, with a negotiable sense of self, whose behaviors are guided primarily by their emotions. Bowen's Western notion of rationality and objectivity in the differentiation of self may not be applicable to many immigrant families within which members' sense of self are guided by the roles ascribed to them by their culture and for whom emotion plays a more accepted, even valued, role in guiding behavior. Sluzki (1979) addressed the inherent conflict between the egalitarian orientation of the Western cultures and the more autocratic orientation of other cultures (e.g., East Indian and Costa Rican). In families from other cultures, "mutual dependence may be equated with loyalty" (p. 388). For example, in Asian immigrant families, rather than an "I" identity, the family members are taught to embrace a "we" identity. Individuals do not stand alone but rather are seen as a product of their family and the generations before them (Lee & Mock, 2005). A therapist who approaches the family with the belief that differentiation is healthy for better adjustment of family members might not be received well by the family, perhaps resulting in premature termination.

Bowen (1978) believed that the family was an "emotionally interdependent unit," which meant that changes in one part of the family system will inevitably result in changes in other parts and ultimately in the whole family. He further claimed that families exert homeostasis, that is, they strongly promote conformity on each member's behaviors to maintain equilibrium (Walsh & McGraw, 1996). Among immigrant families, the differential rates of adaptation and acculturation of parents and adolescents often polarize the family and lead to intergenerational conflicts (Baptiste, 1987; Farver et al., 2002; Landau-Stanton, 1985; Le & Stockdale, 2008; Rumbaut & Portes, 2002). In Asian American immigrant families, one of the major responsibilities of all family members is to avoid bringing shame, or loss of face, to the family. The fear of losing face can be a powerful motivating force for a family member to conform to the family's expectations and may be used to suppress deviation from family norms. Similarly, in immigrant Cuban families, the interests of the family are placed over the interest of an individual and are the basis of traditional Cuban family structure (Bernal, 1982; Queralt, 1984).

Although some immigrant families are mutually interdependent in certain ways that might disadvantage some family members, especially the younger generation, Bowen's ideas about differentiation and taking the "I positions" (Bowen, 1966, 1971, 1978) can be useful in creating different boundaries. Many families have different levels of acculturation even within the family members. For example, first-generation children might be better acculturated or assimilated in the majority culture versus their parents who migrated from the homeland and do not speak English. The "I positions" can be helpful for the family members in understanding where each member is coming from, resulting in healthier communications within the family system. Such an approach, however, should be employed cautiously, as a therapist risks imposing on the family a Western notion of individual expression that might not be appropriate.

Bowenian therapists believe that understanding how family systems operate is more important than techniques. Even though Bowen himself disliked techniques, "one essential technique" in the Bowenian family therapy is that of asking process questions. Process questions are designed to slow people down, diminish reactive anxiety, and start them thinking not just about how others are upsetting them but also about how they participate in the interpersonal problems (Nichols & Schwartz, 1991). There is therefore no attempt to actively change the family but an attempt to enlighten their interactions that result in interpersonal problems. This could be very helpful in gaining trust with the immigrant family who might have a general distrust of "an outsider" (the therapist) not understanding the cultural values of the family but trying to change the family functioning.

Structural Family Therapy

The structural family therapy model, developed by Salvador Minuchin at Philadelphia's Child Guidance Clinic, emphasizes structural change as the main goal of therapy, which is considered more important than the details of individual change. It is a therapy of action with the focus on modifying the present, not on exploring and interpreting the past. Because the past was instrumental in the creation of the family's present organization and functioning, it is conceived as being present now and will be available to change by interventions that change the present (Minuchin, 1974).

Immigrants bring a lot of rich and complex history with them when they seek therapy. Mostly, the presenting concerns are imbedded in or are intimately connected with the history of the family's immigration to the United States. Some of these concerns may include the circumstances that necessitated migration; the values, rules, and roles in the traditional culture left behind; and the process of adjusting to varied differences in the new culture. Without an understanding or knowledge of the losses and changes sustained in the immigration process, the therapist might base interventions solely on the presenting concerns without addressing the context of the immigration process. In so doing, she or he may lose credibility with the family, along with missing important therapeutic opportunities (Levenback & Lewak, 1995). Exploring the immigration history with the family can also help children understand the origins of differences between their and their parents' values and behaviors (e.g., the kind of cultural environment the parents were brought up in, rules and values in parents' home culture).

According to this model, even though no clear lines exist between healthy and unhealthy families, healthy families are seen as able to modify their structure to cope with or accommodate to the changing circumstances. The basic goal of structural family therapy is the restructuralization of the family's system of transactional rules, such that the interactional reality of the family becomes more flexible, with an expanded availability of alternative ways of dealing with each other (Colapinto, 2000).

One of the important techniques in this structural change is that of enactment. In this, the family members are encouraged to deal directly with each other in sessions while the therapist observes and modifies these unhealthy interactions. This technique may not work with some immigrant families for whom roles of the family members are formal and rigid. There might be reluctance on the part of some family members to openly challenge and deal directly with the conflict with other family members, especially in front of the "outsiders." For example, in a majority of East Indian immigrant families, the relationship of the parents with children is formal and vertical with regard to age and gender, and communication and authority flow downward consistent with a hierarchical order of position and status (Baptiste, 2005). East Indian parents accept as their duty the care of their children, and children's reciprocated duty is to unquestionably respect and honor their parents (Baptiste, 2005). A family with such rigidly ascribed roles might be resistant to any structural change, and there is a likelihood of early termination if the parents feel challenged in front of their children by the therapists.

Structural family therapy, however, talks of reestablishing the power hierarchical patterns within families with clear boundaries between the subsystems. For example, the spousal subsystem has clear boundaries with the children, the parents, and other subsystems. The clear boundary enables children to interact with their parents but excludes them from the spousal subsystem (Nichols & Schwartz, 2006). This is a useful concept for many immigrant families with hierarchical family orientations. Jalali (2005), while writing on Iranian families, mentioned that structural and strategic family therapies are two of the most effective techniques with Iranian immigrant families. She further stated that Iranian families usually respond positively to directives and may actually request them. This may be similar for many other immigrant families who see therapy as a venue to receive concrete guidance.

Structural family therapy conceptualizes family as a living open system that is in constant transformation:

> This transformation or evolution is regulated by the interplay of homeostasis and change. Homeostasis designates the patterns of transactions that assure the stability of the system, the maintenance of its basic characteristics as they can be described at a certain point of time; homeostatic processes tend to keep the status quo (Jackson, 1957, 1965). Change is the re accommodation that the living system undergoes in order to adjust to a different set of environmental circumstances or to an intrinsic developmental need. (Colapinto, 2000, p. 145)

For most immigrant families, homeostasis and change are essential and necessary aspects of retaining the cultural values while adjusting to the new culture. In many cultures, roles, rules, and responsibilities are prescribed from a traditional upbringing. For example, in Latino culture *machismo* is the term used to describe the cultural norm for male behavior. *Machismo* refers to the man's responsibility to provide for, protect, and defend his family (Mayo, 1997). When moving to a new country, because of limited economic resources, all members of the family might need to work outside of the home. This can often result in changing gender roles, especially for women, which can present new challenges, including threatening a man's sense of *machismo*. In addition, the second-generation family members may embrace and adapt to the mainstream culture, which can further result in confusion and conflict, hence disrupting the homeostasis of the familial environment.

The therapist's role, according to the structural family therapy model, is somewhat of a paradox; the therapist aims to support while challenging, attack while encouraging, and sustain while undermining the system (Colapinto, 2000). Although this role has some obvious benefits in encouraging the structural change in some immigrant families, there are also some distinctive drawbacks. One of the obvious benefits is that the therapist will be able to experience firsthand the structural functioning of the immigrant family and be able to suggest some changes while being sensitive to the family's cultural values. Some immigrant families, such as those from Vietnam, are reluctant to seek help and prefer to resolve problems among family members by dealing with them within the family circle (Leung & Boehnlein, 2005). For a therapist to take on the paradoxical role of an attacker and an encourager of the system, he or she needs to display both ascribed and achieved credibility (Baptiste, 2005) not only to be able to navigate the system skillfully but also to do so in a culturally knowledgeable way to gain the family's trust and thus the desired structural change. Baptiste (2005) discussed the critical importance of ascribed credibility in working with East Indian immigrant families. This is likely true when working with any immigrant family.

Strategic Family Therapy

The Washington School of Strategic Family Therapy was organized by Jay Haley and Cloé Madanes in the mid-1970s (Keim, 2000). In strategic family therapy, therapy begins when the client makes the first contact with the therapist, followed by the therapist and client working collaboratively. Strategic family therapy has diverse approaches, but all share certain common characteristics (Madanes, 1981). One primary component is that it is the therapist's responsibility to plan a strategy for solving the client's problems (Haley, 1963, 1967, 1976). The clear goals set by the therapist always involve solving the presenting problem that the clients bring into therapy. The emphasis is on designing a strategy for each specific problem rather than applying a particular method (Madanes, 1981).

In this approach, there is an emphasis on hierarchy, with parents in charge of their children, and all cross-generation coalitions, such as one parent siding with a child against another parent, are blocked (Madanes, 1981). Interventions in this family therapy usually take place in the form of directives. Family members are encouraged to do something, both inside and outside the sessions, to change the ways that the members relate to each other. Directives are deliberately planned, with no emphasis on insight and understanding by the family. The general expectation is that with the changes in therapy, families will be able to transfer the learning to other areas of their life and thus continue to change. Essentially, the moment the presenting symptoms subside, the therapy is considered complete.

The approach's brief, pragmatic, and problem-focused emphasis would translate well for many immigrant cultural families who are looking for "solutions" to the presenting problem and do not necessarily want to understand the origins of their concerns for various reasons. Irish immigrants may experience embarrassment about having problems and so may be reticent to let anyone know about them (Donlon-Farry, 1998). So, most likely when Irish immigrants do seek therapy for what they acknowledge as a problem, they might be most comfortable with quick solutions to the presenting concerns. McGoldrick (2005) mentioned that structured therapy, focused specifically on the presenting concern, will be most helpful and least threatening to these clients.

Because of the active, powerful role of the therapist in this approach (Thomas, 1992), this therapy might also be effective with immigrant families with hierarchical family orientations who respond well to directives that come from an expert in the field. Richeport-Haley (1998) found strategic family therapy to be a culturally congruent approach when working with families of Spanish, South American, and Japanese origins. In another study, Soo-Hoo (1999) found this family therapy model to be a culturally good fit when working with Chinese American families. Jalali (2005) mentioned that Iranian families respond well to directives, and strategic family therapy might be one such effective approach.

The nonemphasis on the history of the immigrant family, however, might not be helpful to those whose presenting concerns are embedded in the immigration trauma. Simply getting rid of the presenting concerns might be a short-term approach to longer term issues that might come up, wrapped in a different package, later on. Another danger is that by not addressing the immigration history and its effects on the family, the therapist might lose credibility with the family along with missing important therapeutic opportunities (Levenback & Lewak, 1995).

In this approach, the therapist actively tries to promote change by using directives that are an overt or covert message from the therapist to the client. These directives encourage clients to take an action or make some sort of change in relation to the presenting problem. This approach encourages therapists to consider the cultures and personalities of the clients while delivering the directives (Keim, 2000). According to Griffin and Greene (1999), therapy is most successful when therapists and clients can identify the problem and recognize the interactional patterns surrounding the problem, and the clients are able to *carry out these directives* given by their therapist. For those immigrant families who are hesitant to follow a therapist's directive but who find it difficult to question the "expert," covert messages from the therapist in the form of indirect directives might be useful in bringing about change. An indirect directive also does not put much pressure on the clients to follow through, with a freedom to reject the directive without feeling that it would hurt the therapist's feelings (Keim, 2000).

The Washington School of Strategic Family Therapy believes that therapists should practice in a flexible, humanistic, and skillful fashion (Keim, 2000). The therapy uses the client's own language and metaphors around problems thereby helping therapists establish strong, genuine, and trusting relationships, conducive to constructive change. It is tailored to the unique needs of each client without relying on a "one size fits all" approach. This is especially useful in working with immigrant families whose diverse cultural backgrounds demand unique treatment.

Communication/Validation Process Family Therapy

Satir is arguably the foremother of family therapy, and her communication and validation process therapy served to model for other therapists the central importance of human contact (Satir, Banmen, Gerber, & Gamori, 1991; Satir & Bitter, 2000). She is known for her emphasis on authentic personal presence and her utmost faith in the potential of all people, and her model of family therapy rests on the assumption that people are growth oriented. As such, her communication- and validation-based approach emphasizes a focus on family resources and strengths rather than "problems," per se. Taken even further, what are typically viewed by therapists and families alike as "problems" are not the concern in Satir's model; rather, it is how families cope with these stressors that can cause distress. Indeed, she believed that when families engage with one another congruently (Satir et al., 1991), they use language that accurately captures each member's experience and their verbal and nonverbal communication matches, and they can handle (inevitable) stress without becoming distressed. This style of communication requires an open and honest directness, core to the validation process therapeutic approach.

A central tenet of this model is the notion that anything that happens to upset the balance of the system, dubbed a foreign element, "requires the system to address what will happen in largely unknown territory" (Satir & Bitter, 2000, p. 77). When the family cannot expel the foreign element, "a space, place, or context has to be made to help in receiving what is new to the family process." Such a course aptly explains the immigration process, whereby a family very evidently must adapt to many foreign elements. Although the necessary rearrangement of the family system, according to Satir, is accompanied by chaos, new possibilities can be found out of that confusion. This incorporation of fresh possibilities, whereby newly integrated possibilities become second nature, is similar to the process of integration articulated by Berry (2003).

Goals

Goals of Satir's family therapy include generating hope, building on or creating coping skills, and helping develop options among family members, always focused on growth rather than on "problems." In so doing, Satir saw the personhood or humanness of the therapist as more central than a specific skill set. In particular, the therapist models congruence and responds to any lack thereof among the family members in a nonjudgmental manner. Part of being fully human means utilizing the physical, as well as other, parts of the self. Family sculpting, a well-known family therapy technique popularized by Satir, involves making body postures of the family interaction patterns and can readily incorporate those members not present. In fact, including virtual families or connections (Falicov, 2007), crucial especially in working with transnational families, can naturally extend from Satir's utilization of movement, touch, and other forms of sensory connection.

Another commonly used technique, the family life fact chronology (FLFC), entails chronologically listing all significant events in the family over a set period of time, an intervention that can be particularly helpful in piecing together potentially disjointed pieces of an immigration process. For family members who underwent different immigration processes, the FLFC can afford the family an opportunity to learn about and from their unique and overlapping experiences. Also, metaphor, frequently used to speak symbolically with families, may be useful with certain groups, such as with many Latinos(as), for whom proverb and other symbolically rich language serve as important vehicles for communicating values and norms (Arrendondo et al., 2006). However, it is important to note that with some immigrant families, such as with those from some Asian countries of origin who communicate in more concrete language, the use of metaphor may be less appropriate, confusing, and perhaps even threatening. Dramatic enactments, and other experiential interventions, can help some families express and make sense of family metaphors, struggles, and stories. Falicov (2007) described one school-based, multiple-family group counseling program in Canada in which families collaborated in writing and performing a play characterizing one mother's emigration from the Philippines and later reunion with her spouse and children. They were able to enrich the play with details of the Philippines, the various reasons for the emigration, and the effects on all the family members. This intervention is a good example of the use of drama to chronicle the immigration experience for a family. Moreover, experiential interventions can serve as a creative forum by which therapists can access and utilize the often rich and meaningful support and direction found in religion for so many immigrant families (Falicov, 2000).

Some practitioners may believe that experiential techniques can seem strange to a number of people, thereby potentially creating discomfort for new clients; however, for immigrants who may experience therapy as wholly foreign, such techniques may not be experienced as particularly threatening. On the other hand, for some families who are accustomed to a medical model and view the family therapist as an extension of the medical professional, or as the "expert," introducing experiential interventions such as family sculpting might reduce the therapist's credibility. In discussing therapeutic issues in working with East Indian immigrant families, Baptiste (2005) discussed the difference between ascribed credibility (that which the family assigns, based on therapist knowledge of relevant cultural and familial factors) and achieved credibility (therapist clinical skills). The former, he emphasized, is particularly critical. Not only is it important to be knowledgeable of our clients' worldview to adequately and accurately understand and empathize with them, but Baptiste also suggested that maximizing ascribed credibility can compensate for gaps in our achieved credibility. Of course, multicultural competence also entails knowing what clinical techniques are more likely to be helpful and appropriate for different clients, and becoming familiar with the cultures of origin among clients can help therapists to use culturally fitting clinical skills and techniques. Nevertheless, enhancing clients' perceived credibility of the therapist as trustworthy can go a long way in helping myriad clients become more amenable to a variety of techniques (e.g., family sculpting).

Although Satir had a positive reputation for being able to work effectively with families from varying ethnic backgrounds, her emphasis on direct, clear, and very open communication may not be appropriate for all immigrant families. For instance, such open sharing of feelings is discouraged in many Asian cultures (Wong & Mock, 1997). In addressing family separations as part of the immigration experience for many families, Falicov (2007) discussed how "controlling or resigning oneself by blocking affect may ... in many ethnic groups ... be reinforced by culture, religion, or social class circumstances" (p. 162). She went on to suggest that "a middle ground that encourages clients to maintain connections through actions, however tenuous, is a plausible therapeutic compromise between encouraging open expression of painful affects and complete avoidance of remembrance by blocking of feelings" (p. 162), a fitting approach that modifies Satir's push for fully open and direct communication. To be sure, for families who maintain a high-context communication style, wherein more relative reliance is placed on nonverbal and contextual cues for communication, encouraging a complete openness could be culturally inappropriate. However, others of Satir's techniques might succeed precisely where this particular therapeutic focus may fall short. Specifically, for families who engage in high-context communication styles, the use of metaphors, images, body postures, and dramatic enactments are likely to be welcomed and quite useful.

Seeing the family as internally resourceful may be very empowering to an immigrant family that might experience disempowerment, including a common, explicit lack of recognition for their existing culture-based sources of strength, in the new country. Because the family members may have a different worldview that may obscure them, helping them identify these resources can be challenging for an American therapist. Doing so, however, can be quite validating to the family members who might expect more of the same disregard for their cultural practices from an American therapist as that experienced in the larger, new culture. Exploring and focusing on the family members' attributes, talents, environmental strengths, and aspirations can be empowering for a family who might be accustomed to Americans (at their best) wanting to "help" them. Nonetheless, immigrants, especially those who have recently immigrated, may not have all the tangible knowledge and skills needed to thrive in the new country, so providing some external resources (e.g., information on enrolling children in school, instruction on utilizing public transportation) may be helpful and, at times, necessary.

Narrative Family Therapy

Narrative family therapy is grounded in postmodern theory, which views all knowledge as narrative or story. Rather than language representing some external and fixed reality, separate from the language itself, it is said to always reflect a dynamic, coconstruction of meaning. In other words, narrative family therapy is concerned with how families construct their social realities, their identities, and their stories. Their social realities are not created in isolation from one another or from the communities, cultures, and periods of time within which they engage. Somewhat similar to Satir's approach to family therapy, narrative family therapy does not focus on pathology or dysfunction. Instead, narrative therapists fully participate with families in deconstructing how a particular "problem" became storied into existence and cocreating a different story. This new "storying" can entail challenging the status quo, which may have gone unquestioned up until that point. The therapist, then, collaborates with the family in deconstructing restrictive or oppressive realities and coconstructing new ones by melting "the system of languaged interaction that had coalesced around the problem issues" (Kogan & Gale, 2000, pp. 216–217).

Perhaps not surprisingly, a narrative family therapist adopts a not-knowing posture toward the clients. Indeed, the therapist engages with the family in an ongoing questioning of any taken-for-granted body of knowledge. As such, the therapist helps elucidate how the "problem … got talked into being, and how it might be related to cultural stories" (Kogan & Gale, 2000, p. 217). As the new client stories are constructed, the therapist remains attentive to the dominant social discourses at play within the client's life outside of as well as inside the therapy room.

Indeed, although all reality, and so all narrative, is seen as nonessential (i.e., is socially constructed), it is not constructed in a vacuum, separate from dominant discourses. All meaning is considered to be intimately connected to systems of power. The production of meaning attached to acculturation, then, is tied to systems of power in the United States. Not all identities, stories, and experiences are accorded equal legitimacy. For immigrant families, for whom English is usually either a second language or not known at all and whose cultural practices, values, and styles of dress may differ from the dominant norms of the United States, their narratives are not the dominant stories, and their stories do not garner the same level of recognition, acceptance, or legitimacy as the dominant narratives. Desires for a family's story to be accepted may lead family members, in particular adolescents and children, to find ways to gain a voice. Narrative therapy is one medium by which they can begin to do this.

A very commonly used technique in narrative work is that of externalization. When working with immigrant families, a therapist can utilize the externalizing of the problematized narrative to create some distance between it and the possibility of burgeoning new stories. In so doing, the therapist can explore exceptions to the problem-saturated family narrative, helping to identify discourses that contributed to the development of this narrative as well as alternative stories (Monk, 1996). Similarly, "restorying" the past, including the immigration process, can help prioritize preferred narratives that may have become clouded by current predicaments.

Given the prevalence of transnational connections among today's immigrants, family members may engage in what Turner (1991) described as "a circular, connecting and reconnecting pattern between two places, bridging geographical locations and distinctive meaning systems" (p. 407), creating a reality involving dominant stories from (at least) two different contexts. As discussed, narrative therapy provides a lens through which new stories can be constructed. Perhaps most pertinent, the narrative approach to family therapy appositely lends itself to an integration of multiple stories, stories from multiple cultures or contexts. Such an integration is useful for all immigrant families, and perhaps particularly so for those who maintain transnational relationships. Despite that there are better outcomes for families who maintain some level of integrated biculturalism (Berry, 1990), many family therapists continue to focus on helping families adapt to the new culture. A narrative approach can encourage and provide an avenue for the therapist to join the family in bridging these stories and cocreating new ones in the process.

Conclusion

With the ever-increasing diversity among immigrant families in the United States, each with distinct cultural norms and values, varying migration, and living arrangements, as well as unique familial patterns, the validity and usefulness of traditional models of family therapy may be outdated, at least when universally applied. Family therapists are finding it increasingly necessary to both select relevant techniques among various models and fit their approaches to the needs of the clients rather than the other way around (Nichols & Schwartz, 2006).

Even though some immigrant families might not bring migration history as one of their explicitly stated presenting concerns, it is an important, often life-changing, experience that impacts the emotional well-being of most immigrant families. As such, regardless of the approach or combination of approaches used in family therapy, it is important that the therapist addresses not only the circumstances surrounding the migration but also the factors that led to it. This understanding can assist the therapist in helping the immigrant family negotiate the balance of adapting to a new culture while preserving ties with the family and community of origin (Levenbach & Lewak, 1995).

Family therapists need to be flexible in their therapeutic approaches, displaying an understanding of the need, and a willingness, to modify or integrate them. For example, many families from a host of different cultures place considerable value on religion and spirituality (Baptiste, 2005) and indigenous treating agents (Fadiman, 1997). In those families, it is important that therapists both have an understanding of the particular role that religion or spirituality plays in the family and incorporate indigenous agents appropriately in their treatment of the presenting concerns.

Lastly, culturally specific considerations are critical in successful counseling with immigrant families (Marsella, 1993). Sometimes, an immigrant family's cultural values and norms are very different from those of the therapist, which necessitates an approach based on informed knowledge of the culture and background of the clients. Family therapists need to be careful, however, not to generalize cultural stereotypes to their clients. Therefore, it is crucial that we allow these known cultural norms to inform our working hypotheses when working with immigrant families while also maintaining a self-awareness of how our own beliefs and customs influence our assumptions.

References

Ainsworth, M. D. S. (1968). Object relations, dependency, and attachment: A theoretical review of the infant–mother relationship. *Child Development, 40*, 969–1025.

Arrendondo, P., Aviles, R. M. D., Zalaquett, C. P., Grazioso, M. D. P., Bordes, V., Hita, L., & Lopez, B. J. (2006). The psychohistorical approach in family: Counseling with Mestizo/Latino immigrants; A continuum and synergy of worldviews. *The Family Journal: Counseling and Therapy for Couples and Families, 14*(1), 13–27.

Baptiste, D. (1987). Family therapy with Spanish heritage immigrant families in cultural transition. *Contemporary Family Therapy, 9*(4), 229–251.

Baptiste, D. A. (2005). Family therapy with East Indian immigrant parents rearing children in the United States: Parental concerns, therapeutic issues, and recommendations. *Contemporary Family Therapy, 27*(3), 345–366.

Beckerman, N. L. & Corbett, L. (2008). Immigration and families: Treating acculturative stress from a systemic framework. *Family Therapy, 35*(2), 63–81.

Bernal, G. (1982). Cuban families. In M. McGoldrick, J. K. Pearce, & J. Giordano (Eds.), *Ethnicity and family therapy* (pp. 187–207). New York: Guilford.

Berry, J. W. (2001). A psychology of immigration. *Journal of Social Issues, 57,* 615–631.

Berry, J. W. (2003). Conceptual approaches to acculturation. In K. M. Chun, P. B. Organista, & G. Marín (Eds.), *Acculturation: Advances in theory, measurement and applied research* (pp. 17–37). Washington, DC: American Psychological Association.

Berry, J. W. (1990). Psychology of acculturation: Understanding individuals moving between cultures. In R. W. Brislin (Ed.), *Applied cross-cultural psychology* (pp. 232–253). Newbury Park, CA: Sage.

Berry, J. W., Kim, U., & Boski, M. (1988). Acculturation and mental health: A review. In P. Dassen, J. W. Berry, & N. Satorius (Eds.), *Cross-cultural psychology and health* (pp. 207–236). Newbury Park, CA: Sage.

Berry, J. W., Kim, U., Power, S., Young, M., & Bujaki, M. (1989). Acculturation attitudes in plural societies. *Applied Psychology, 38,* 185–206.

Bowen, M. (1966). The use of family theory in clinical practice. *Comprehensive Psychiatry, 7,* 345–374.

Bowen, M. (1971). Family therapy and family group therapy. In H. Kaplan & B. Sadok (Eds.), *Comprehensive group psychotherapy* (pp. 384–421). Baltimore: Williams & Wilkins.

Bowen, M. (1978). *Family therapy in clinical practice.* New York: Jason Aronson.

Chia, R. C., Chaung, C. J., Cheng, B. S., Castellow, W., Moore, C. H., & Hayes, M. (1985). Attitudes toward marriage roles among Chinese and American college students. *Journal of Social Psychology, 126*(1), 31–35.

Chung, R. H. G. (2001). Gender, ethnicity, and acculturation in intergenerational conflict of Asian American college students. *Cultural Diversity and Ethnic Minority Psychology, 7*(4), 376–386.

Coatsworth, J. D., Maldonado-Molina, M., Pantin, H., & Szapocznik, J. (2005). A person-centered and ecological investigation of acculturation strategies in Hispanic immigrant youth. *Journal of Community Psychology, 33*(2), 157–174.

Colapinto, J. (2000). Structural family therapy. In A. M. Horne (Ed.), *Family counseling and therapy* (3rd ed., pp. 140–169). Itasca, IL: F. E. Peacock.

Darvies, L. G., & McKelvey, R. S. (1998). Emotional and behavioral problems and competencies among immigrant and non-immigrant adolescents. *Australian and New Zealand Journal of Psychiatry, 35*(5), 658–665.

Donlon-Farry, E. (1998). A profile of recent Irish immigrants and their cross-cultural adaptation difficulties: Clinical and service implications. *Journal of Multicultural Social Work, 6*(3), 93–109.

Espin, O. (1987). Psychological impact of migration on Latinas: Implications for psychotherapeutic practice. *Psychology of Women Quarterly, 11*(4), 489–503.

Fadiman, A. (1997). *The spirit catches you and you fall down.* New York: Farrar, Straus, & Giroux.

Falicov, C. J. (2000). *Latino families in therapy: A guide to multicultural practice.* New York: Guilford.

Falicov, C. J. (2007). Working with transnational immigrants: Expanding meanings of family, community, and culture. *Family Process*, *46*(2), 157–171.

Farver, J. A. M., Narang, S. K., & Badha, B. R. (2002). East meets West: Ethnic identity, acculturation, and conflict in Asian Indian families. *Journal of Family Psychology*, *16*(3), 338–350.

Griffin, W. A. & Greene, S. M. (1999). *Models of family therapy: The essential guide.* Philadelphia: Taylor & Francis.

Haley, J. (1963). *Strategies of psychotherapy.* New York: Grune and Stratton.

Haley, J. (1967). *Advanced techniques of hypnosis and therapy: The selected papers of Milton H. Erickson.* New York: Grune and Stratton.

Haley, J. (1976). *Problem-solving therapy: New strategies for effective family therapy.* San Francisco: Jossey-Bass.

Hojat, M., Shapurian, R., Foroughi, D., Nayerahmadi, H., Farzaneh, M., Shafieyan, M., & Parsi, M. (2000). Gender differences in traditional attitudes toward marriage and the family. *Journal of Family Issues*, *21*(4), 419–434.

Hsu, E., Davies, C. A., & Hansen, D. J. (2004). Understanding mental health needs of Southeast Asian refugees: Historical, cultural, and contextual challenges. *Clinical Psychology Review*, *24*(2), 193–213.

Jackson, D. D. (1957). The question of family homeostatis. *Psychiatric Quarterly Supplement*, *31*, 79–90.

Jackson, D. D. (1965). The study of the family. *Family Process*, *4*, 1–20.

Jalali, B. (2005). Iranian families. In M. McGoldrick, J. Giordano, & N. Garcia-Preto (Eds.), *Ethnicity and family therapy* (pp. 451–467). New York: Guilford.

Keim, J. (2000). Strategic family therapy: The Washington School. In A. M. Horne (Eds.), *Family counseling and therapy* (pp. 170–207). Itasca, IL: F. E. Peacock.

Kogan, S. M. & Gale, J. E. (2000). Taking a narrative turn: Social constructionism and family therapy. In A. M. Horne (Ed.), *Family counseling and therapy* (3rd ed., pp. 208–242). Itasca, IL: F. E. Peacock.

Landau-Stanton, J. (1985). Adolescents, families, and cultural transition: A treatment model. In M. Mirkin & S. Koman (Eds.), *Handbook of adolescent and family therapy* (pp. 363–381). New York: Gardner Press.

Le, T.N. & Stockdale, G. (2008). Acculturative dissonance, ethnic identity, and youth violence. *Cultural Diversity and Ethnic Minority Psychology*, *14*(1), 1–9.

Lee, E. & Mock, M. R. (2005). Asian families. In M. McGoldrick, J. K. Pearce, & J. Giordano (Eds.), *Ethnicity and family therapy* (pp. 269–289). New York: Guilford.

Leung, P. K. & Boehnlein, J. K. (2005). Vietnamese families. In M. McGoldrick, J. Giordano, & N. Garcia-Preto (Eds.), *Ethnicity and family therapy* (pp. 363–373). New York: Guilford.

Levenback, D. & Lewak, B. (1995). Immigration: Going home or going to pieces. *Contemporary Family Therapy*, *17*(4), 379–395.

Madanes, C. (1981). *Strategic family therapy.* Washington, DC: Jossey-Bass.

Main, M., Tomasini, L., & Tolan, W. (1979). Differences among mothers of infants judged to differ in security. *Developmental Psychology*, *15*, 472–473.

Marsella, A. J. (1993). Counseling and psychotherapy with Japanese Americans: Cross-cultural considerations. *American Journal of Orthopsychiatry*, *63*, 200–208.

Mayo, Y. (1997). Machismo, fatherhood and the Latino family: Understanding the concept. *Journal of Multicultural Social Work, 5*(1), 49–61.

McGoldrick, M. (2005). Irish families. In M. McGoldrick, J. Giordano, & N. Garcia-Preto (Eds.), *Ethnicity and family therapy* (pp. 595–615). New York: Guilford.

Minuchin, S. (1974). *Families and family therapy.* Cambridge, MA: Harvard University Press.

Monk, G. (1996). How narrative therapy works. In G. D. Monk, J. Winslade, K. Crockett, & D. Epston (Eds.), *Narrative therapy in practice: The archaeology of hope* (pp. 3–31). San Francisco: Jossey-Bass.

Nichols, M. P., & Schwartz, R. C. (2006). *Family therapy: Concepts and methods* (7th ed.). Boston: Allyn and Bacon.

Pottinger, A. M., Stair, A. G., & Brown, S. W. (2008). A counseling framework for Caribbean children and families who have experienced migratory separation and reunion. *International Journal for the Advancement of Counseling, 30*(1), 15–24.

Queralt, M. (1984, March–April). Understanding Cuban immigrants: A cultural perspective. *Social Work,* 115–121.

Richeport-Haley, M. (1998). Ethnicity and family therapy: A comparison of brief strategic family therapy and culture-focused therapy. *American Journal of Family Therapy, 26,* 77–90.

Rumbaut, R. G. & Portes, A. (2002). *Ethnicities: Coming of age in immigrant America.* Berkeley: University of California Press.

Satir, V. M. Banmen, J., Gerber, J., & Gamori, M. (1991). *The Satir model: Family therapy and beyond.* Palo Alto, CA: Science & Behavior Books.

Satir, V. M. & Bitter, J. M. (2000). The therapist and family therapy: Satir's human validation process model. In A. M. Horne (Ed.), *Family counseling and therapy* (3rd ed., pp. 62–101). Itasca, IL: F. E. Peacock.

Sluzki, C. E. (1979). Migration and family conflict. *Family Process, 18,* 379–390.

Smith, A., Lalonde, R., & Johnson, S. (2004). Serial migration and its implications for the parent–child relationship: A retrospective analysis of the experience of the children of Caribbean immigrants. *Cultural Diversity and Ethnic Minority Psychology, 10*(2), 107–122.

Soo-Hoo, T. (1999). Brief strategic family therapy with Chinese Americans. *Journal of Family Therapy, 27,* 163–179.

Strier, D. R. (1996). Coping strategies of immigrant parents: Directions for family therapy. *Family Process, 35*(3), 363–376.

Thomas, M. B. (1992). *An introduction to marital and family therapy.* New York: Macmillan.

Turner, J. E. (1991). Migrants and their therapists: A trans-context approach. *Family Process, 30*(4), 407–419.

Van IJzendoorn, M. H. & Sagi, A. (2008). Cross-cultural patterns of attachment: Universal and contextual dimensions. In J. Cassidy & P. Shaver (Eds.), *Handbook of attachment: Theory, research and clinical application* (2nd ed., pp. 713–734). New York: Guilford.

Vega, W. A., Kolody, B., Valle, R., & Weir, J. (1991). Social networks, social support, and their relationship to depression among immigrant Mexican women. *Human Organization, 50*(2), 154–162.

Walsh, W. M. & McGraw, J. A. (1996). *Essentials of family therapy: A therapist's guide to eight approaches.* Denver, CO: Love.

Wong, L. & Mock, M. (1997). Developmental and life cycle issues of Asian Americans: Asian American young adults. In E. Lee (Ed.), *Working with Asian Americans: A guide for clinicians* (pp. 196–207). New York: Guilford.

Chapter 4

Working With Hispanic/Latino(a) Immigrant Families

Adam Zagelbaum

Contents

Hispanic (Latino) groups are described by the U.S. Census Bureau (2000) as Mexican, Mexican American, Puerto Rican, Cuban, Central or South American, or other Hispanic and represent the largest ethnic group in the United States. The number of Latino/Hispanic immigrants is also steadily increasing (Passel & Cohn, 2008). It is actually very difficult to determine accurate census numbers for Hispanic/Latino groups, as unauthorized emigration has continued to be an issue for the United States. A 2008 report by the Pew Research Center estimated that 11.9 million unauthorized immigrants lived in the United States. According to Tienda and Mitchell (2006), despite their common language and ancestral ties to Spain, Hispanics are highly diverse. Altogether they represent 20 Spanish-speaking nationalities, both recent immigrants and families that date back to the first Spanish settlements in what is now the United States. The term *Latino* has emerged within the past decade or so as a more popular and positively accepted term used by this immigrant group as opposed to the more European-influenced and government-developed term of *Hispanic*.

It is also important to note that older Hispanic and Latino(a) individuals compose one of the largest ethnic minority groups in the United States and are expected to be the largest ethnic minority group by 2028 (Federal Interagency Forum on Aging Related Statistics, as cited by Cruza-Guet, Spokane, Caskie, Brown, & Szapocznik, 2008). The potential for multigenerational conflicts within immigrant households, in addition to acculturative stress and other life circumstances, poses further concerns for such families. The need for counseling services in addition to health care support can be one of the greatest challenges for these families to face (Cruza-Guet et al., 2008; Melendez & McDowell, 2008). However, it has been shown that high levels of social support, especially for older Latino(a) clients, can reduce levels of psychological distress and systemically improve family dynamics (Cruza-Guet et al., 2008). This showcases not only a need for counseling professionals to assist these families but also a reciprocal effect that family members can have on one another when provided with effective counseling services. The reasons that these families immigrate to the United States indicate that psychological distress is almost unavoidable as acculturation and adjustment occur.

Reasons for Migrating

The main reasons associated with why residents migrate to other countries include extreme poverty (often due to high rates of unemployment), political and/or religious persecution, and/or lack of opportunities to pursue adequate levels of education or vocational training to improve social and/or economic status. The presence and severity of these types of issues often pressure immigrants to make the difficult choice of coming to the United States illegally. Immigration and documentation issues often cause stress among Latino families as they strive to meet their basic needs and get ahead. This stress may put family members at greater risk of socioemotional problems (Melendez & McDowell, 2008).

It is important to be aware of how the immigration experience has influenced and affected the Latino immigrant community. There is so much that occurs even before an individual or family actually arrives in the United States. Often, it is these earlier experiences that may be responsible for the current socioemotional challenges being faced by individuals (Falicov, 2007). A professional working with such a client will need to decipher this type of history in a caring, respectful, and diplomatic manner. Professionals who focus on getting this information will be giving their clients a gift that is rarely made available to them: the opportunity to talk about and share what their life was like before coming to this country and how it has affected them to leave that life behind to begin anew in the United States. Beyond this, which in itself has the potential to strengthen the professional's bond with a client, there will be an opportunity to address any pertinent experiences that the client has had during the actual emigration to the United States.

Counseling Within Latino(a) Culture

Much of counseling within the Latin American culture places significant emphasis on family and systemic relationships. In countries like Portugal, however, such services are not prominent or available in high quantity. When counseling does occur, it takes fair amounts of time, as opposed to brief therapy sessions, because of the systemic nature that often involves several relationships and perspectives to be examined (Zagelbaum, 2009).

Another factor that influences how counseling is offered is spirituality. Portuguese clients seek out services called *consellerio*. This practice explains why professional counseling services are largely nonexistent in some Latin American cultures. It is more important to address personal matters through religious and spiritual guidance, as opposed to a licensed professional (Rollins, 2006). Clients from Portugal who immigrate, however, do turn to mental health and welfare professionals to facilitate action plans that can help them acculturate into the host culture. The same can be said of Peruvian clients. The focus of counseling is more community based and is considered to be action focused (Bloemraad, 2006; Melendez & McDowell, 2008). Also, community-based institutions such as schools, government agencies, and religious organizations provide counseling services because of the communal norms of the culture, though socioeconomic factors can often limit who has access to such services (Melendez & McDowell, 2008; Rollins, 2006).

When most youths seek counseling services, it is largely for vocational guidance purposes. Furthermore, the Spanish verb for counseling, *aconsejar*, translates into the English phrase "to tell someone what to do" (Espin & Renner,

1974). Even within recent years, research studies have shown that Latin American immigrant clients often seek counseling services that are used to facilitate social connections with members of the community and various peer groups (Page-Gould, Mendoza-Denton, & Tropp, 2008; Yeh & Inose, 2003). Although counseling is not necessarily designed to uncover deep-rooted psychological issues that may impact clients on a subconscious or unconscious level, it takes on a form of action and productivity that is designed to move clients forward and create social dynamics that allow for issues to be worked through. The same principle applies to adult clients.

Although many Latin American clients migrate because of political pressure or socioeconomic stress that does not provide enough support for their families, narrative approaches used to uncover emotional trauma are not the dominant treatment modalities that are used throughout the counseling process (Hernandez, 2002). The focus on taking action allows for clients to appropriately address issues of trauma without dwelling on negatives to the point by which fear and anger-based emotions do not overpower the positive momentum of counseling. It is important for counselors who are to work with Latin American immigrant clients to recognize the importance of emphasizing thoughts and behaviors.

At the same time that thoughts and behaviors are emphasized, research has supported the notion that Latinos/(as) are less likely than Caucasians to view psychological issues such as depression from a biological perspective (Givens, Houston, Van Voorhees, Ford, & Cooper, 2007). Counseling is preferred over medication, though this does not mean that medication should never be considered as part of a client's treatment. In terms of what Latino(a) clients appear to believe about psychological issues, there is a strong belief that these matters can be optimistically handled through either therapy or encouragement of self-regulation and personal care (Cabassa, Lagomasino, Dwight-Johnson, Hansen, & Xie, 2008). Thus, examining each family member's issues seems essential to establishing a systemic support network during the counseling process and allows for each client's thoughts and behaviors regarding the acculturation and adjustment process to be effectively examined and explored.

Acculturation and Adjustment Issues

One of the most significant stressors associated with Latino(a) immigrant family adjustment issues is economic and career establishment. Data have long suggested that Hispanic men within the United States are often employed in laborer, operator, and production services as opposed to Caucasian men who often serve in supervisory, professional, and managerial roles (Zapata, 1995). Also, they tend to hold the lowest wage jobs out of all full-time workers (Houvourus, 2001; Melendez & McDowell, 2008). Likewise, non-Hispanic women are often employed in managerial and professional occupations, whereas their Hispanic female counterparts within the United States are not. Furthermore, full-time working Hispanic women have been identified as having the lowest income of any population subgroup (Zapata, 1995). Though these income issues are prevalent and similar among Latino(a) immigrants, the psychological impacts are quite different.

Men's Issues

Latino men are heavily influenced and impacted by *hombria*, *machismo*, and other concepts of gender associated with the definition of manliness (Melendez & McDowell, 2008; Mirande, 1997; Perilla, 1999). Within Latin American culture, men are expected to have professional identities that reflect their ability not only to work but also to provide for their families. The sense of being relevant and valued by society comes from both family and career-oriented productivity. Money and economic survival are, more often than not, why Hispanic/Latino men tend to immigrate to this country alone before attempting to bring their families. Unless the financial means exist, the heads of families attempt to establish themselves first, even if it takes several years. If the head of a family is not in the new country legally, this process can take even longer, if it happens at all. Most Hispanic/Latino men, with possible variations among those from some countries of origin or subgroups, feel the great responsibility of providing for their families, whether they include parents, younger siblings, and/or spouses and children. Often men, including those with higher levels of education, are willing to do any type of work they can find in their new or host country to establish some sort of financial and residential foundation. A minority of men and women emigrate with the guarantee of a job or career, but this does not often balance the stresses and strains that occur as adjustment to the host culture occurs. There is a high degree of stress among these men who are often facing many hardships, including intolerance and discrimination from some natives of the host country (Melendez & McDowell, 2008).

There are many immigrants from Latin America, such as Peruvians (Melendez & McDowell, 2008), who do not have their professional training or educational backgrounds recognized in their host countries, which can create several barriers when seeking employment. Family demands, coupled with lack of income, can create significant levels of stress and depression for Latino men. These issues can manifest in many forms and are believed to be one contributing factor to how some Latino(a) immigrant families experience conflict (Schofield, Parke, Kim, & Coltrane, 2008) and domestic violence (Belknap & Sayeed, 2003; Perilla, 1999).

Women's Issues

Latina women are frequently viewed as primary caregivers within Latino(a) culture and are expected to provide significant attention and resources to children and elders within the family (Larson & Richards, 1994). This is not to say that fathers do not have these responsibilities but rather to say that Latin American households tend to have fathers who serve as primary regulators of rules and not necessarily as emotional caregivers and nurturers (Mirande, 1997). Traditionally, Hispanic/Latina women have stayed behind in their countries of origin, either waiting for a parent to come back for them or caring for children and aging family members while waiting for their husbands or other family members to come back and either bring earnings to share or bring them back to the new country. Over the years, there has been a growing trend whereby more and more women are emigrating on their own for the same traditional reasons as the men before them. Whichever circumstance a woman faces, it often involves having to take on nontraditional responsibilities when left behind in their native country. This reality, as embodied in having to parent and care for children and families alone, while facing the normal day-to-day stressors of staying behind can take its toll. Yet, once women do make it to a new or host country, they have a whole new set of issues to face.

Recent reports have indicated that many female immigrants have never been married and do not have children, which was not a significant proportion from groups of female immigrants of the past (Fry, 2006). Although some Latin American societies are providing more educational and career opportunities for women than was the case many years ago, the family role of Latina women has largely remained the same (Melendez & McDowell, 2008). Also, reliance on other family, friends, and community members help such women develop fairly egalitarian parental relationships and seek out some independent roles away from the household (Kummerer, Lopez-Reyna, & Hughes, 2007; Melendez & McDowell, 2008). However, the responsibilities of engaging their children in school and language development appear to be largely associated with the mother's relationship(s) with schools and speech and language therapy programs (Kummerer et al., 2007).

The stressors often experienced by Latina immigrant women appear to relate to loss of financial resources and limited availability of additional family and community members to provide social support (Melendez & McDowell, 2008). Also, when children struggle with acculturation and school-based demands that arise within the host country, mothers often feel a sense of shame and frustration that contributes to stress and psychological issues (Huynh & Fuligni, 2008; Schwartz & Zamboanga, 2008). Latin Americans often rely on family, relatives, and friends in their community, especially in times of crisis. Immigrants can often be shocked and frustrated by the relatively independent dynamics that unfold when such crises occur in many U.S. communities. The lack of social networks can be difficult and can impact ways in which issues such as depression are handled (Cabassa et al., 2008). Women will seek services and support when struggling with psychological issues and stress, but it also appears important for them to have a sense of connectedness with other community agencies such as churches to find sources of inspiration and empowerment that further enhance their adjustment to the host country (Melendez & McDowell, 2008).

It is also important to note that domestic violence can often be an issue that impacts Latino(a) immigrant families, frequently involving the women as victims (Almeida & Durkin, 1999; Melendez & McDowell, 2008). Even though an accurate number is difficult to officially report, it is clear that Latino groups compose one of the highest rates of domestic violence incidents, especially among immigrant women (Fedovskiy, Higgins, & Paranjape, 2008; Galanti, 2003). Many of these women may not recognize that physical abuse and domestic violence are illegal acts in the United States, which may complicate matters when it comes to reporting these incidents in the first place. When coupled with a marginalized status and perceptions of discrimination by members of the host culture, Latina immigrant women who are victims of domestic violence present significant concerns that require effective counseling services (Melendez & McDowell, 2008). They may also have exacerbated symptoms of post-traumatic stress disorder, because the act of abuse may remind them of past traumas experienced in their native county (Fedovskiy et al., 2008). As difficult as this may sound, however, there are instances where it is believed that engaging these women in social and legal services that address the issues of domestic violence can allow them to find both support and educational opportunities in the host culture as well as their personal power to stand up for their rights (Melendez & McDowell, 2008). These outcomes do not justify the occurrence of domestic violence, but they do show the importance of providing Latina immigrant women and their families effective and accessible counseling services.

Issues of Youths

Children and adolescents within Latino(a) immigrant families can also experience a range of issues as they adjust and acculturate to the host country. The issues facing Hispanic/Latino children and adolescents immigrating to a new or host country mirror those of their elders but also involve unique nuances associated with their age(s) and the expectations from parents or guardians, as well as the new culture(s) they encounter. For younger children, the changes may be a bit more subtle and easier to adjust to in the best scenarios. Older children and adolescents, however, often face more complicated social and peer-relational issues that tend to play out in the school settings they are introduced to in the new country. One of the more prominent issues reported in research literature involves academic struggles and high dropout rates from school institutions (Huynh & Fuligni, 2008; Vazquez-Nuttall, Li, & Kaplan, 2006). Some of these struggles can be due to language and literacy issues (Kummerer et al., 2007), difficulties in balancing home and school responsibilities (Gnaulati, 2002), and challenges faced from perceived racial discrimination and mental health issues (Hwang & Goto, 2008).

Huynh and Fuligni (2008) reported that although Latin American adolescents often experience racial discrimination, the extent to which parents prepare their children for this bias is not well known. Furthermore, when discrimination is experienced by children and adolescents, it is not clear whether immigrant parents are aware of how it is manifesting. Some of these perceptions may stem from misunderstanding whether the discrimination is considered a form of peer "teasing" or social pressure, adult power dynamics, or something beyond the scope of these social and developmental relationships (Greene, Way, & Pahl, 2006). What appears clear is that parental involvement within the home life and school life of children and adolescents helps to mediate some of these stressors, promote academic success and achievement, and allow for greater trust to be established between peer and adult networks (Vazquez-Nuttall et al., 2006).

When trust and perception of support are missing from school and home environments, Latino(a) immigrant youths and young adults appear to experience increased levels of psychological distress, suicidal ideation, state and trait anxiety, and clinical depression (Hwang & Goto, 2008). College-age Latinos(as) have also reported greater feelings of being accused of doing something wrong such as stealing, cheating, not doing an equitable share of expected work, or breaking the law when this perception of discrimination exists without proper channels of support, especially when compared to other immigrant and culturally diverse counterparts (Hwang & Goto, 2008). Sometimes, this pressure can result in intragroup marginalization, whereby interpersonal distance is created and acculturating individuals display behaviors and/or attitudes that differ from their heritage's group norms and identities (Castillo, Conoley, Brossart, & Quiros, 2007). Latino(a) students often report that family conflict due to acculturation would often center around issues associated with language; not speaking or understanding Spanish, coupled with not being active participants in Latino customs or traditions, are often behaviors that manifest from this process (Castillo et al., 2007). This can also create stress and tension among peers who may accuse these individuals of acting like the host culture (e.g., "acting White"), and these youths may be subjected to pressure and ridicule that continue to isolate and alienate them as they struggle with their identity and adjustment to the host culture (Castillo et al., 2007). Though there are assessments and measures that allow for Latino immigrant youths to be screened for these possible issues, such as the Multidimensional Acculturative Stress Scale (Rodriguez, Myers, Mira, Flores, & Garcia-Hernandez, 2002), what also appears to be helpful for many of these struggling youths is belonging to some ethnic student organizations (Negy & Lunt, 2008). Some reports of cross-group friendships appear to have similar benefits for certain Latino(a) clients as well (Page-Gould et al., 2008). The sense of support and community can provide a safe space for such youths to develop academic, emotional, and social outlets within school and college campuses, and this systemic approach can often be useful in connecting individuals to others who may otherwise feel disconnected and/or marginalized within school and family settings. It should also be noted, however, that cultural socialization may keep Latino(a) immigrant students engaged in school because they have fewer socioeconomic resources and a strong sense of pride. It is resiliency developed through a seemingly paradoxical process to mainstream culture; as long as mistrust of other groups is not prominent, academic motivation can become stronger out of a need to survive and advance into career and social networks (Huynh & Fuligni, 2008). There can be a sense of independent strength that grows from seeds of stress.

The importance of the parent–child relationship, however, cannot be stated enough when it comes to working with Latino(a) immigrant families. Acculturative stress levels can often increase the frequency and amount of parent–child conflicts, especially in Latino(a) households (Schofield et al., 2008). However, parent–child relationship quality has been found to moderate the imbalances between parent–child acculturation gaps and child adjustment. In other words, even when acculturative stress is experienced within Latino(a) immigrant households, family members who report having close and effective relationships with one another experience fewer disruptions and conflicts between parents and children (Schofield et al., 2008). Interestingly, Schofield et al. found this effect especially significant for father–child relationship gaps, which could again come from the notion that men and boys within Latino(a) households provide more of a work-based function, whereas women and girls tend to take on more nurturing roles that allow for greater bonding and emotional regulation. Regardless of what struggles children and adolescents face, however, a skilled and culturally competent counselor must pay particularly close attention as to how the parent–child relationship is impacting the functionality of the system.

It is not unheard of for members of the same family to be at different stages of English-language acquisition and use. The same can often be true about stages and levels of acculturation. Such varying degrees of adjustment within a family can cause even more stress among family members. Counselors working with such clients will need to find creative methods and strategies for helping such individuals and families. There are, however, some techniques that have been consistently used and reported as effective.

Recommended Techniques

Narrative approaches appear to be one of the most frequently applied and effective techniques that counseling professionals use when working with Latino(a) immigrant families (Falicov, 2007). The ability to tell one's story in terms of pre- and postmigration status not only allows for the counselor to understand the essence of the client, his or her homeland, and family but also allows the client to feel validated and connected to the counselor because of the sense of importance and willingness to listen that the attention paid during this narrative process displays. There are three contexts that Falicov recommended for counselors to pay attention to while listening to narratives: the relational context, the community context, and the cultural and sociopolitical context.

The relational context refers to the intimate connections that people have as a result of personal connections with family and close, intimate friendships. People who have been separated from family as they relocated to the United States, for example, can share memories about their native country from this perspective and context. Presenting letters or sharing phone calls with these individuals can be one way that narratives are presented during the course of counseling sessions (Falicov, 2007).

The community context refers to the network of people that connect with clients through neighborhood and cultural/ethnic relationships. This context can be developed in the host country or maintained via communications with the country of origin. Community venues such as churches, hospitals, and schools are often places where immigrant clients can be encouraged to join or volunteer their services. Not only does this sense of community allow for family members to enter their community in a physical sense, but also it allows for social capital and peer networks to be established with members who can empathize with their situation and provide homogeneous connections with other immigrants (Falicov, 2007).

The cultural and sociopolitical context represents the larger venue of what is also referred to as social justice. It involves exploring immigrants' opinions of the host culture in terms of how it impacts family gender and generational relationships (Falicov, 2007). The exploration of family values, and how they have shifted as a result of the opportunities that are or are not accessible as a result of existing within the host culture, often leads to a growth and learning process that can allow for family members to connect with one another, as well as with the counselor, as issues associated with parenting, spiritual practice, and ways of obtaining social and economic resources are uncovered. Counselors and family therapists are strongly cautioned, however, to be mindful that immigrant clients may make attempts to hide experiences and feelings about discrimination within the host country out of fear that they may be seen as unappreciative of or resentful about existing within the current home venue (Falicov, 2007). It is for reasons such as this that some indigenous resources of Latino(a) culture are also used in the counseling process with these clients.

Cuentos (stories) therapy is another counseling strategy to consider with this population. This form of therapy originated in Puerto Rico and is based on indigenous folktales (Ramirez, Jain, Flores-Torres, Perez, & Carlson, 2009). The stories used contain healing themes and models of behavior such as self-transformation and endurance through adversity. Cuentos is used primarily to help Hispanic children recover from depression and other mental health problems related to leaving one's homeland and living in a foreign culture. There are also opportunities to use these stories when engaging children and adolescents in conflict resolution processes (Thayer, Updegraff, & Delgado, 2008) and some forms of sibling therapy (Gnaulati, 2002). Helping clients cope with loss and frustration are often the themes that come from this work, but with the use of culturally sensitive material as the base of this work, immigrant clients may feel more able to learn and grow from this counseling process as a result.

Another example of a culturally infused technique involves the use of *dichos* or sayings that impart a message that could then be brought back to the presenting issue(s) at hand. Sometimes, metaphors can be used as well, so that clients are able to better comprehend the messages (Bernal & Saez-Santiago, 2006). Even if a counselor is not bilingual or bicultural, efforts can be made to become more knowledgeable about the best strategies and approaches to use with this varied population. In some appropriately arranged circumstances, a trusted and highly bilingual interpreter could be enlisted to assist in the initial evaluation stage of counseling, or the counselor could make an effort to learn some of the more common phrases in Spanish that would help establish a positive counseling experience. This last goal is something that has been found to go hand in hand with another cultural tradition known as *personalismo*, which describes the positive nature that amicable relationships can be based on and built on (Soto-Fulp & DelCampo, 1994). This has been found to be a positive indicator of continued counseling relationships and more effective outcomes when the clients perceive it is present in the counseling relationship.

There are also significant types of interviewing and questions that counselors are recommended to use when working with Latino(a) immigrant families, which have been previously discussed in prior texts and adapted for individual, couples, and family counseling (Zagelbaum, 2009). Mitrani, Santisteban, and Muir (2004, as cited in Zagelbaum, 2009) proposed specific questions to be asked to particular family members within the Latino family. Many of their experiences with clients often involve single parent families, usually single mothers, who have separated from their children to establish a better financial and emotional space within the United States. Parents are often asked to describe the reasons they came to the United States, along with the particular hopes they had for their family. Also included in this questioning are details about how difficult it was to make the decision to immigrate, find a job, and settle into the host culture. In addition, engaging in a narrative about the most difficult aspects of relocating to a new country, in many cases by oneself, also helps to enrich the therapeutic discourse among family members.

Child and adolescent clients are often asked to speak about the people with whom they were left with back home as their parent came to the United States, the quality of the relationship with these people at the time of the separation, the explanation they received as to why the separation occurred, what they were told about their parent, the image they had of the parent during the period of separation, and the reactions to the level and type of contact they had with one another during the years of separation (Mitrani et al., 2004). This dialogue engages parent and child in a fundamental understanding of emotional concerns, as well as issues of perception versus reality during the transitional period.

When the parent and child have been reunited and have revealed their feelings and beliefs about their individual experiences, there are questions posed to the family. These questions consist of the following (Mitrani et al., 2004): How was the reunion different from what you expected it to be? How is life here different from that in your country? What do you like and dislike about living here? How would you like your family to be now? What can we [including the therapist] work toward? The family is reunited literally in the sense that the therapeutic discourse focuses on all members as a collective unit but also figuratively in the sense that everyone has had a chance to hear and expound on each other's ideas during the therapeutic process. Within many Latin American families, this process is a template for what ideal family patterns of communications should look like. Therefore, counselors are advised to approach these types of clients in this way because of how these systemic interventions tap into the collective strengths of the family unit.

Conclusion

The family stresses and strains associated with family dynamics are complex enough, let alone how complicated they can become when undergoing the immigration and acculturation processes. Though Latino(a) immigrant families are one of the largest groups of immigrants, if not the largest group, within the United States, this does not mean that they have plentiful resources and social networks to work with or social services that are readily available. Whether working with parent–child, spouse–spouse, sibling–sibling, parent–elder, entire family, or any possible combination in between, a skilled counseling professional must recognize the importance of using a systemic perspective when working with these clients. They also must recognize the need to provide action-based services that actively engage these clients in work beyond the scope of the therapy office, extending into community churches, schools, and neighborhoods. Building alliances and allowing open and honest discussions about discrimination to occur are not easy tasks, but the use of narrative techniques and culturally appropriate resources that tap into the strengths and resiliencies of these immigrant clients can allow for positive outcomes to occur, with the counseling professional serving as an instrumental agent who allows for these families to thrive and empower others within the communities they reside.

Discussion Questions

1. Is the ability to discuss life experiences, cultural heritage, family systems, and historical background of identified Latino(a) immigrant clients necessary as part of an effective counseling treatment plan? Why or why not?
2. How can acculturation affect psychological processes such as personality formation, vocational choices, emotional disorders, and help-seeking behaviors with Latino(a) immigrant clients?
3. Explain how Latino(a) populations' religious and/or spiritual beliefs and values, including attributions and taboos, affect worldview, social functioning, and expressions of emotional stress.
4. How do the sociopolitical and economic influences experienced by Latino(a) immigrants impact the counseling process?
5. How might counseling practitioners advocate at institutional and community levels on behalf of Latino(a) immigrant clients?

References

Almeida, R. & Durkin, T. (1999). The cultural context model: Therapy for couples with domestic violence. *Journal of Marital and Family Therapy, 25,* 313–324.

Belknap, R. & Sayeed, P. (2003). Te contaria mi vida: I would tell you my life, if only you would ask. *Health Care for Women International, 24,* 723–747.

Bernal, G. & Saez-Santiago, E. (2006). Culturally centered psychosocial interventions. *Journal of Community Psychology, 34*, 121–132.

Bloemraad, I. (2006). *Becoming a citizen: Incorporating immigrants and refugees in the United States and Canada.* Berkley: University of California Press.

Cabassa, L., Lagomasino, I., Dwight-Johnson, M., Hansen, M., & Xie, B. (2008). Measuring Latinos' perceptions of depression: A confirmatory factor analysis of the Illness Perception Questionnaire. *Cultural Diversity and Ethnic Minority Psychology, 14*, 377–384.

Castillo, L., Conoley, C., Brossart, D., & Quiros, A. (2007). Construction and validation of the Intragroup Marginalization Inventory. *Cultural Diversity and Ethnic Minority Psychology, 13*, 232–240.

Cruza-Guet, M.C., Spokane, A.R., Caskie, G.I.L., Brown, S.C., & Szapocznik, J. (2008). The relationship between social support and psychological distress among Hispanic elders in Miami, FL. *Journal of Counseling Psychology, 55*, 427–441.

Espin, O. & Renner, R. (1974). Counseling: A new priority in Latin America. *Personnel and Guidance Journal, 52*, 297–301.

Falicov, C. (2007). Working with transitional immigrants: Expanding meanings of family, community, and culture. *Family Process, 46*, 157–171.

Federal Interagency Forum on Aging Related Statistics. (2000). *Older Americans 2000: Key indicators of well-being.* Hyattsville, MD: National Center for Health Staistics.

Fedovskiy, K., Higgins, S., & Paranjape, A. (2008). Intimate partner violence: How does it impact major depressive disorder and post-traumatic stress disorder among immigrant Latinas? *Journal of Immigrant and Minority Health, 10*(1), 45–51.

Fry, R. (2006). Gender and migration. *Pew Hispanic Research Report*, 1–42. Retrieved July 25, 2009, from http://pewhispanic.org/files/reports/64.pdf

Galanti, G.A. (2003). The Hispanic family and male-female relationships: An overview. *Journal of Transitional Nursing, 14*, 180–185.

Givens, J., Houston, T., Van Voorhees, B., Ford, D., & Cooper, L. (2007). Ethnicity and preferences for depression treatment. *General Hospital Psychiatry, 29*, 182–191.

Gnaulati, E. (2002). Extending the uses of sibling therapy with children and adolescents. *Psychotherapy: Theory/Research/Practice/Training, 39*, 76–87.

Greene, M., Way, N., & Pahl, K. (2006). Trajectories of perceived adult and peer discrimination among Black, Latino, and Asian American adolescents: Patterns and psychological correlates. *Developmental Psychology, 42*, 218–238.

Houvouras, S. (2001). The effect of demographic variables, ethnic prejudice, and attitudes toward immigration on opposition to bilingual education. *Hispanic Journal of Behavioral Sciences, 23*, 136–152.

Hernandez, P. (2002). Trauma in war and political persecution: Expanding the concept. *American Journal of Orthopsychiatry, 72*, 16–25.

Huynh, V. & Fuligni, A. (2008). Ethnic socialization and the academic adjustment of adolescents from Mexican, Chinese, and European backgrounds. *Developmental Psychology, 44*, 1202–1208.

Hwang, W. & Goto, S. (2008). The impact of perceived racial discrimination on the mental health of Asian American and Latino college students. *Cultural Diversity and Ethnic Minority Psychology, 14*, 326–335.

Kummerer, S., Lopez-Reyna, N., & Hughes, M. (2007). Mexican immigrant mothers' perceptions of their children's communication disabilities, emergent literacy development, and speech-language therapy program. *American Journal of Speech-Language Pathology, 16*, 271–282.

Larson, R.W., & Richards, M.H. (1994). Family emotions: Do young adolescents and their parents experience the same states? *Journal of Research on Adolescence, 4*, 567–583.

Melendez, T. & McDowell, T. (2008). Race, class, gender, and migration: Family therapy with a Peruvian couple. *Journal of Systemic Therapies, 27*, 30–43.

Mirande, A. (1997). *Hombres y machos: Masculinity and Latino culture.* Boulder, CO: Westview.

Mitrani, V., Santisteban, D., & Muir, J. (2004). Addressing immigration-related separations in Hispanic families with a behavior-problem adolescent. *American Journal of Orthopsychiatry, 74*, 219–229.

Negy, C. & Lunt, R. (2008). What college students really think about ethnic student organizations. *Journal of Diversity in Higher Education, 1*, 176–192.

Page-Gould, E., Mendoza-Denton, R., & Tropp, L. (2008). With a little help from my cross-group friend: Reducing anxiety in intergroup contexts through cross-group friendship. *Journal of Personality and Social Psychology, 95*, 1080–1094.

Passel, J. & Cohn, D. (2008). *Trends in unauthorized immigration: Undocumented inflow now trails legal inflow.* Hispanic Pew Center. Retrieved from http://pewhispanic.org/reports/report.php?ReportID=107

Perilla, J. (1999). Domestic violence as a human rights issue: The case of immigrant Latinos. *Hispanic Journal of Behavioral Sciences, 21*, 107–133.

Pew Research Center. (2008). *U.S. population projections: 2005–2050.* Retrieved from http://pewhispanic.org/reports/report.php?ReportID=85

Ramirez, S., Jain, S., Flores-Torres, L., Perez, R., & Carlson, R. (2009). The effects of cuento therapy on reading achievement and psychological outcomes of Mexican-American students. *Professional School Counseling, 12*(3), 253–262.

Rodriguez, N., Myers, H.F., Mira, C.B., Flores, T., & Garcia-Hernandez, L. (2002). Development of the Multidimensional Acculturative Stress Inventory for Adults of Mexican Origin. *Psychological Assessment, 14*, 451–461.

Rollins, J. (2006). Getting a global perspective: A glimpse of the counseling profession in 27 countries. *Counseling Today, 1*, 1–34.

Schofield, T., Parke, R., Kim, Y., & Coltrane, S. (2008). Bridging the acculturation gap: Parent–child relationship quality as a moderator in Mexican American families. *Developmental Psychology, 4*, 1190–1994.

Schwartz, S.J., & Zamboanga, B.L. (2008). Testing Berry's Model of Acculturation: A confirmatory latent class approach. *Cultural Diversity and Ethnic Minority Psychology, 14*, 275–285.

Soto-Fulp, S. & DelCampo, R. (1994). Structural family therapy with Mexican-American family systems. *Contemporary Family Therapy, 16*, 349–362.

Thayer, S., Updegraff, K., & Delgado, M. (2008). Conflict resolution in Mexican American adolescents' friendships: Links with culture, gender, and friendship quality. *Journal of Youth Adolescence, 37*, 783–797.

Tienda, M. & Mitchell, F. (2006). *Hispanics and the future of America*. Washington, DC: National Academies Press.

U.S. Census Bureau. (2000). *United States Census 2000*. Washington, DC: Author.

Vazquez-Nuttall, E., Li, C., & Kaplan, J. (2006). Home–school partnerships with culturally diverse families: Challenges and solutions for school personnel. *Journal of Applied School Psychology, 22*, 81–102.

Yeh, C., & Inose, M. (2003). International students' reported English fluency, social support, satisfaction, and social connectedness as predictors of acculturative stress. *Counseling Psychology Quarterly, 16*, 15–28.

Zagelbaum, A. (2009). Counseling new citizens. In C. Ellis & J. Carlson (Eds.), *Cross cultural awareness and social justice in counseling*. New York: Routledge.

Zapata, J. (1995). Counseling Hispanic children and youth. In C. Lee (Ed.), *Counseling for diversity: A guide for school counselors and related professionals*. Boston: Allyn and Bacon.

Chapter 5

Working With European Immigrant Families

Gregg Kuehl, Adam Zagelbaum, and Jon Carlson

Contents

Europe is made up of approximately 50 states on the second smallest continent in the world. The Council of Europe is made up of 47 countries, and the European Union currently has 27 member countries. The European Union was founded in 1993. Europe is split not only between individual nations with their own languages but also between European Union and non–European Union. According to the United Nations, the population of Europe was estimated to be 731 million people. That is slightly more than one ninth of the world's population. The multicultural and multilingual nature of the European continent provides a challenge when considering the many immigrants from this region of the world (Lunt, 1998).

Europe can also be divided into Eastern and Western Europe. Eastern Europe is usually considered to be the land extending from Greece in the south to Finland in the north, bounded on the west by Italy and Germany and on the east by Russia. Most of the Eastern European nations share a history in that they were identified by communism and the Soviet Union's domination after the Second World War. The strong communist influences have left Eastern Europe less urban and less industrialized than Western countries.

Like in other regions of the world, people emigrate from Europe for a variety of reasons. They might move to the United States to seek employment or educational opportunities. Europeans may move because of political upheaval in their home country, a natural disaster, or any number of other reasons. Declining opportunities at home and the hope for a better future have motivated millions of immigrants to move from their country of origin to the United States (Strom et al., 1983).

A family might move from Europe for greater business opportunity. For example, one could imagine a Finnish man whose company bought a factory in a Midwestern city in the United States. This man might have a wife and two children to consider before he decides to move to the United States to move up within his company. He might travel to the United States first to start the job and to look for housing while his family waits in Finland. Once he has established residence in the United States, he would then send for his family to come and live with him.

Another family might move because of some political upheaval in the country of origin. For example, a family of five might have fled Kosovo because of conflict there. The family might decide to flee to the United States and has to move rather hastily. The father and mother might have had to make a decision to move quickly and leave behind friends and belongings. Such a family could end up in the United States with little or no money and have a much harder time acculturating.

There may also be certain Europeans who have a migrant personality that compels them to move (Boneva & Frieze, 2001). There may be certain individuals who are more likely to leave than to stay in their home countries. In one study (Frieze et al., 2004) researchers looked at the difference between those who had the desire to stay in their country of origin and those who wanted to leave. The study focused on individuals from Croatia, the Czech Republic, Poland, Russia, and Slovenia. All of those countries had been socialist countries that were transitioning to a more capitalist system and were experiencing economic difficulties at the time of the study. The researchers found that people from those countries who were more likely to emigrate considered work more central for them than those who wanted to stay. Their data support the idea that in the emigration process, a country loses some of its citizens who are strongly involved with their job or career (Boneva & Frieze, 2001).

In addition, Frieze et al. (2004) found that more family-oriented individuals would be less willing to leave their country of origin and resettle in a different country. There might be cultural differences in terms of importance of family for immigrants. For example, for Eastern Europeans, the social support from the extended family is the most valuable one (Robila, 2007). In times of need, people in Eastern Europe reach out to their parents and grandparents for help (Robila, 2004). This support is solicited especially in regard to child-rearing duties. Counselors must be aware that the decision to emigrate involves family and in many cases separation from family.

Whatever the reason Europeans move from their country of origin to the United States, moving is always a complex and stressful experience. Immigration is typically accompanied by a deep sense of loss (Mirsky, 1991). In many cases the immigrant loses touch with his or her family and friends. The immigrant leaves behind the homeland, and all that was familiar to him or her is gone, including the culture and language. Moving into a new culture is a stressful event. It is a major life transition that involves profound physical, psychosocial, and cultural changes that all challenge prior modes of adaptive functioning (Vercruysse, 2002). Moving stretches the immigrant's ability to cope in many areas of life, and it also puts stress on the family.

The Finnish family in the previous example could be experiencing stress due to separation from the familiar environment. They would be leaving behind family, friends, and the environment that they are accustomed to in order to pursue economic opportunity. The family might experience separation while the father is away establishing himself in the United States. The mother might be left to raise the children on her own or with the help of extended family members while waiting to travel to join her husband in the new country. The family members would then experience a reunion in the new, as yet unknown, environment away from the support that they have known. The family would then go through an acculturation process as a whole and as individual members. Each step along the way is a new stressor on the family.

Despite the inherent stress associated with the immigration process and the rapid diversification of the United States, relatively few resources have been developed to address the specific needs of America's immigrant population. In addition, little research can be found on White European immigrant groups in the general counseling and psychology literature (Ponterotto et al., 2001). Information can be generated from the multicultural literature and the limited literature on European immigrants and how it affects family systems.

Counselors working with European immigrant families must understand the particular needs of those families, the mental health issues that they may have prior to their move, the particular stress that immigrating can have on the individuals and on the families, and the acculturation stress and its impact on those families. Counselors must also be aware of the attitudes that Europeans have toward the profession of counseling and how that attitude might affect their help-seeking behavior. With this knowledge, counselors can better understand the specific needs of European immigrant families, and the mental health profession can then best serve European immigrant families.

Europe is considered the birthplace of Western culture. Europe is also where modern psychology originated; however, it has been largely dominated by American psychology most recently (Lunt, 1998). Europeans have had exposure to psychology and the counseling profession. Chen and Mak (2008) found in their research that the trend in help seeking was associated with Western influences. They found that individuals exposed to and influenced by Western norms and practices held more positive attitudes toward seeking professional help and actually used more mental health services.

Underutilization of mental health services has been a prevalent and severe issue across the globe (Chen & Mak, 2008). In the United States only about 15% of individuals with mental health problems actually seek out professional help. A similar gap of underutilization of services was found in European countries. In European countries, around one fifth of the individuals who sought help for mental health services were actually receiving them (Alonso et al., 2004). Underutilization of mental health services is true of the indigenous population in the United States, so it is no surprise that immigrants also underutilize counseling services.

Immigrants may not be aware of what counseling services are available to them. Immigrant populations also tend to attach a stigma to mental and emotional dysfunction and thus do not seek out mental health services (Primm, Lima, & Rowe, 1996). Another barrier for immigrants with regard to seeking mental health services is a pervasive xenophobic sentiment toward immigrant groups combined with economic difficulties in the United States (Nikelly, 1997). No matter from where the immigrant family comes, they have taken a risk to uproot and start a life in an unfamiliar country.

Moving into a new culture is a stressful event that affects the individual emotionally, behaviorally, and physically. The stress can impact the family, and it can impact individual family members differently. The level of acculturation can impact the stress level of the immigrant, and it can also impact that individual's view of seeking help. For example, Ponterotto et al. (2001) looked at attitudes toward counseling among Italian and Greek Americans of varying acculturation levels.

Ponterotto et al. (2001) found that among Italian American college and university students, women had a greater recognition of personal need for counseling and were more confident in counseling's potential usefulness than did men.

They found similar results for the Greek American sample. High-acculturated women were more open regarding personal problems than were high-acculturated men. These findings suggest that at least among Italian and Greek clients, women are more likely to recognize the need for counseling services and are more likely to seek out such services.

In addition, Ponterotto et al. (2001) found that low-acculturated Greek and Italian Americans preferred to see an ethnically similar counselor to deal with their personal problems. That was true for both men and women. However, the most important counselor characteristic for both Italian and Greek Americans was an advanced degree. So although ethnic similarity was seen as important to both groups, seeing their counselor as an expert was more important.

It is important for counselors and counseling professionals when working with European immigrant families to understand who in the family initiated the contact with counseling services. Ponterotto et al. (2001) found some gender differences in Greek and Italian Americans in terms of attitudes toward counseling. However, they suggested more focused follow-up research was needed. In addition, more research is needed with regard to other countries in Europe and gender differences with regard to attitudes toward counseling. Regardless it is important for the counselor to explore with the immigrant family whose idea it was to come to counseling.

Acculturation of European Families

When a European family immigrates to the United States, there is a process in which the family becomes acclimated to the new culture, and that process is known as acculturation (Brilliant, 2000). During this process immigrants experience a number of changes and a number of losses. They typically experience feelings of denial, confusion, anxiety, helplessness, irritability, anger, and sadness (Vercruysse, 2002). Several theoretical models have been proposed to describe the process of adjustment that people go through when they transfer to a new culture. The U-shaped curve has received the most attention in the literature. The U-shaped curve predicts that the immigrant initially has a stage of optimism, believing that things will be better in the new location. The initial stage is usually followed by a low or crisis in which the immigrant realizes that there are more difficulties than he or she had anticipated. Eventually in the last stage the immigrant has a gradual coming to terms with the new culture. The U-shaped curve predicts a honeymoon stage, followed by a disorganization stage, finally leading to a recovery and adjustment stage.

Immigration places stress on family relationships. The level of stress in acculturation is moderated by a number of factors (Brilliant, 2000). Some factors that affect the level of stress in acculturation include the nature of the larger society, the characteristics of the acculturating group, the phase of acculturation, and the characteristics of the individual. Marginalization and separation are modes of acculturation that are associated with higher levels of stress. Assimilation and integration are modes of acculturation associated with lower levels of stress.

The phases of acculturation include contact, conflict, crisis, and adaptation (Brilliant, 2000). In the first phase, the immigrant overestimates what he or she can accomplish. The immigrant has an initial excitement about new possibilities. If an immigrant moved to the United States for employment opportunities or educational opportunities, the hope and excitement are high in this phase. The new immigrant may take on more responsibility than he or she can reasonably handle at this point. The immigrant may appear arrogant during this initial phase of acculturation and believe that anything is possible.

Immigrants low in acculturation, that is, those in the early phase, have been recently uprooted. They left their traditional supportive interpersonal networks in their society of origin and have not yet had the time to construct such networks in the new society (Rogler, Cortes, & Malgady, 1991). There are a number of strains during this time that impinge on everyday life in unpredictable ways. It is during this time that the immigrant without certain skills, such as knowledge of English, keeps the unfamiliar world from becoming familiar and controllable. This situation lowers self-esteem and eventually gives rise to symptomatic behavior.

The middle phase of acculturation, conflict and crisis, is usually made up of those immigrants who have been in the United States from three to five years (Brilliant, 2000). During this phase immigrants often experience depression. The initial hope and confidence in the bright future is replaced by the challenges and struggles of immigration. Immigrants face the obstacles that they thought would be easily overcome. They had anticipated being ahead of where they are currently in the process. Many times the immigrant is not completely fluent in the language yet, they have not yet begun their careers, and they may have menial jobs to make do, or they may be on welfare. Immigrants at this phase are frustrated and impatient.

Ironically, increases in acculturation cause stress and additional problems for the immigrant. As the person increases in acculturation to the new society, that person is alienating him- or herself from the traditional supportive primary groups (Rogler et al., 1991). Increased acculturation also facilitates the internalization of host-society cultural norms, which could include damaging stereotypes and prejudicial attitudes toward one's own group. Increases in acculturation stress the person's coping skills and expose him or her to the risk of increased alcohol and drug abuse.

The last phase of acculturation is adaptation (Brilliant, 2000). It is in this phase that realistic expectations can be accepted and pursued. The immigrant in this phase has come to the realization that the new life cannot be achieved without experiencing the painful loss. The immigrant also must abandon the fantasies that were held and were used to ease the pain of the transition so that there can be realistic, productive growth and success. Good mental health stems from the optimal combination of retaining the supportive traditional cultural elements and learning the host society's instrumental cultural elements (Rogler et al., 1991).

Another factor that could affect the European immigrant family is a discrepancy in acculturation status within the family. This discrepancy between immigrant parents and youth is known as the acculturation gap and has been hypothesized to impact normal parent–child generational differences (Hwang, 2006). The acculturation gap may increase intergenerational family conflict, which in turn leads to greater distress for parents and for children. The acculturation gap could lead to greater frustration, depression, and feelings of inadequacy for the immigrant. It could also lead to doubts about the decision to immigrate and feelings that a mistake was made. According to Hwang (2006) direct tests of the acculturation gap hypothesis are lacking.

Effective counseling interventions differ with each phase of acculturation. According to Brilliant (2000), the primary task in the beginning is to identify realistic boundaries while accepting that there will be some resistance to recognizing those boundaries. In the next phase, the immigrant needs support, encouragement, and coping tools to help ease feelings of hopelessness. There is also a period of mourning as losses are recognized and accepted. When the immigrant has successfully moved through all of the phases, the focus of counseling can shift to enhancing opportunities for optimal performance.

Counseling European Immigrant Families

When counselors are given the opportunity to work with European immigrant families, it is important for them to familiarize themselves with the family's country of origin. They must also become familiar with any special circumstances surrounding the reasons for immigrating to the United States. Was it for a job opportunity, to go to school, or to join other family members already here, or were the reasons more dramatic such as political upheaval or some other catastrophe? This information could help the counselor understand the family members' acculturation and the particular stress that they may be under.

It is also essential that a counselor assess the family's language use and preference. Most immigrants encounter difficulties in mastering the new language. The loss of the mother tongue in immigration is accompanied by a deep sense of loss of self-identity (Mirsky, 1991). Children typically learn a new language more easily than do adults. Counselors need to be aware that this may be a humiliating situation for the parent (Nikelly, 1997). Children who learn English quickly often may act as translators for their parents. The children in many cases are torn between the world of their parents and the American culture.

In working with European immigrants, counselors must be aware of their worldview. The worldview held in the traditional values of Europe like that of North America exalts personal control and responsibility, the achievement of recognition and power, self-interest, autonomy, and self-sufficiency (Nikelly, 1997). On the basis of these values, counselors working with these immigrants maintain professional distance and emotional independence from their clients. They treat their clients in a businesslike manner when providing their expertise. Through this model the expectation is that the immigrants will assume responsibility for whatever happens to them. It is assumed that they will develop survival skills and will be able to succeed without relying on others.

Counselors working with European immigrant families must also consider the age of the children within the family. If there are adolescents in the family, there could be more stress that the family faces. Family relationships have been shown to play a significant role in adolescents' psychological well-being. Greenberger and Chen (1996) found that family relationships contribute less to the explanation of depressed mood in a college sample than in early adolescence. This may be due to the fact that there is an increased importance in extrafamilial relationships in older adolescents.

European American adolescents studied by Greenberger and Chen (1996) perceived both of their parents as being warmer and more expressive of positive emotions than did Asian American adolescents. Greenberger and Chen found that parental warmth and low conflict with parents appear to contribute to well-being throughout the entire early-to-late adolescent period. They found in the sample of European Americans that there was also significantly less depression among the adolescents when there was more parental warmth and less conflict in the family relationships.

For a counselor to help European immigrants during the period of stress that is marked by having adolescent children in the home, the counselor must first educate the family on the struggle for autonomy in adolescence. The counselor could then help the family with basic communication skills to help deal with conflict that might emerge during this time. The counselor could also help the immigrant parents set more realistic standards for their children, especially given the parallel acculturation issues that might be occurring for the children.

In terms of health matters, the CDC (2002) reported that the 10 leading causes of death for European Americans in 2002 consisted of heart disease, cancer, stroke, chronic lower respiratory disease, unintentional injuries, diabetes, influenza/pneumonia, Alzheimer's disease, nephritis/nephritic syndrome/nephrosis, and suicide. It is interesting to note that suicidal behavior is among one of the top 10 causes of death, because it appears logical to assume that mental health and wellness issues are important mediating factors that apply to this statistic. The National Institute of Mental Health (NIMH, 2006) reported that an estimated 26.2% of Americans ages 18 and older suffer from a diagnosable mental disorder in a given year. When applied to the 2004 U.S. Census data, the number of people who meet this condition totals 57.7 million individuals. Furthermore, mental disorders are said to be the leading cause of disability in both the United States and Canada for people ages 15 to 44 (World Health Organization, 2004). Also, it should be known that many types of mental illnesses and conditions are found within the European American population. However, the most significant conditions that appear to relate to European Americans are major depression, schizophrenia, bipolar disorder, obsessive-compulsive disorder, panic disorder, and post-traumatic stress disorder (NIMH, 2001).

One other important demographic finding is that women within this population are more likely than men to have feelings of hopelessness and worthlessness (NIMH, 2001). This is not to say that European American women are more likely than European American men to experience mental illness and/or mental health conditions, but it is worth noticing that women within this population are more likely to report feelings and conditions that are strongly correlated with suicidal ideation. It is for this reason that strong attention should be paid to examining the strengths and challenges that this population possesses when it comes to working with its members as clients in a mental health setting.

Strengths (That Contribute to Resilience)

One of the greater strengths that appear to contribute to the psychological resilience of European Americans is a sense of individualism. The notion of being able to independently approach problems, gain a sense of identity, and implement solution-based behaviors has long been a characteristic of this population. This is not to say that European Americans are largely selfish people but rather to stress a point that having a strong self-focus allows for members of this population to largely focus on personal contributions regarding their problems and the steps they need to take to address such problems. This sense of control has been shown to significantly contribute to how individuals view stressful situations as approachable and manageable tasks (Gentry, 1984). It also correlates to how individuals believe that their life activities and pursuits have personal meaning, interest, value, and significance (Kobasa, 1979). Furthermore, it relates to how individuals view the notion of making change. Individuals who tend to have a sense of control and commitment in their lives also tend to view change as a process that is normal and positive, as opposed to a sign of illness and/or failure

(Kobasa, 1979). It has been demonstrated that although European Americans are more likely than African Americans to report episodes of depression, anxiety, fear, health concerns, and an inability to express feelings to others, European Americans are more likely to engage in greater activities that promote health habits and do not involve the use of tobacco, alcohol, and drugs (Harris, 2004). One explanation of these data relates to the fact that although European Americans are more likely to experience mental health issues, they are more likely to label their issues as relevant to their mental health and engage in a course of treatment that promotes healthy lifestyle behaviors. In fact, Harris (2004) managed to find an association between this variable of control and health habits. Also, composite findings of psychological hardiness, commitment, and control were associated with low levels of anxiety, anger, depression, and stress within a sample of European Americans (Harris, 2004). It is this type of thinking and emotional regulation that has been shown to make most individuals able to counteract negative emotions and self-defeating thoughts that often surface in moments of stress and thus contribute to greater psychological resilience and successful adaptation to stressful events throughout the life span (Ong, Bergeman, Bisconti, & Wallace, 2006). Thus, European Americans appear to have a strong sense of how to adapt to psychosocial stressors because of their ability to focus on themselves and their personal thoughts, feelings, and behaviors during difficult periods.

Another strength that appears relevant to European American youths and middle-aged adults is the ability to assimilate into various types of groups. Though European Americans have dominated the cultural landscape of the United States for much of its history, there have also been various accounts to show how they have blended in with other groups that have also settled into the landscape (Gladding, 2000). There have been increasing amounts of intergroup marriages and multicultural relationships that have occurred between European Americans and various other populations (Sue, Ivey, & Pedersen, 1996), which provide some evidence to support the notion that interpersonal communication and assimilation skills are positive qualities that European Americans have used for effective socialization. In a broader sense, these skills are also related to social competency, which is a specific strength that has been applied to European American youths and their African American cohorts (Caplan et al., 1992). In social situations, it appears that most European American youths are able to learn effective ways of communicating and establishing social networks because of the fact that they are able to effectively learn components of character education and interpersonal management skills (Caplan et al., 1992; Goldstein & McGinnis, 1983). Modeling techniques and approaches appear to be effective learning tools for these children because of the independent learning styles and task-oriented approaches that European American students often employ (Gladding, 2000). This is not to say that other cultural groups are unable to demonstrate these same characteristics but rather to say that effective social competency has been observed among European Americans who have been exposed to this specific task-oriented style of learning (Caplan et al., 1992). Teachers often report fewer mental health problems for European American students than they do for their Hispanic American and African American counterparts (Zimmerman, Khoury, Vega, Gil, & Warheit, 1995). Though these data may be culturally biased, it suggests that within the educational environment, European Americans may be perceived as having a well-functioning and adaptive style that allows for effective learning and communication to occur. Again, this is not a statement designed to show that other cultural groups do not have these capabilities but rather a way of showcasing perceived strengths of European American students.

Another perceived strength of European American populations relates to their analytical and empirical worldview (Gladding, 2000). Being that European Americans seem particularly able to analyze their problems, it appears that they are more likely to objectively define their problems and goals associated with treatment. Though there may be a smaller threshold by which European American caregivers, as opposed to those from other cultural groups, view an issue as a behavioral and/or mental health problem, European American caregivers are willing to consider using these labels in what appears to be an attempt to address problematic behaviors (Roberts et al., 2005). There are many explanations that have been used to address why this process occurs. One explanation is that European Americans perceive the cost–benefit ratio of labeling problems with a behavioral and/or mental health focus as a positive option that allows for an effective mental health treatment system to facilitate the helping process (Roberts et al., 2005). Another explanation is that the openness and expression of difficulties within European American families appears to be of greater intensity than within other family systems (Roberts et al., 2005). Though openness is certainly a strong characteristic of African American and Latino(a) American families, the authoritarian roles that parents often play within these systems may not allow for youths and young adults to openly express and talk about perceived problems related to behavioral and mental problems (Ortega & Alegria, 2002). One other hypothesis as to why European Americans and European American caregivers are able to use labels of behavioral and mental health problems more frequently than other cultural and ethnic groups is that many individuals within this population do not view the use of these labels as a poor reflection on their caregiving and social skills (Roberts et al., 2005). As previously noted, European Americans are highly individualistic and independent thinkers. Thus, when an individual is analyzing problematic thoughts and/or behaviors, his or her potential to create the problem can also be viewed as a reason to believe that he or she can take steps toward alleviating it. An individual who has a problem has the ability to address it, and though it may not allow for the family system to feel good about the fact that someone within the family is struggling with an issue, it does not ultimately result in a collective shame about why the individual has developed a problem. European American children and adolescents are usually referred to counseling and mental health services via parents and related caregivers, which may reflect the fact that these parents believe that their children can benefit from these services independently (Roberts et al., 2005). It is through this form of logic and reasoning that European Americans are believed to have a fairly good propensity for embracing counseling and theoretical approaches that correlate well with their analytical and independent thinking style (Gladding, 2000). In one study, European American adults were two times as likely as their African American and Latino(a) American counterparts to use any outpatient services, two and a half times more likely to see a mental health professional, two times as likely to see a primary care physician for mental health problems, and one and a half times more likely to see a primary care physician for mental problems (Roberts et al., 2005), and European American youths were one and a half times more likely to use school-based mental health counseling and/or therapy than were African American and Latino(a) American youths (Roberts et al., 2005). There appears to be decent data to suggest that European Americans bring several strengths and positive beliefs to counseling and mental health relationships when such services are sought. However, some of these same characteristics that bring them to the therapeutic relationship can also serve as significant challenges to mental health professionals who attempt to facilitate the therapeutic process.

Weaknesses (That Serve as Challenges to Mental Health)

Though it is certainly encouraging to know that many European Americans are able to seek mental health services, it is also important to bear in mind that European Americans are more likely to label behaviors and issues as those that require mental health service or intervention as opposed to members of other ethnic/racial groups (Harris, 2004; Roberts et al., 2005). Studies have shown that African American mothers, for example, reported less anxiety in their children than European American mothers, even though their children exhibited highly similar symptoms regarding depression and anxiety disorders (Walton, Johnson, & Algina, 1999). In another study, European Americans were more likely than African Americans and Latino(a) Americans to rate the mental health of their adolescents as fair or poor, with European Americans also being twice as likely to believe their adolescents were having problems stemming from drug or alcohol use, emotional issues, or behavior issues during the previous year in which the study was conducted (Roberts et al., 2005). It is not just the caregivers referring to their children and adolescents, however, that demonstrates the tendency for European Americans to label matters as requiring behavioral and mental health treatment.

In a study where European American and African American college students were asked to evaluate their psychological, mental, and physical health, European Americans reported a greater average frequency of episodes of depression, anxiety, fear, self-directed anger, anger directed at others, inability to express feelings to others, concerns about health status, and experiences with unusual amounts of stress (Harris, 2004). Thus, even when dealing with self-reports, it appears that European Americans are more likely to view tendencies and behaviors as threats to their health and well-being. Similar behaviors and tendencies do not necessarily carry this meaning within other cultural and ethnic groups (Roberts et al., 2005). It is important for a counselor and/or mental health professional to recognize that this tendency to focus on problems may act as an enabling behavior that may not inspire or motivate some European American clients to engage in the change process.

Another significant weakness relates to the concept of individualism. Though European Americans are largely focused on independence and rugged individualism in terms of approaching problems and enacting change (Gladding, 2000), this does not always aid in the change process. Within family dynamics, individualism can often prevent members from disclosing deep issues and/or emotions that can often allow for greater levels of support and comfort to occur (Johnson, 2003). It is often difficult to engage in an effective change process when social supports do not reinforce the notion of change, and European Americans may be at particular risk for this type of struggle because of the fact that problems are often viewed as the primary responsibility of the individual to resolve (Mahoney, 1991). Such dynamics have been studied with teenage girls (Johnson, 2003), adolescent and teenage boys (Goldstein, 1995), and young adults (Ambert, 1997). Although the concept of individualism for European Americans is often a considerable strength (Gladding, 2000), the astute counselor and/or clinician must be aware of the fact that ignoring the systemic context in which change occurs can lead to a difficult pattern by which some individuals may not be able to further adapt to other changes that occur throughout the life span (Jopp & Rott, 2006).

This pattern of egocentrism and self-focused thinking can often be viewed as a form of resistance, especially when European Americans are working with diverse individuals who do not necessarily come from an individualistic culture (Diamondstone, 2002). Though resistance in some forms is not always considered a negative factor, people who value collectivistic and nondirective communication can view individuals who resist certain ideas and communications as disinterested in common goals. It can appear that egocentric individuals are pushing their own agendas onto others, even if such individuals are attempting to work in a collaborative manner (Diamondstone, 2002). This may be particularly significant for European American males, who are often viewed by mainstream society as task-oriented individuals who often do not have a strong propensity for sensitivity and/or strong emotional intelligence (Englar-Carlson & Stevens, 2006). Although there has been a movement toward new masculinity that involves greater sensitivity and understanding of men's issues, the notion of being a strong, independent human is often associated with European American values and can make the counseling process quite challenging for males who are likely to view the discussion of personal issues and feelings as a sign of weakness. What a mental health professional must do, therefore, to promote effective change and participation in therapy is to provide European American clients with incentives and ideas that harness their perceived strengths and positive qualities that allow for progress to be made. Several techniques and theoretical approaches can aid in this task.

Harnessing the Strengths of European American Clients

Being that many European American clients effectively use logic and analytical reasoning, it is not surprising that most counseling and clinical interventions follow a scientist-practitioner model. The general procedure of gathering background information about a client, defining his or her problem, formulating a hypothesis to attempt a resolution to said problem, engaging in the problem-solving process, and evaluating the outcome of this approach is strongly recommended. In other words, using the scientific method helps to form a structure for therapy, and many children and young adults within the European American population thrive on structure and organization. Many theoretical approaches that have been effectively applied to working with European American clients, such as rational-emotive behavior therapy and cognitive behavioral therapy, are based on a systematic and meticulous manner by which information about a client and his or her issues is gathered and applied to treatment (Brown & Lent, 2000; Gladding, 2000). This sense of predictability and organization can lead to the perception that a problem can be controlled, which directly taps into the internal locus of control that many European American clients utilize in their everyday lives.

The use of empirical data and information provides another outlet for the effective mental health worker to harness the therapeutic strengths of the European American client. Because European Americans value their individualism so strongly, they may not be able to recognize the fact that there are many individuals who share several issues that they also possess. This is evident in many cases where children and adolescents believe in the notion of an imaginary audience that will harshly judge and/or exploit them if they show any signs of weakness and/or ineffectiveness regarding how they perform in school and among peer groups (Santrock, 2004). Unless presented with information about the fact that they are not the only people who suffer with such issues, many young clients may feel overwhelmed and/or consumed by the idea that their problems are greater than their ability to control them; this is a form of learned helplessness that comes from an internal locus of control. However, when provided with the information that there are many individuals who share common elements and factors related to personal problems, European American clients can often harness their ability to assimilate into groups and engage in a program and/or group modality that allows for effective intervention to take place. In other words, this information allows these clients to gain a sense of hope and relief that comes from being able to join with others who share common characteristics and problem-solving goals (Kim, Ng, & Ahn, 2005). Numerous research studies and intervention reports appear to back up this notion for European American clients who have difficulties with social skills (Goldstein & McGinnis, 1983), anger management (Goldstein, 1995), various forms of anxiety and depression, and various other issues that relate to behavioral and mental health.

Another way that mental health professionals can effectively engage European American clients in the treatment process is to use alternative thinking strategies. Because these clients are more apt to label their behaviors and issues as problems than as strengths, an effective mental health counselor needs to challenge European American clients to find positive reframes and conceptualizations that can not only normalize many of their concerns but also empower them to systematically apply this alternative thinking strategy to future concerns that may come their way. One of the most difficult elements of the counseling process is the initial stage whereby clients are asked to define their problems and set their goals (Brown & Lent, 2000). For many European American clients, especially young children through middle adulthood, this can serve as a form of admission that indicates failure and/or inability to independently function (Johnson, 2003). Younger clients are often referred to counseling by their caregivers and/or significant authority figures (Walton et al., 1999). The effective mental health counselor can reframe this initial part of the process right away by pointing out to such clients that although they have been referred for treatment, they managed to follow through with this referral. All too often, the notion of seeking mental health services can be associated with weakness and inability to maintain a sense of personal control. A counselor can use this information in a slightly revised manner, which can show clients that they are actually strong and capable individuals who have managed to recognize that a problem exists and can be worked through by personally engaging in the counseling process. This is a demystification strategy that can often allay fears and concerns many clients may have if they seek counseling service.

One clinical example that best showcases how to harness the strengths of European American is the case of Bob (a 13-year-old middle school student) and his family: mother Jane (age 35) and father John (age 65). (These names have been altered from the actual case records.) All of these individuals were only children within their families of origin and had no other biological relatives living within their Midwestern community. This multigenerational Midwestern family was referred to counseling via their family physician, for the purposes of dealing with anxiety. Bob was born with a deformed pituitary gland that resulted in somewhat stunted growth. Both of his parents were working-class individuals with high school educations. All three family members had been exposed to medical advice and intervention throughout their lives because of Bob's development, Jane's weight issue, and John's smoking habits. They were very concrete thinkers who were very good at following doctor's orders but were also likely to view everything as a potential crisis. For example, because of Bob's inability to quickly form blood clots, Jane was encouraged to monitor her child's physical activity very closely so in case of emergency, she would be able to administer necessary injections that would prevent further damage from occurring. Jane became so consumed by this information that it dominated her thinking and behavior. She would need to be present for any encounters that her son would have, and he was often not permitted to leave their home out of her fear that something would happen to him. John did not view himself as an effective person who could administer the necessary treatment, primarily because of his age, and Bob would not even be allowed to gather the mail from the family mailbox located no more than 50 feet away from their home. Bob was a dutiful son, being that he would constantly obey his mother and father's requests. However, as Bob began to enter adolescence, he began to make closer connections with peers and desired the ability to visit them at their homes. Though Jane and John knew that these days would come, they were not comfortable with the idea of letting their child out of their sights. They found themselves in a position where any information they encountered about the social world would be viewed as a threat to their son's well-being. For example, they saw a news story about a swarm of killer bees that was expected to migrate to the United States, and they used this as a reason to believe they could not visit distant relatives. Not only were these killer bees not expected to come into contact with any parts of the country where friends and loved ones resided, they never came. This was not enough to convince John and Jane, however, that some of their behaviors and beliefs may have been irrational. After all, Bob had grown into a relatively healthy 13-year-old boy who never encountered any serious medical trauma apart from his original diagnosis. He even entered into middle school with decent grades in his specialty courses and appeared to be well liked by teachers and peers. On the basis of their levels of anxiety, their family physician recommended that they seek counseling and mental health services.

Jane admitted that much of her behaviors and beliefs were patterns that she adapted after being raised by parents who were very extreme thinkers. Though there were no reports of physical or sexual abuse, Jane stated that many of her mother and father's manners by which they would deal with certain situations appeared "very strict." For example, she spoke of a time when she was a child, and there was a tornado warning in effect for her state county. She recalled her parents marching down into the basement of their home and remaining there until the warning had passed. The tornado did not pass through the county and did not come into contact with many of the immediate places around her neighborhood. Even though she viewed these actions as extreme to some degree, she believed her parents were providing excellent care and that they expressed love through these protective measures. This may have explained why Jane did not socialize very much with her peers and eventually ended up marrying someone who was nearly twice her age, out of a conscious and/or unconscious need to remain in a relationship with a father figure. Her main goal for therapy was to watch her child become more able to see himself like a "normal" boy and to not feel anxious herself about whether he would grow up into a "normal" adult.

John admitted that he was also from a very strict upbringing. He believed that he was supposed to be more of a "doer" than a "feeler." Although he knew his wife was an anxious person, he believed that as long as she was able to follow the doctor's orders and closely monitor Bob, she was doing what needed to be done. He did not reveal much about his past during the course of therapy, and he initially believed that much of the responsibility associated with looking out for his son's safety was for his wife. He was either working or visiting doctor's offices for his personal health issues most of the time, and though he valued the paternal role that he had within the family, he did not view himself as a person who could get very involved with some of the caretaking issues. His main goal for therapy was to see his child and wife feel more stable on a daily basis.

Bob was presented as a pleasant young man who had many fears about things he had heard or seen from his parents and the media. Some of this information was confusing to him, because his peers would not always agree with the same data. For example, he reported watching a movie with his mother where the characters were trapped in an elevator, and though the movie was based on fiction, he was not able to completely tell that this scenario was not likely to happen in everyday life. His mother confirmed the fact that this event is a plausible occurrence and avoided using elevators for a period of time after seeing the movie. Bob did not report feeling angry or anxious about his mother's actions but wondered if his friends were correct. This appeared to be the main theme in

Bob's life: Was he a bad person for not always agreeing with his mother, and how would either parent take the news if he were to take the words of friends and/or other authority figures over theirs? Bob's main goal for therapy was to not feel scared about certain issues in his life all of the time.

The family initially reported to session as a group, whereby data were gathered on all three individuals in the presence of one another. After discovering that all family members had specific goals, it was determined that subsequent sessions would involve all three members for one half of the time, followed by just the counselor and Bob for the remainder. Both of the parents would remain in the waiting area so as to encourage them to allow for Bob to remain with a stranger while they were within the immediate vicinity but not in direct sight and earshot. This intentional modeling procedure served as a way of encouraging Bob to independently explore his issues while at the same time encouraging his parents to remain outside of his personal space. Sessions were videotaped in case there were concerns about what was taking place during the course of counseling. Parents were also asked to assess their level of anxiety as a result of their presence outside of Bob's personal space, and this activity was encouraged outside of the therapy office as well. Both parents complied.

Much of the work that took place between Bob and his counselor centered around the idea of feeling comfortable with asking people for help and/or getting information from others if he was not certain about certain facts. Bob was not comfortable with making mistakes around his parents because he would observe them reacting to many of his behaviors with anxiety and overcompensation. As a result, Bob believed that he was making things difficult for his mother and father. In actuality, both parents expressed deep levels of love and appreciation for Bob but were so consumed with making sure that he was physically safe that they simply did not focus on emotional well-being. Bob's counselor praised him for being open about his feelings and concerns. Bob also engaged in various role-plays whereby his counselor would model what it would be like to ask a teacher, peer, or family member for help. Bob was shown specific steps to take to determine if he should ask for help, how he should approach someone he was willing to ask, and what things he could say. By actively engaging in these simulation exercises, Bob not only was praised for his positive efforts but also managed to normalize and reframe what it means to ask for help. Instead of viewing this behavior as a weakness and/or fault, Bob eventually came to an understanding that it is a normal behavior that people exhibit when they have curiosities. Ironically, this behavior was one of the operational definitions Bob's mother provided as a way of knowing that her son could function as a "normal" child. The family dynamics improved dramatically between Jane and Bob as a result.

Jane had always believed that her son was capable of being a child "just like any other kid." However, her fears and anxieties surrounding her perceptions of having a physically ill child distorted much of this basic belief. When she was asked by her counselor to give a detailed description of what a "normal" child would behave like, she produced numerous insights into the way in which she could reframe her perception of Bob. At first, there was some resistance on the part of Jane to believe that many of the operational definitions she used to define a "normal" child could apply to her son. She also used information regarding her son's illness and her husband's older age to suggest that there were too many "abnormalities" that existed within the family system to ensure that some of these "normal" experiences would be able to occur. This negative labeling allowed for one of the strongest interventions to occur during the course of therapy.

Jane believed that a "normal" young man would be able to bond well with his father. John presented himself as a fairly strict individual within the family system and did not signify to Jane or Bob that he was open to developing emotional rapport. One of the more interesting disclosures that came out of therapy was the fact that John did not believe in letting his son win at certain games, such as checkers. John was convinced that letting Bob win would not be an accurate way by which he would be able to learn how to perform things the "right" way. After some disclosure to his counselor, along with a more open dialogue between him and his wife, John agreed to set up an opportunity to let Bob win one game. John was willing to consider this idea because he agreed with the idea that it would be very difficult for Bob to have a drive for success if there was no model in place for him to understand exactly what success looked and felt like. Bob and John played this game in a separate room of the counseling clinic while Jane observed the interaction on videotape. Jane became tearful as she observed her son experience the joy of winning a game of checkers, and she appreciated the fact that her husband remained a good sport about this event. However, it was even more encouraging when they returned the following week to report that Bob actually won a game of checkers against his father without this assistance. This was an unexpected event for everyone but Bob. However, this is precisely what makes the strengths of European American clients fairly easy to harness. If clients are given a model for success and a systematic approach toward understanding what steps need to be taken to enact this model, they can adopt a worldview by which their actions can improve their self-efficacy, self-talk, and thoughts and feelings about how they are able to function. Bob was working off a model of success that his family was previously uncertain about using out of fear and concern for his safety. If he would gain a false sense of hope about gaining success, Bob could set himself up for further disappointment if he were to eventually fail. However, when Bob was presented with a model for success, he was able to take it at face value and independently engage in actions that led to future successes because he was able to concretely understand what steps needed to be taken to maintain this momentum. His parents also learned that the limitations they were placing on Bob were contributing to the very anxieties and negative labels that were disrupting the family's comfort in the first place. All of these pieces of data were systematically observed, questioned, and addressed during each session so that all family members could gain a concrete understanding of what changes needed to be made to reach the goals they had set. This European American family showcases the importance of using the reframing approach whenever possible. All of the thoughts, feelings, and behaviors that these clients were using were based on the notion of care and concern for each other. Bob was trying to be a dutiful son so as not to disappoint his parents. Jane was trying to be a protective parent to ensure the safety of her son along with a reduced burden of responsibility for her husband. John was trying to be a solid authority figure within the family system so that rules and norms could be maintained. By approaching these clients with the fundamental understanding that their actions, feelings, and thoughts were based on this notion of care made for solid rapport within the therapeutic environment as well as a justifiable manner by which reframes and challenges to these clients could be made. Being that the clients were primarily focused on negatives and problematic elements of their lives, giving them a model for focusing on positives and alternative strategies by which they could attain their goals allowed for effective change to take place. Furthermore, it also allowed for these clients to take these new beliefs and behaviors outside of the therapy room and into the community, which further enhanced their mental and behavioral health.

How to Build an Alliance With the Client's Community

In terms of how to build an alliance with the European American client's community, the same process that is used in the counseling process can be applied. Bob and his family were aware of people who existed in their community but did not appear certain as to why they needed to socialize with these individuals. For Jane, getting close to members of the community involved exposing negative characteristics about herself as a parent and woman that she believed would ultimately create more stress for her to deal with. After the counselor provided Jane with information about how there were parenting groups, women's groups, and social meetings that took place on a regular basis for people like her who struggle with issues of maintaining a significant home and social life, Jane felt not only more able to attend these meetings but also more aware of the fact that she was not exposing herself as a "bad" person. She was able to see that by demonstrating the same social skills and actions that she shared in the counseling room to people within the community, she was able to form meaningful connections with others. She formed mentoring relationships with people whom she felt connections with, and she served as a role model for other family members regarding how to become socially engaged with other people. Jane managed to join a women's social group, which afforded her the opportunity to gather appropriate space between herself and her family responsibilities. Though she was apprehensive about first leaving her son's side, Jane was able to see after a few encounters that her husband was supportive of her and that her son was capable of handling her absence. It also afforded Bob and John time to further develop a stronger father–son bond that was often not expressed, possibly because of the fact that it was something they did not feel comfortable displaying in the presence of the matriarch. Also, by having Jane join in with more social activities, she became more aware of how her son would benefit from having some time to visit friends of his own. Though Jane would still supervise these visits, she allowed her son to visit local neighborhood children at their homes. This process was important not only for Bob but also for Jane because it allowed her to gain a sense of trust with other members of the community with whom she felt unable to communicate with in the past. Eventually, it was hoped this would extend opportunities for other community members to visit her home.

Theoretical Orientations

We hope it is evident from the aforementioned data that reality/choice theory, rational-emotive behavior therapy (REBT), cognitive behavioral therapy (CBT), Adlerian theory, and solution-focused brief therapy (SFBT) all appear to be the most effective theoretical orientations that counselors who work with European American clients use. Many of these theories are synthesized with each other, such as SFBT and Adlerian theory (McCurdy, 2006) and reality/choice theory and CBT (Kastner, 2006; Merrick & Dattilio, 2006). These theories also appear to be easily adapted for individuals at different developmental levels. For example, CBT is often adapted to child and adolescent populations as well as adult populations (Lopata, Thomeer, Volker, & Nida, 2006). The same applications have been used with reality/choice theory (Kastner, 2006) and SFBT (Lethem, 2002). Furthermore, the fact that each of these theoretical approaches have been successfully applied to populations with clinical mental health issues also makes them significantly relevant treatments to employ when working with European American clients because of the fact that they are likely to suffer from some of these issues. CBT is one of the most powerful forms of intervention for clients who are clinically depressed (Merrick & Dattilio, 2006), and SFBT has received favorable outcomes when used on clients who suffer from emotional problems (Maree & Fernandes, 2003). Each theory also seems to have particular strengths that aid European American clients during the course of therapy.

Reality/choice theory appears to be strongly related to favorable counseling outcomes with European Americans because it examines factual conditions while giving clients the empowerment and independence to alter these conditions. This notion of having personal choice and personal freedom is well received by European American clients because of their tendency to favor individualistic thinking. Also, because of the tangible and systematic nature of approaching client goals, reality/choice theory does not appear to overwhelm many European American clients by focusing on details that may veer away from the immediate construction of an action plan (Kastner, 2006). The direct and individually focused manner by which this theory operates helps encourage European American clients to work toward change and instills a sense of hope that positive actions can be taken toward turning these changes into realities.

The same organization process that applies to reality/choice theory also makes REBT and CBT effective theoretical approaches for European American clients. REBT and CBT provide a structured framework for both client and counselor to approach issues and a systematic way in which feelings, thoughts, and behaviors can be analyzed. This need for order and structure is greatly appreciated by most European American clients and one of the major strengths that CBT and REBT bring to therapy. It is not surprising that they are among the most preferred forms of treatment that clients and mental health workers use (Merrick & Dattilio, 2006).

Another frequently used theoretical approach by mental health workers who assist European American clients is Adlerian theory. The positive approach and use of encouragement speaks to the sense of independence and determination that European Americans value and to which many of these clients strongly adhere. Reliance on family dynamics and interpersonal understanding of the community also allow for clients to gain a sense of connectedness to others in a way that inspires European Americans to seek out these connections. The value of this insight allows for lifestyle change, as opposed to simplistic behavioral change (McCurdy, 2006). Thus, Adlerian theory helps European American clients systematically analyze issues, but the end result extends beyond adjusting of behaviors; it is a shift in perspective and new lifestyle approach that allows for changes to be made.

Changes are also essential to the theoretical approach known as SFBT (Lethem, 2002). This approach is also structured and systematic, but by not specifically focusing on the origin of a particular problem, clients can feel encouraged to overcome issues that have readily accessible solutions that are within their control. Considering that many European American clients are used to analyzing problems and relying on diagnostic labels that usually confirm biases toward obstacles and/or symptoms related to clinical issues, SFBT encourages clients to focus on the exceptional factors in their lives that are more related to strengths and resiliency. This principle aligns well with the rugged individualism and focus on action that many European Americans value. Furthermore, with the managed care system set in place by many mental health agencies and private practices, SFBT allows clients with limited funding and propensity to rely on efficient use of time by which they can seek help. This relatively modern approach appears to be a well-matched theoretical perspective that aligns with European American values.

Principles and Guidelines

Based on review of literature and examination of case studies that relate to European American clients, it appears that each of the aforementioned theoretical approaches follows these specific principles and guidelines. The first three (Reality/Choice theory, Rational-Emotive Behavior Therapy, Cognitive-Behavioral Therapy) speak to ways by which a mental health worker can decrease negative functioning of European American clients, whereas the latter two (Adlerian Theory, Solution-Focused Brief Therapy) refer to ways by which positive functioning can be increased. The skilled mental health worker is encouraged to follow all of these concepts, regardless of the theoretical orientation to which he or she adheres:

1. Take the client seriously (they perceive labels in a concrete and factual manner).
2. Normalize their extreme feelings whenever possible by providing reality checks and/or information.
3. Be concrete and direct so as not to give a sense of confusion.
4. Be structured and organized so that people can see the predictable, authentic nature of your work.
5. Balance a feeling dialogue with a behavioral and cognitive one.
6. Use encouragement and positive reinforcement to assure clients that they are doing well.
7. Provide reframing techniques to show clients how their negative concepts can actually have positive meaning.
8. Use "I" statements and model other social skills so that clients can actively engage in a more positive pattern of interaction that can be generalized outside of the therapy room.
9. Come up with concrete goals and/or steps for clients to take so that they are able to see that problems have solutions.

10. Be able to use the data to accentuate positives (call attention to the progress you have seen).

Future Recommendations

As was mentioned previously, there is a dearth of scholarly literature devoted to White European immigrant groups (Ponterotto et al., 2001). Much of the multicultural literature has focused on American minorities and on Hispanic and Asian groups. Europe has generally been lumped in with North America and has been considered part of Western culture. When it has been examined more closely, Europe has typically been taken as a whole and not examined in terms of the cultural differences between countries or even between regions within countries. Counselors and counseling professionals need to consider that just as the culture in the Midwestern United States is different from that in the Atlantic and Pacific coasts, different regions of European countries may also be culturally different.

As Cohen (2009) suggested, counselors need to explore more kinds of variation among more kinds of cultures. When it comes to European immigrants, it is not enough to simply say that the immigrant family is European. Counselors and counseling professionals need to look at the many forms of culture within Europe and how those influence the individual and family. Europe, like North America, is becoming more and more diverse. With modern mobility people are migrating across Europe and into different nations. Different religious groups such as Muslims have also been growing in Europe, which can have an impact on the culture of the continent.

Counselors and counseling professionals need to also look at the nation that the immigrant family comes from in terms of whether it is Eastern or Western European. The Eastern European nations have relatively recently split off from the Soviet Union and are developing their own independent nations. Researchers should look to see how nations such as those affect the family and how therapists can help families from those nations. They might also look at if and how those families differ from families from Western European nations, and how those differences affect them as immigrants.

Another area for future focus for counselors and counseling professionals is to identify European immigrants' preferences for multicultural counseling competencies. Fraga, Atkinson, and Wampold (2004) looked at preferences of Asian American, European American, and Hispanic undergraduate students. They wanted to know if ethnic minorities underutilized outpatient and college counseling centers because they perceived counselors to not be competent to address their culturally related issues. They found in their study that European

American participants had a high preference for competencies that seem to be more related to ethnic minorities, such as a strong preference for a counselor who is willing to interact with institutions on behalf of racial/ethnic minorities and respect clients' indigenous helping practices and minority help-giving networks. The researchers suggested that the results may have been due to the fact that the sample was taken from ethnic-specific courses at the university where the study was done. It would be good for researchers to replicate these findings but to also include European immigrants in the study for further analysis.

Counselors and counseling professionals need also to look at what they can do as professionals to help facilitate the transition of European families to the United States. There is little scientific evidence to validate the widely held belief that moving has any long-term negative impact on average people (Vercruysse, 2002). It is nevertheless important for counseling professionals to keep in mind that for some, moving into a new culture can be associated with any number of stress-related reactions that do require early interventions from qualified professionals.

Vercruysse (2002) presented a community help service that has been in service in Brussels since 1969 that is worth looking at for counselors working with European immigrants. The service provides a broad range of support services that contribute to the well-being of relocated individuals, couples, and families. The services she described could be utilized in the United States to help relocated European families, including the provision of mental health information, a 24-hour information and crisis telephone service, a counseling center staffed by professional therapists, and the pursuit of ongoing research, consultation, and training in the broader community. This could be a model for counselors and counseling professionals to utilize, especially in areas where there are high concentrations of European immigrants.

Discussion Questions

1. How might you change your approach if you were counseling an immigrant family from Western Europe or from Eastern Europe?
2. How might you change your approach if you were counseling an immigrant family who was from a country that is a member of the European Union or a family who is from a country that is not in the European Union? Would it matter?
3. What considerations might you have when conceptualizing an immigrant family other than the fact that the family is from European origin?
4. How might you help a European immigrant family successfully move through the phases of acculturation?

5. How might you work with a European immigrant family whose members are at different acculturation levels?

References

Alonso J., Angermeyer, M.C., Bernert, S., Bruffaerts, R., Brugha, T.S., Bryson, H., et al. (2004). Use of mental health services in Europe: Results from the European Study of Epidemiology of Mental Disorders (ESEMeD) project. *Acta Psychiatrica Scandinaviaca, 109 (suppl.420)*, 47–54.

Ambert, A. (1997). *Parents, children and adolescents: Interactive relationships and development in context.* New York: Haworth Press.

Boneva, B. S. & Frieze, I. H. (2001). Toward a concept of migrant personality. *Journal of Social Issues, 57*, 477–491.

Brilliant, J. J. (2000). Issues in counseling immigrant college students. *Community College Journal of Research and Practice, 24*, 577–586.

Brown, S. & Lent, R. (2000). *Handbook of counseling psychology.* New York: John Wiley & Sons.

Caplan, M., Weissberg, R., Grober, J., Sivo, P., Grady, K., & Jacoby, C. (1992). Social competence promotion with inner city and suburban young adolescents: Effects on social adjustment and alcohol use. *Journal of Consulting and Clinical Psychology, 60*, 56–63.

Center for Disease Control. (2002). Ten Leading Causes of Death: 2002. Atlanta, GA: Author. http://webappa.cdc.gov/sasweb/ncipc/leadcaus10.html.

Chen, S. X. & Mak, W. W. S. (2008). Seeking professional help: Etiology beliefs about mental illness across cultures. *Journal of Counseling Psychology, 55*(4), 442–450.

Cohen, A. B. (2009). Many forms of culture. *American Psychologist, 64*(3), 194–204.

Diamondstone, J. (2002). Keeping resistance in view in an activity theory analysis. *Mind, Culture, and Activity, 9*, 2–21.

Englar-Carlson, M. & Stevens, M. (2006). *In the room with men: A casebook of therapeutic change.* Washington, DC: American Psychological Association.

Fraga, E. D., Atkinson, D. R., & Wampold, B. E. (2004). Ethnic group preferences for multicultural counseling competencies. *Cultural Diversity and Ethnic Minority Psychology, 10*(1), 53–65.

Frieze, I. H., Boneva, B. S., Sarlija, N., Horvat, J., Ferligoj, A., Kogovsek, T., Miluska, J., Popova, L., Korobanova, J., Sukhareva, N., Erokhina, L., & Jarosova, E. (2004). Psychological differences in stayers and leavers: Emigration desires in Central and Eastern university students. *European Psychologist, 9*(1), 15–23.

Gentry, W. (1984). *Handbook of behavioral medicine.* New York: Guilford.

Gladding, S. (2000). *Counseling: A comprehensive profession* (4th ed.). New York: Merrill/Prentice Hall.

Goldstein, A. (1995). *Understanding and managing children's classroom behavior.* New York: John Wiley & Sons.

Goldstein, A. & McGinnis, E. (1983). *Skillstreaming in childhood: Teaching prosocial skills to the secondary school child.* New York: McNaughton & Gunn.

Greenberger, E. & Chen, C. (1996). Perceived family relationships and depressed mood in early and late adolescence: A comparison of European and Asian Americans. *Developmental Psychology, 32*(4), 707–716.

Harris, S. (2004). The effect of health value and ethnicity on the relationship between hardiness and health behaviors. *Journal of Personality, 72,* 379–412.

Hwang, W. (2006). Acculturation family distancing: Theory, research, and clinical practice. *Psychotherapy: Theory, Research, Practice, Training, 43*(4), 397–409.

Johnson, N. (2003). On treating adolescent girls: Focus on strengths and resiliency in psychotherapy. *Journal of Clinical Psychology, 59,* 1193–1203.

Jopp, D. & Rott, C. (2006). Adaptation in very old age: Exploring the role of resources, beliefs, and attitudes for centenarians' happiness. *Psychology and Aging, 21,* 266–280.

Kastner, B. (2006). Choice theory as it applies to different backdrops: A case study. *International Journal of Reality Therapy, 26,* 20–22.

Kim, B., Ng, G., & Ahn, A. (2005). Effects of client expectation for counseling success, client–counselor worldview match, and client adherence to Asian and European American cultural values on counseling process with Asian Americans. *Journal of Counseling Psychology, 52,* 67–76.

Kobasa, S. (1979). Stressful life events, personality and health: An inquiry into hardiness. *Journal of Personality and Social Psychology, 37,* 1–11.

Lethem, J. (2002). Brief solution focused therapy. *Child and Adolescent Mental Health, 7,* 189–192.

Lopata, C., Thomeer, M., Volker, M., & Nida, R. (2006). Effectiveness of a cognitive-behavioral treatment on the social behaviors of children with Asperger disorder. *Focus on Autism and Other Developmental Disabilities, 21,* 237–244.

Lunt, I. (1998). Psychology in Europe: Developments, challenges, and opportunities. *European Psychologist, 3*(2), 93–101.

Mahoney, R. (1991). *Human change processes: The scientific foundations of psychotherapy.* Chicago: Basic Books.

Maree, J. & Fernandes, P. (2003). The impact of emotional intelligence on solution-focused therapy with an adolescent. *Early Child Development, 173,* 499–508.

McCurdy, K. (2006). Adlerian supervision: A new perspective with a solution focus. *Journal of Individual Psychology, 62,* 141–153.

Merrick, P. & Dattilio, F. (2006). The contemporary appeal of cognitive-behavior therapy. *New Zealand Journal of Psychology, 35,* 117–119.

Mirsky, J. (1991). Language in migration: Separation individuation conflicts in relation to the mother tongue and the new language. *Psychotherapy: Theory, Research, Practice, Training, 28*(4), 618–624.

National Institute for Mental Health. (2001). The numbers count: Mental disorders in America. Washington D.C.: U.S. Department of Health and Human Services. http://www.nimh.gov/health/publications/the-numbers-count-mental-disorders-in-america/index.shtml.

National Institute of Mental Health. (2006). The numbers count: Mental disorders in America. Washington D.C.: U.S. Department of Health and Human Services. http://www.nimh.gov/health/publications/the-numbers-count-mental-disorders-in-america/index.shtml.

Nikelly, A. G. (1997). Cultural Babel: The challenge of immigrants to the helping professions. *Cultural Diversity and Mental Health, 3*(4), 221–233.

Ong, A., Bergeman, C.S., Bisconti, T., & Wallace, K. (2006). Psychological resilience, positive emotions, and successful adaptation to stress in later life. *Journal of Personality and Social Psychology, 91*, 730–749.

Ortega, A. & Alegria, M. (2002). Self-reliance, mental health need and the use of healthcare among island Puerto Ricans. *Mental Health Services Research, 4*, 131–140.

Ponterotto, J. G., Rao, V., Zweig, J., Rieger, B. P., Schaefer, K., Michelakou, S., Armenia, C., & Goldstein, H. (2001). The relationship of acculturation and gender to attitudes toward counseling in Italian and Greek American college students. *Cultural Diversity and Ethnic Minority Psychology, 7*(4), 362–375.

Primm, A. B., Lima, B. R., & Rowe, C. L. (1996). Cultural and ethnic sensitivity. In W. R. Breakey (Ed.), *Integrated mental health services: Modern community psychiatry* (pp. 146–159). New York: Oxford University Press.

Roberts, R.E., Alegria, M., Roberts, C.R., & Chen, I.G. (2005). Mental health problems of adolescents as reported by their caregivers: A comparison of European, African, and Latino Americans. *The Journal of Behavioral Health Services and Research, 32*, 1–13.

Robila, M. (2004). Families in Eastern Europe: Context, change, and variations. In M. Robila (Ed.), *Families in Eastern Europe*, 1-14, New York: Elsevier.

Robila, M. (2007). Eastern European immigrants in the United States: A socio-demographic profile. *The Social Science Journal, 44*, 113–125.

Rogler, L. H., Cortes, D. E., & Malgady, R. G. (1991). Acculturation and mental health status among Hispanics: Convergence and new directions for research. *American Psychologist, 46*(6), 585–597.

Santrock, J. (2004). *Life-span development.* New York: McGraw-Hill.

Strom, R., Daniels, S., Wurster, S., Betz, M. A., Graf, P., & Jansen, L. (1983). Childrearing attitude assessment as a prelude to integrating foreign families. *Journal of Marriage and the Family, 45*, 961–963.

Sue, D., Ivey, A. & Pedersen, P. (1996). *A theory of multicultural counseling and therapy.* Pacific Grove, CA: Brooks/Cole.

Vercruysse, N. (2002). Report from Euroland: Assisting individuals, couples, and families on the move. *European Psychologist, 7*(2), 149–152.

Walton, J., Johnson, S., & Algina, J. (1999). Mother and child perceptions of child anxiety: Effects of race, health status, and stress. *Journal of Pediatric Psychology, 24*, 29–39.

World Health Organization. (2004). *The world health report 2004: Changing history, Annex Table 3: Burden of the disease in DALYs by cause, sex and mortality stratum in WHO regions, estimates for 2002.* Geneva: Author.

Zimmerman, R., Khoury, E., Vega, W., Gil, A., & Warheit, G. (1995). Teacher and parent perceptions of behavior problems among a sample of African American, Hispanic, and non-Hispanic White students. *American Journal of Community Psychology, 23*, 181–197.

Chapter 6

Working With African Immigrant Families

Robyn Brammer

Contents

Africa composes over 20% of the Earth's land mass, holds a billion people, and contains 53 separate countries. It is the second largest of the Earth's seven continents, and it possesses amazing diversity. Mount Kilimanjaro in Tanzania rises 19,340 feet, while Lake Assal in Djibouti rests 502 feet below sea level (Zijlma, 2009). Africa has the world's second largest freshwater lake (Lake Victoria), second deepest freshwater lake (Lake Tanganyika), the longest river (Nile), and the lake containing the most diverse species of fish (Lake Malawi). Africa holds the world's oldest desert and the only desert in Africa inhabited by elephant, rhino, giraffe, and lion ("Africa," 2009).

Africa also possesses a huge range of people. Egypt's capital city, Cairo, is the largest city in Africa, with an estimated 17 million people living in the metropolitan area (Demographia, 2009). Nigeria, the most populated country in Africa, has an estimated population between 125 and 145 million people (National Population Commission of Nigeria, 2005). At the world's biggest hospital (Baragwanath Hospital in Soweto, South Africa), nearly 2,000 patients pass through the gates each day (Johnson, 2003). Concentrations such as these tell just part of the story. There are at least 3,000 distinct ethnic groups in Africa, with more than 2,000 spoken languages. When combined, the Arabic dialects compose the most common language, with 170 million speakers, mostly living in North Africa and the Horn of Africa (Zijlma, 2009).

With so many people ranging across so many different cultures, African immigrants face considerable challenges. There are still too few research studies and systematic theories applied to African immigrants and refugees (Warriner, 2007). In addition, Black immigrants include more than those coming from the African continent. There are substantial cultural differences between West Indians (i.e., Blacks from the Caribbean), Black African Americans, and Africans in the United States. It is important to note that more than a quarter of African immigrants are White, Arab, or generally non-Black (Obiakor & Afoláyan, 2007). It would take more than a chapter to fully articulate these differences, so this book will emphasize the largest group of immigrants.

Definition of the Native Culture

Though African immigrant families come from a large and diverse geographical region, there are some common concerns. To understand these, it is important to grasp the issues currently affecting the African regions. One of the most pressing concerns, which affects every country to different degrees, is disease (Othieno, 2007). AIDS is a primary concern, as millions have already died of the disease, and more than 22 million people in Africa are HIV positive. AIDS is projected to kill half of all 15-year-olds in Zimbabwe, Botswana, and South Africa by 2012 without substantial interventions (Cichocki, 2007).

According to Kanabus, Fredriksson-Bass, and Pembrey (2009), sub-Saharan eastern Africa has more HIV and AIDS cases than any other region of the world. The scope of the problem is difficult to fathom. In 2007, the AIDS epidemic in Africa claimed the lives of 1.5 million people in this region. It orphaned over 11 million children. The magnitude of the crisis not only overwhelms the health care sector but also affects education, industry, agriculture, transport, human resources, and the economy in general in countries such as Botswana, Lesotho, Namibia, South Africa, Swaziland, Zambia, and Zimbabwe, where 15–26% of adults are infected with HIV.

For counselors, the reasons for the disease's spread are as important as knowing the rates of infection. Some of the commonly discussed reasons include inadequate distribution of condoms, limited voluntary testing offices, and HIV-infected mothers nursing their children. The latter has led to over two million sub-Saharan children becoming HIV positive. This represents more than 85% of all children living with HIV worldwide (Kanabus et al., 2009). Some of the less discussed reasons are equally important and even more alarming. In South Africa, infant and toddler rape occurs at a low but consistent level. Two reasons for this include socialization influences from the country's violent apartheid past, as well as virgin cleansing myths (Chiroro, Bohner, Viki, & Jarvis, 2004). From my experiences in Malawi, the latter is the more common rationale. Some men believe the blood of a virgin is curative. When they learn they are infected with HIV, they rape young girls to cure themselves. Education involving condoms, breast-feeding, and cleansing myths is an important intervention needed throughout AIDS-infected countries.

Malaria has also affected much of Saharan Africa. As many as 3,000 children under the age of five die each day from malaria in Africa. Depending on the country, 1–5% of GDP in Africa covers costs of malaria control and lost labor. This results in a stunning loss of income (Ssemakula, 2001). Africa might have amassed $100 billion if malaria had been eradicated 10 years ago.

In addition to diseases, Africans face crises in several other areas. Many African countries have only recently begun to view education as a right rather than a privilege. Having public ownership of programs, improving literacy learning, and empowering learners in Africa are still in their nascence (Maruatona, 2006). Related to educational weaknesses, language differences are holding Africa back. One of the main issues preventing Africa from emerging as a superpower is the lack of language unity. Despite a sustained campaign to rally support from political leaders to unify African languages, little substantial growth has occurred (see Owino, 2002). Political leaders across many countries have also dogged rumors of corruption.

John Mukum Mbaku (1998) explained that many developing countries fail in their attempt to minimize bureaucratic corruption. Africans, he argued, have tried societal, legal, market, and political strategies, but all of these attempts to manipulate outcomes put too much confidence in the change agents themselves. For many African countries, the judiciary systems and police forces operate outside the laws they are supposed to defend. Corrupt change agents cannot produce a functional system.

Why Do Africans Come to America?

When Africans immigrate to America, they do so to avoid the conflicts mentioned above, but they also come for the economic opportunities, to escape oppression, to improve their education, and to provide financial support to family remaining in their home countries. Despite a global trend of falling poverty and income inequality, African poverty rates are increasing. In 1970, over 80% of the world's poor lived in east and south Asia. By the year 2000, 67.8% of the world's poor lived in Africa (Sala-i-Martin, 2006). This means almost 300 million Africans are impoverished, roughly 50% of the African population. During the same time, poverty rates in Asia declined to just 3%. Within Africa, poverty head counts increased in all countries with the exception of Botswana, the Republic of Congo, the islands of Mauritius, Cape Verde, and the Seychelles. Poverty was once an Asian problem; now it is an African tragedy driven by stunted economic growth (Sala-i-Martin, 2006).

As Africans leave the country, they create what has been called a "brain drain," which further exacerbates the problems (Obiakor & Afoláyan, 2007). Haider (1997) focused on Somalia's brain drain and how this problem steals talent from an impoverished developing country. The migration of highly educated people removes physicians, scientists, professors, economists, computer programmers, and engineers from the areas in most need of them. This undermines the economic development process. Technology, preventive health care, and housing are often the most immediate losses. In 2002, a group of technology firms, nonprofit organizations, and UN agencies launched a network to reverse the loss of professional skills from Africa. The program has achieved some success, but failing economies, high unemployment, human rights abuses, armed conflict, and limited health and education services tend to dissuade people from returning (Mutume, 2003). Immigrants also tend to find good jobs in America, which allows them to provide financial support to family remaining in their home country (Takougang, 1995).

When in America, Africans often struggle to find a corporate identity. Most do not identify with the African American culture, which is unique and separate from most African ways of life (Wamwara-Mbugua, Cornwell, & Boller, 2008). They also struggle against prejudice and find it confusing that White Americans categorize them with African Americans.

Second-generation immigrants often face an even greater struggle. Unlike their parents, who come with a clear cultural identity, children born to immigrants often lose the ability to speak their native language. They do not fully understand all the traditions and cultural aspects of their heritage, and they do not fully belong to the African American culture. As such, these immigrant children face unique challenges and will require special interventions.

Definition of Counseling Within the Native Culture

To understand African counseling, it is important to understand traditional healing practices. Berg (2003) did an excellent job introducing some of the important concepts in African healing. To begin with, Western therapists and physicians lack a clear understanding of healers' training. Sometimes called "witch doctors" (an inaccurate and deceptive term), healers undergo an initiation process requiring rigorous preparation and ancestral approval. They are, as Berg noted, skilled psychotherapists.

One reason why traditional healers play a role in African societies is a shared socioreligious philosophy. This worldview differs from Western and Eastern perspectives and defines many African beliefs and customs. According to van Dyk (2001), the traditional African worldview is based on a holistic and anthropocentric ontology. To understand the world, people must start by looking at themselves, their tribe, and their community. Many Africans believe in a unified force of nature, which animates all living things. God is the source of this force, but spirits play a role (Vontress, 1991). With God running all things, he is somewhat withdrawn from the daily role of people's lives. Ancestors and spirits of the dead are more likely to intercede in effecting change (van Dyk, 2001). Africans ascribe most illnesses, diseases, conflicts, misfortunes, or accidents to the spirit level. Chance, luck, and fate play no role. From a traditional African point of view, every illness or problem has an intention and a cause. To combat the illness, the individual must understand who or what caused the disease (Sow, 1980; van Dyk, 2001).

The most common reason for seeing a healer is to gain favor for an upcoming event or social concern; for example, winning a soccer game, passing a test, interviewing for a job, and so on. The healer works to bring harmony between the individual seeking help and the spirits associated with the events in question. Vontress (1991) discussed five common types of healers: the herbalist (who prescribes teas, wraps, and edible herbs), the juju man (who manipulates great powers through dance, music, mascots, lotions, amulets, or spells), the medium (who transmits messages from the dead to the living), the healer (who is a generalist and involves treatments from many of the other specialties), and the sorcerer (who is imbued with powers that can harm, destroy, or kill). Given the lack of Western medical and psychiatric services available in much of Africa, these healers are often the first line of defense against medical, psychological, and social problems. There are pros and cons to this. Kahn and Kelly (2001) found that psychiatric nurses were willing to refer several types of clients to healers, specifically those dealing with *thwasa* (an illness that calls one to become a healer), those dealing with traditional customs, patients with "cultural" problems, those with *amafufunyana* (evil spirit possession), and those under the effects of *ukuthakatha* (witchcraft). A sizable minority of these nurses would refer patients to healers for schizophrenia (28% would refer), family trouble (27%), alcoholism (21%), or drug abuse (12%). There was also consensus that healers varied in training and skills, and the government should regulate the profession.

When healers intervene with psychological or counseling-related issues, they rely on several techniques. They will use dream interpretation (often to discern what is happening in the spirit world around the individual), possession dances (which last for days, focus on healing a single family, but usually involve the community as a means of combating evil spirits), pharmacotherapy (both to evoke direct cures and to produce symbolic results—sometimes a purgative is prescribed to cause vomiting to expel an evil spirit), shock therapy (this may involve dipping someone into a cold river or simply scaring them by dressing in war outfits and brandishing knives), exorcisms (the most dangerous form of this involves smoking out the demon by forcing smoke into orifices such as the mouth or vagina), and music (Herring & Salazar, 2002). The latter is common in almost all native practices. It is difficult to imagine African healing without it.

The role of African healers and traditional medicine has become even more important of late, as additional studies continue to show the value of services for several mental-health-related issues. Havenaar, Geerlings, Vivian, Robertson, and Collinson (2008) found that traditional healers were occasionally sought specifically for mental health problems such as alcoholism or violent outbursts. More often, South Africans visited healers for disturbing dreams, "fits," job loss, physical ailments, and cultural concerns.

Whether Africans seek traditional or Western aid for mental health, family plays an essential role in most interventions. Many individuals are reluctant to make important decisions without consulting fathers or uncles (Vontress, 1991). When the African client is away from family, it is common for them to con-sult their "American family," which may involve friends or coworkers who have come from their native country. Counselors should avoid forcing clients to make immediate decisions in sessions and instead provide them with time to seek guidance from family.

Opinions About Those Who Seek Counseling

Seeking Western-style counseling raises the most concerns among African immi-grant women and may partly account for underutilization of mental health care services by disadvantaged women (Nadeem, Edge, Fongwa, & Belin, 2007). In their study, Nadeem et al. (2007) included 15,383 low-income women who were screened for depression in county entitlement services. They found that immigrant African and Caribbean women were nearly 50% less likely to desire

Western mental health services than Black women born in the United States. Stigma played a significant role in this difference. Many African immigrants see counseling as something reserved for people with serious psychiatric problems.

A secondary but possibly larger obstacle involves immigrants' perception of counselors. Cultural mistrust exists for mental health professionals and the medical establishment. Part of this distrust stems from a lack of appreciation of African culture, but there are other issues as well. Africans have great respect for authority figures, especially those who provide needed services. But they are also suspicious of people who appear programmed for politeness (Vontress, 1991). White culture tends to emphasize pleasantries, smiling, and light conversation. When such presentations appear contrived, African immigrants are likely to view the professional with caution. It is important for counselors to be genuine and honest with such clients. Emphasizing formulaic interventions is unlikely to work effectively, as would interventions where no advice or information is given. For these reasons, even African counselors shy away from Western techniques such as cognitive behavioral interventions (Kagee, Suh, & Naidoo, 2004).

A final barrier for immigrants seeking help involves an inability to reach available services. Immigrants struggle with poverty, limited insurance, lack of transportation, no child care, institutional racism, discrimination, and stigma associated with mental illness. They are also less likely to receive Medicaid or other forms of public assistance (Lear, 2005). Such stressors are paradoxically likely to decrease an individual's desire for help. Obasi and Leong (2009) found a negative relationship between psychological distress and positive attitudes toward professional psychological services. The more psychological distress individuals have, the worse they feel about mental health services.

Description of Acculturation Issues

When immigrants do seek counseling services, they come with a variety of needs. African immigrant families exist between two worlds. Their gender roles, marital traditions, child-rearing techniques, and sociocultural traditions are all in flux. The typical African immigrant family faces immense pressure to survive economically and maintain cultural pride (Obiakor & Afoláyan, 2007). Because of these issues, gender plays a significant role in presenting issues.

When men come for counseling, they tend to struggle most with issues of alienation. This is especially true if they are single or without children (Nwadiora, 1995). Issues of aggression, often out of frustration regarding the discrimination African men face in the States, also become apparent over time and may require intervention (Stevenson, 2002). African men may also seek services when negative emotions from their work environment spill over into family relation-ships (Donald & Linington, 2008).

Because women are more likely to identify with traditions associated with home, African women are significantly more likely to require mental health ser-vices than men. For women emigrating from Africa, language, racial identity, class struggles, gender identity and roles, and international politics all affect their transition. For example, in many parts of Africa, a woman without chil-dren is considered barren, and marriages are unlikely to survive (Nwoye, 2006). If women are single and supporting themselves financially, they are also likely to face daily challenges earning a livable wage (Warriner, 2007). Black women on welfare are also at high risk of depression (Coiro, 2001).

Despite the significant connection between low income and depression, mar-riage counselors working with African women should realize that some financial sacrifices may be necessary to preserve mental health. For example, across most African countries, culture dictates large, festive weddings. Hosting a private or small wedding would be considered not only rude but also offensive. Friends and relatives expect not only to receive wedding invitations but also to play a role in the ceremony ("Africa," 2009). Wedding culture and the various parties and cel-ebrations around the event have also been linked to community and individual mental health (Guerin, Elmi, & Guerin, 2006).

Obiakor and Afoláyan (2007) addressed the problem of cultural discon-tinuity, where families integrate elements of their new culture while clinging to some of the traditions from their past. They do not overromanticize their homelands. They are aware of the political and economic struggles they left, but they still miss "home." The Yoruba (an ethnic group) has an adage that relates to this: "The child's home even if it is dung is always a palace away from home." No matter where the family moves outside of Africa, it will always struggle to adjust.

Acculturation for Children

Immigrant children face the greatest and most complex obstacles when coming to the States. A primary consideration relates to handling the loss of their native culture (Obiakor & Afoláyan, 2007). Obiakor and Afoláyan (2007) argued that multicultural strategies (e.g., infusing native linguistic and cultural identities into instructional techniques) enhance academic achievements. They recom-mended practitioners and teachers do the following to succeed at this.

Encourage Parental Involvement. As discussed earlier, most African cultures are family and tribal centric. Involving parents in the lives of their children rein-forces cultural continuity. African immigrant children are also likely to respond with anger when playmates speak derogatorily of their parents, hit a brother or sister, or otherwise discriminate against family members (Nwoye, 2006).

Recognize Age-Appropriate Cultural Expectations. In most parts of Africa, children are instructed rather than disciplined. There is no expectation on children before they are taught, so there is no need to discipline them for not understanding. When children are informed what to do, it is usually an activity related to the family or tribe. Children cooperate within the family structure rather than conform to it. When a child reaches adulthood (which may be between age six or college age, depending on the culture), the individual is expected to fully belong to the community. This is a time of increased responsibility rather than freedom. Adulthood is an opportunity to contribute to rather than escape from a family or tribe (Jenkins, 2007). Despite such comments, there is also inadequate monitoring of child abuse in Africa. In America, immigrants will likely see the ordinary discipline of European Americans as harsh, but they may also be surprised by the involvement of Child Protective Services for cases of neglect. In many African countries, child abuse and neglect are highly underreported (Osagie & Akande, 2001).

Understand Responses to School Success. Schools become a social group for African children. When the system accepts immigrants' cultural identity, immigrants are more likely to bridge the two worlds.

Avoid Unnecessary Acculturation of Immigrant Children. Seeing the African culture through Western eyes is likely to create cultural discontinuity or conformity. For example, in many parts of Africa, corporal punishment of any kind is viewed as physical abuse. Slapping a child's wrist in public would be viewed as cruel. When counselors are constructing effective discipline strategies, they should consider such cultural distinctions. Such differences are especially important because child care concerns are primary reasons why African immigrant parents seek counseling (Obeng, 2007).

When working with children who were adopted from Africa, counselors encounter another set of concerns. I worked with a family who had already seen another counselor. The European American parents had adopted a daughter from Zambia and went to counseling to help with the transition. The parents expressed concern over their lack of knowledge regarding African culture, but the counselor told them to "treat her as they would their own child." The girl was four years old, and the counselor assumed she would be too young to remember anything about her homeland. Mohanty and Newhill (2008) noted that although the number of international adoptees has risen dramatically over the past decade, we still lack an agreed-on framework for counseling such children. With the AIDS pandemic creating millions of orphans, the number of children needing homes is likely to rise even further. This, in itself, changes the culture of Africa, as African countries never had orphans in the past. Children who lost their parents were raised within extended family systems (Foster, 2002). However, most researchers (e.g., Freundlich, 2000; Roby & Shaw, 2006; Serbin, 1997) agree that racial and cultural identity for internally adopted children is extremely important.

Roby and Shaw (2006) argued that transcultural, international adoptions should be considered only when kinship and community efforts fail to find safe and loving families for children. They also argued that all international adoptions should maintain a respect for the history and culture of the child's African origins.

What Should Counselors Do for These Families?

When a counselor is working with a family, his or her first consideration should be the greeting or, as Vontress (1991) called it, establishing prerapport. For Europeans, a simple handshake and a nod are normative. For Africans, greetings are more elaborate and significant. The first few seconds of a meeting could significantly determine the counselor's sensitivity to African issues.

Jenkins (2007) recommended the following in regard to greetings. First, take time to greet everyone who attends, starting with the male leader of the family. Shake hands with every family member. The method of shaking hands is different in various parts of the continent. Some areas emphasize touching palms, bowing, or making multiple movements. For example, in many parts of eastern and southern Africa, a triple shake is common. The movement begins as a European handshake, slides upward until the fingers rest against the base of the thumb, then slide back to the European grasp. Children are often hugged, and Africans are likely to be suspicious of someone who appears rigid around kids.

Once greetings are established, therapy should begin with stories. When conducting an assessment with a European American, many counselors attempt to gather facts. They march through a list of details they predetermined as important, then check off which concerns exist for a particular individual or family (Jenkins, 2007). The primary purpose for this search is diagnostic. Counselors want to ascertain *what* is happening within the family. For African immigrants, the primary concern is not *what* the problem is but *how* they can improve the situation.

For African immigrants, the investigation should be more spiritual. Africans see all things as connected. Nothing exists separate from anything else. When something negative occurs, a solution will also appear. Because of this harmony, the client's narrative must be coconstructed with the therapist, and counselors need to work on several types of active listening. Because of this, narrative therapy is often the recommended intervention for African families (Semmler & Williams, 2000).

Nwoye (2006) suggested that counselors engage in five types of listening when working with African families: empathetic listening (show solidarity with a client's feelings), credulous listening (give the client the unhurried time to tell his or her story), deconstructive listening (explore other possible data that might not have been covered by the client's story), unpacking (cross-check the narrative's controversial or negative issues), and hermeneutic listening (identify the personal meanings or interpretations that the client gives to the events).

Nwoye (2006) also recommended that counselors, while listening to the story, separate parents to allow each person to tell his or her story. In this structure, African (patrilineal) culture dictates first interviewing the father, then the mother, then the children. Such an approach is not compatible with Minuchin's (1974) notion of having children confront parents in the here and now. African culture requires deference and respect to parents, which makes the Western model of confrontation inappropriate.

Once the stories are gathered, counselors should look for common metaphors, dreams, or stories. If at all possible, the counselor should also come prepared with common African stories to bring into the session. For example, if working with a couple who engages in frequent arguments in front of their children, the counselor could have them discuss the African proverb "When two elephants fight, the grass gets hurt."

In this context, narrative counseling could also involve the client's spiritual beliefs (Banks-Wallace, 2004). Some native healers treat mental health issues through washing, steaming, inducing vomiting, singing, or dancing (Mzimkulu & Simbayi, 2006). Counselors might ask clients to release anger by washing their hands in a sink and saying, "I release the anger from my hands." They could help a child with motivation for a test by playing the child's favorite music during the session and getting him or her "pumped up" for the exam. Steaming is also used in Native American culture and is a useful metaphor for sweating out toxins in the system. In all of these examples, care should be taken not to act as a traditional healer but to show solidarity with the client's worldview (Obiakor & Afoláyan, 2007).

Another technique used by traditional healers involves ancestral breathing. Edwards (2008) described how Zulu diviners (*izangoma*) and doctors (*izinyanga*) refer to this process as *selapha ngamandla amadlozi*. Contemporary indigenous Zulu view breathing exercises as a connection between the individual and the supernatural force of one's ancestors. When visiting a healer, the diviner will contact the spirit of the ancestors and channel this power into divinatory bones. Clients sometimes inhale this ancestral spiritual breath (or energy) from the bones. Sometimes, the diviner may sense an evolutionary history of lions in the spirit and roar with power. Sometimes, the breath is like a python and quiet. Usually, the breath is associated with a departed ancestor who has appeared in the client's dreams. The process involves breath-coordinated movement involving rhythmic hand clapping, singing, music, and dancing.

Although channeling ancestral energies would not be appropriate for a mental health counselor to do, breathing exercises may be adapted to fit into the African spiritual worldview (Edwards, 2008). In the exercises above, inhaling is considered healing, and exhaling is the release of negative energy. Counselors can tap into this by asking clients to think of the positive spiritual forces they believe in (e.g., Christian, ancestral, etc.) and imagine the spiritual force filling them with each breath. Upon the release, counselors can have clients picture the negative energy they wish to expel (e.g., fear, depression, anxiety, etc.).

Spiritual breathing exercises are most likely to work with adults who can appreciate the metaphorical value of the activity, but most families coming for therapy are not seeking anxiety management techniques. Instead, they are likely to come when their children face struggles integrating into American society. Parents will see the counselor as a consultant, and they will want specific guidelines. All of this starts by the counselor building an effective relationship with children. Parents will trust a therapist who can connect and build rapport with their kids.

When counselors are working specifically with children, African games may be used in play therapy. Kekae-Moletsane (2008) advocated the use of Masekitlana, which is a traditional Sotho game played by children in South Africa. The game is a monologue, played by one person at a time while other children listen. During play, the speaker usually relates stories about issues or concerns. It might involve actual events, wishes, feelings, dreams, or anything else. There are no specific rules, no formal structure, and no competitive element. Even shy children enjoy the experience.

To play Masekitlana, the children need two small stones. With one stone, the player repeatedly strikes the other as the story progresses. Depending on the emotions conveyed, the pace, frequency, and strength of the collision will vary. During sad, angry, or frustrating parts of the story, players hit the stones hard and frequently. During positive and uplifting parts of the story, the speaker's tone usually softens, and the stones are hit gently and rarely. Players often get very involved in their stories, often to the point of shouting or crying (Kekae-Moletsane, 2008).

The nondirective component of Masekitlana is not accidental. African culture tends to avoid "directive" or administrative tones. A camaraderie will be more successful than an authoritative style of leadership (Jenkins, 2007). Direct confrontation will seldom result in positive change.

Clearly, the depth of cultural differences is immense, and learning the thousands of African cultures would take a lifetime. Because of this, when working with African families, counselors should gain advice or consultation from someone familiar with the culture. Counselors who are not of African descent should also ask clients how they feel about working with someone from a different ethnic group. Treat these investigations seriously, and pay careful attention to nonverbal cues. Many Africans may feel threatened by a European therapist and will comply with therapy without actually feeling safe. They may state that they are comfortable with their counselor but maintain poor eye contact, position themselves several feet away, and speak in a quiet voice. These behaviors do not necessarily imply tension in the relationship, but they should be explored with sensitivity (Brammer, 2004).

Contraindications or Limitations

The narrative therapy approach recommended in this chapter is not insight oriented. The goal is not to let the client come to his or her own conclusions in a vacuum. African clients come to therapy for specific suggestions and help. They are usually aware of their feelings before coming to therapy, but they hope to obtain specific exercises to help them deal with their plight (Brammer, 2004).

It is also important for counselors to avoid appearing overly friendly or problem free. African immigrants have often come from areas where prejudice and discrimination are intense and dangerous. They are able to identify the slightest nonverbal cues of discomfort or evasiveness. If the counselor notices the client pulling back or reacting to a nonverbal cue, it is crucial for the counselor to self-examine and take responsibility for whatever just occurred. For African culture, professionalism is not scientific expertness; it is a relationship where the trained party helps as a friend.

Recommendations and Advocacy

Advocacy issues for Africans are far-reaching and extend across a number of domains. Globalization is changing the way the world interacts, especially as it relates to using national resources (Buchan et al., 2009). Global warming could devastate west Africa over the next 20 years. A UN report (Bates, Kundzewicz, Wu, & Palutikof, 2008) projected that the amount of arid and semiarid land in Africa may increase by 231,661 to 347,492 square miles. To put this into context, the country of Malawi is 45,000 square miles. If global warming continues at its current pace, within the next 70 years, the Sudan may see its agricultural production potential decrease by 56%. Senegal may experience as 52% reduction (Cline, 2007). Both countries have already been devastated by political and economic instability. It is imperative for clean water supplies to increase in eastern and western Africa before such draughts come, or millions will die. When global warming concerns are coupled with an international movement to fight against Africa's "brain drain," the next generation of immigrants is likely to have lower levels of education or financial resources.

By far, the most prevalent battle for Africa and African immigrants involves the fight against disease. Youth have started becoming active in this battle against AIDS (Campbell, Gibbs, Maimane, Nair, & Sibiya, 2009), and related matters of substance abuse must also be taken more seriously (Simmons et al., 2008). Global warming has already changed the areas affected by malaria, with the disease now reaching higher into the mountains than ever before. The larger topic of finding cures for African diseases and health care for this population is also a matter of importance (Tucker & Makgoba, 2008).

Advocacy for domestic issues is also an important role counselors should address. As mentioned earlier, child abuse and inadequate reporting will require active interventions by counselors. Domestic violence and aggression offer unique challenges as well (Hampton, LaTaillade, Dacey, & Marghi, 2008; Miller, 2008). American culture views older people differently than African culture does. Battling ageism and finding a place for elder Africans will also become more important in the coming generation (McKay, 2008).

Discussion Questions

1. How could you infuse music into a family counseling session?
2. Are you aware of how African kinesics (gestures, movements, and positions) differs from the kinesics common in your culture?
3. How do Africans greet each other? Do you think shaking someone's hand differently can change rapport and relationships?
4. How can you find a friend or informant who would be willing to serve as your cultural guide?
5. African art and music are deeply ingrained in the culture. How could you gain an appreciation and understanding of these disciplines?
6. What role do you think counselors should play in advocating for the natural resources of Africa?
7. Would you feel comfortable playing Masekitlana by yourself in practice for a play therapy session? Do you think you would play this the same way an African child would play it?
8. African immigrants are less likely to seek mental health care services than African Americans who have lived in the States for multiple generations. What could be done to correct this?

9. Narrative therapy is the recommended intervention for African immigrants. What are the active forms of listening associated with this approach? How would you base your recommendations or advice at the end of such sessions?

10. Traditional healers use active techniques when combating mental health issues. How could you employ similar techniques your sessions?

References

Africa. (2009). In *Encarta*. Retrieved August 23, 2009, from http://encarta.msn.com/encyclopedia_761572628/Africa.html

Banks-Wallace, J. (2004). It's all sacred: African American women's perspectives on spirituality. *Issues in Mental Health Nursing, 25*, 25–45.

Bates, B. C., Kundzewicz, Z. W., Wu, S., & Palutikof, J. P. (Eds.). (2008). *Climate change and water*. Retrieved August 2, 2009, from UN Intergovernmental Panel on Climate Change Web site: http://www.ipcc.ch/

Berg, A. (2003). Ancestor reverence and mental health in South Africa. *Transcultural Psychiatry, 40*, 194–207.

Brammer, R. (2004). *Diversity in counseling: Exploring ethnic and gender issues*. Pacific Grove, CA: Brooks/Cole.

Buchan, N. R., Grimalda, G., Wilson, R., Fatas, E., Foddy, M., & Brewer, M. (2009). Globalization and human cooperation. *PNAS Proceedings of the National Academy of Sciences of the United States of America, 106*(11), 4138–4142.

Campbell, C., Gibbs, A., Maimane, S., Nair, Y., & Sibiya, Z. (2009). Youth participation in the fight against AIDS in South Africa: From policy to practice. *Journal of Youth Studies, 12*, 93–109.

Chiroro, P., Bohner, G., Viki, G. T., & Jarvis, C. I. (2004). Rape myth acceptance and rape proclivity: Expected dominance versus expected arousal as mediators in acquaintance-rape situations. *Journal of Interpersonal Violence, 19*(4), 427–441.

Cichocki, M. (2007). *HIV and oral sex: Is oral sex a safe alternative?* Retrieved August 23, 2009, from http://aids.about.com/cs/safesex/a/oralsex.htm

Cline, W. R. (2007). *Global warming and agriculture: Impact estimates by country*. Washington, DC: Center for Global Development.

Coiro, M. J. (2001). Depressive symptoms among women receiving welfare [Special issue]. *Women and Health, 32*, 1–23.

Demographia. (2009, April). *World urban areas and population projections: 5th comprehensive edition*. Retrieved July 22, 2009, from http://www.demographia.com/db-worldua.pdf

Donald, F. & Linington, J. (2008). Work/family border theory and gender role orientation in male managers. *South African Journal of Psychology, 38*(4), 659–671.

Edwards, S. D. (2008). Breath psychology: Fundamentals and applications. *Psychology and Developing Societies, 20*, 131–164.

Foster, G. (2002). Supporting community efforts to assist orphans in Africa. *New England Journal of Medicine, 346*, 1907–1911.

Freundlich, M. (2000). *Adoption and ethics: The role of race, culture, and national origin in adoption*. Washington, DC: Child Welfare League of America.

Guerin, P., Elmi, F. H., & Guerin, B. (2006). Weddings and parties: Cultural healing in one community of Somali women. *Australian e-Journal for the Advancement of Mental Health, 5*(2), 105–112. Retrieved August 1, 2009, from http://www.ausei-net.com/journal/vol5iss2/guerin.pdf

Haider, A. (1997). *Brain-drain from Somalia: Potentials of the educated Somalis abroad*. Frederiksberg, Denmark: Somali Activation Project.

Hampton, R. L., LaTaillade, J. J., Dacey, A., & Marghi, J. R. (2008). Evaluating domestic violence interventions for Black women. *Journal of Aggression, Maltreatment and Trauma, 16*, 330–353.

Havenaar, J. M., Geerlings, M. I., Vivian, L., Robertson, B., & Collinson, M. (2008). Common mental health problems in historically disadvantaged urban and rural communities in South Africa: Prevalence and risk factors. *Social Psychiatry and Psychiatric Epidemiology, 43*, 209–215.

Herring, R. D. & Salazar, C. (2002). Non-Western helping modalities. In J. Trusty, E. J. Looby, & D. S. Sandhu (Eds.), *Multicultural counseling: Context, theory and practice, and competence* (pp. 283–318). Hauppauge, NY: Nova Science.

Jenkins, O. B. (2007). *Dealing with cultural differences: Contrasting the African and European worldviews*. Limuru, Kenya: Communication Press. Retrieved August 2, 2009, from http://www.orvillejenkins.com/langlearn/pdf/dealdiffbooklet.pdf

Johnson, S. (2003, December 1). *Just another day at the world's biggest hospital: On the frontlines of the AIDS epidemic in Soweto, South Africa*. National Public Radio. Retrieved July 22, 2009, from http://www.npr.org/

Kagee, A., Suh, E.-J., & Naidoo, A. V. (2004). South African counsellors' attitudes towards cognitive behavioural techniques to ameliorate trauma: Effects of a training workshop. *International Journal for the Advancement of Counselling, 26*, 313–320.

Kahn, M. S. & Kelly, K. J. (2001). Cultural tensions in psychiatric nursing: Managing the interface between Western mental health care and Xhosa traditional healing in South Africa. *Transcultural Psychiatry, 38*(1), 35–50.

Kanabus, A., Fredriksson-Bass, J., & Pembrey, G. (2009). *HIV and AIDS in Africa*. Retrieved July 23, 2009, from http://www.avert.org/aafrica.htm

Kekae-Moletsane, M. (2008). Masekitlana: South African traditional play as a thera-peutic tool in child psychotherapy. *South African Journal of Psychology, 38*(2), 367–375.

Lear, J. G. (2005, February 25). Children in immigrant families. *In Focus*, pp. 1–4.

Maruatona, T. (2006). Adult literacy education and empowerment in Africa: Problems and prospects. In S. B. Merriam, B. C. Courtenay, & R. M. Cervero (Eds.), *Global issues and adult education: Perspectives from Latin America, Southern Africa, and the United States* (pp. 344–355). San Francisco: Jossey-Bass.

Mbaku, J. M. (1998). Bureaucratic corruption in Africa: The futility of cleanups. *The CATO Journal, 16*(1). Retrieved July 27, 2009, from http://www.cato.org/pubs/journal/cj16n1–6.html

McKay, C. (2008). Anew consciousness trudging toward leadership. *Educational Gerontology, 34*, 670–690.

Miller, J. (2008). Violence against urban African American girls challenges for feminist advocacy. *Journal of Contemporary Criminal Justice, 24,* 148–162.

Minuchin, S. (1974). *Families and family therapy.* Cambridge, MA: Harvard University Press.

Mohanty, J. & Newhill, C. (2008). A theoretical framework for understanding ethnic socialization among international adoptees. *Families in Society, 89,* 543–550.

Mutume, G. (2003). New initiatives tap skills of African expatriates. *Africa Recovery, 17*(3), 1–5. Retrieved July 27, 2009, from www.africarecovery.org

Mzimkulu, K. G. & Simbayi, L. C. (2006). Perspectives and practices of Xhosa-speaking African traditional healers when managing psychosis. *Human Research Council, South Africa International Journal of Disability, Development and Education, 53,* 417–431.

Nadeem, E., Edge, D., Fongwa, M., & Belin, T. (2007). Does stigma keep poor young immigrant and U.S.-born Black and Latina women from seeking mental health care? *Psychiatric Services, 58*(12), 1547–1554.

National Population Commission of Nigeria. (2005). *Facts and figures.* Retrieved July 22, 2009, from http://www.population.gov.ng/factsandfigures.htm

Nwadiora, E. (1995). Alienation and stress among Black immigrants: An exploratory study. *Western Journal of Black Studies, 19,* 58–71.

Nwoye, A. (2006). A narrative approach to child and family therapy in Africa. *Contemporary Family Therapy: An International Journal, 28*(1), 1–23.

Obasi, E. M. & Leong, F. T. L. (2009). Psychological distress, acculturation, and mental health-seeking attitudes among people of African descent in the United States: A preliminary investigation. *Journal of Counseling Psychology, 56,* 227–238.

Obeng, C. S. (2007). Immigrants families and childcare preferences: Do immigrants' cultures influence their childcare decisions? *Early Childhood Education Journal, 34*(4), 259–264.

Obiakor, F. E. & Afoláyan, M. O. (2007). African immigrant families in the United States: Surviving the sociocultural tide. *The Family Journal, 15,* 265–270.

Osagie, J. E. & Akande, A. (2001). Perspectives on a new strategy for child protection in Africa. *Early Child Development and Care, 166,* 135–148.

Othieno, J. (2007). Twin cities care system assessment: Process, findings and recommendations. *Journal of Health Care for the Poor and Underserved, 18,* 189–213.

Owino, F. R. (Ed.). (2002). *Speaking African: African languages for education and development.* Cape Town, South Africa: CASAS.

Roby, J. L. & Shaw, S. A. (2006). The African orphan crisis and international adoption. *Social Work, 51,* 199–210.

Sala-i-Martin, X. (2006, October). Falling poverty and income inequality: A global phenomenon. *Fraser Alert,* pp. 1–7.

Semmler, P.L. & Williams, C.B. (2000). Narrative therapy: A storied context for multicultural counseling. *Journal of Multicultural Counseling and Development, 28,* 51–62.

Serbin, L. A. (1997). Research on international adoption: Implications for developmental theory and social policy. *International Journal of Behavioral Development, 20,* 83–92.

Simmons, R., Ungemack, J., Sussman, J., Anderson, R., Adorno, S., Aguayo, J., Black, K., Hodge, S., & Tirnady, R. (2008). Bringing adolescents into substance abuse treatment through community outreach and engagement: The Hartford Youth Project. *Journal of Psychoactive Drugs, 40,* 41–54.

Sow, I. (1980). *Anthropological structures of madness in Black Africa.* New York: International Universities Press.

Ssemakula, J. K. (2001). *Malaria: No longer the forgotten epidemic.* Retrieved July 24, 2009, from http://medilinkz.org/

Stevenson, H. C. (2002). Wrestling with destiny: The cultural socialization of anger and healing in African American males. *Journal of Psychology and Christianity, 21*(4), 357–364.

Takougang, J. (1995). Recent African immigrants to the United States: A historical perspective. *Western Journal of Black Studies, 19,* 50–57.

Tucker, T. J. & Makgoba, M. W. (2008). Public–private partnerships and scientific imperialism. *Science, 320,* 1016–1017.

Van Dyk, A. C. (2001). Traditional African beliefs and customs: Implications for AIDS education and prevention in Africa. *South African Journal of Psychology, 31*(2), 60–66.

Vontress, C. E. (1991). Traditional healing in Africa: Implications for cross-cultural counseling [Special issue]. *Journal of Counseling and Development, 70,* 242–249.

Wamwara-Mbugua, L. W., Cornwell, T. B., & Boller, G. (2008). Triple acculturation: The role of African Americans in the consumer acculturation of Kenyan immigrants. *Journal of Business Research, 61*(2), 83–90.

Warriner, D. S. (2007). Language learning and the politics of belonging: Sudanese women refugees becoming and being "American." *Anthropology and Education Quarterly, 38*(4), 343–359.

Zijlma, A. (2009). *Facts about Africa.* Retrieved July 22, 2009, from http://goafrica.about.com/

Chapter 7

Working With Asian Immigrant Families, Part I: Far East, Southeast Asia, and Pacific Islands

A. Zaidy MohdZain

Contents

The term *Asian* refers to those having origins of the native people of the Far East, Southeast Asia, and Indian subcontinent (U.S. Census Bureau, 2004b). The U.S. Census Bureau (2004b) included Cambodia, China, Bangladesh, Burma (now known as Myanmar), India, Indonesia, Japan, Laos, Korea, Malaysia, Pakistan, Philippines, Taiwan, Thailand, and Vietnam. Another common term used is *Pacific Islander*, which refers to those having origins in any original people of Hawaii, Guam, Samoa, or other Pacific Islands such as Fiji or Tahiti. Within the

121

United States, it is common for these two groups to be lumped together, as the term often appears *Asian and Pacific Islander*. For the purpose of this chapter, we are referring to those immigrants whose ancestors or origins come from both the Asian continent and the Pacific Islands as Asian immigrants. The term *Oriental* is outdated, and many Asian American clients may perceive it as an insult or insensitive. They may in return view the counselors using the term as culturally uninformed, which jeopardizes the counselors' own rapport-building efforts. A more acceptable term, *Asian American*, is represented by some 43 different ethnic groups of people originated from a large geographic area. As a group, Asian Americans lack homogeneity, and there are large within-group differences as exemplified by the very concept of diversity (Kim, Yang, Atkinson, Wolfe, & Hong, 2001; U.S. Department of Health and Human Services, 2001).

Demographic Description

According to the U.S. Census Bureau, in March 2002, there were about 12.5 million Asian and Pacific Islanders who lived in the United States. This represents some 4.4% of the total population (U.S. Census Bureau, 2003). In the United States, Asian Indian, Chinese, Filipinos, Korean, and Vietnamese together made up about 80% of the Asian American population. Chinese was the largest group, representing some 24% of the Asian American population, followed by Filipinos, Asian Indian, Vietnamese, and Korean. In terms of the location in which Asian Americans lived in the United States, the U.S. Census Bureau (2004b) stated that 51% of them lived in the West, 19% lived in the South, 12% lived in the Midwest, and 19% lived in the Northeast. Nearly 95% of all Asians lived in metropolitan areas, and some 76% of Asian Americans are foreign born. Asian Americans alone constitute more than a quarter of the foreign-born population in the United States (U.S. Census Bureau, 2004b; U.S. Department of Health and Human Services, 2001).

The Chinese were among the first Asians who came to the United States in the 1850s to build the transcontinental railroad or work in the gold mines, mainly in California. About at the same time period, Japanese came to work in the sugar plantations of Hawaii, and some moved on to California. They were followed by Koreans and Filipinos. Asian Indians started coming to the United States in the early 1900s. Vietnamese and other Southeast Asians came in the late 1970s; many of them had to flee their countries in the aftermath of the Vietnam War (U.S. Department of Health and Human Services, 2001).

Asian Americans, whether they are immigrants, refugees, or American born and have been in the United States for generations, are still struggling with racism and discrimination issues. As an extreme example, this author was fortunate to run into Dr. Ronald Takaki, a renowned professor of multicultural education and best-selling author. He shared his personal experience of how some in his audience of public lectures came backstage to commend him on his ability to speak English with no foreign accent and the shock they had when he informed them that he is a sixth-generation American (R. Takaki, personal communication, April 14, 1999). Perhaps it was because his physical appearance, look, and demeanor were exemplified as "Oriental." The issues of having the feeling or perception of not being accepted as "full Americans" and continuing to be regarded as "foreigners" by society at large continue to play into the psychic of many Asian Americans to this day. Sue and Sue (2008) revealed the result of a survey of a representative sample of some 1,000 adults undertaken by the Committee of 100 to determine their attitudes toward Asian Americans. The dominant perception of adult Americans, as revealed by the survey about Chinese Americans, is that Chinese Americans would be more loyal to China than to the United States, with the examples of over half of the people surveyed believing that Chinese Americans would pass secret information to China, a quarter of the sample would disapprove someone in their family to marry an Asian American, and some 17% would be upset if Asian Americans moved into their neighborhood. Recognizing the institutional racism, the California legislature approved a bill on July 17, 2009, to apologize to the state's Chinese American community for racist laws enacted as far back as 1849 (Liu, 2009).

However, on the flip side of the coin, Asian Americans are also hailed as a "model minority" in affirming and realizing the widely held concept of achieving the "American dream." Kluger (2009) reported a presentation at the annual convention of the American Sociological Association in San Francisco of research by Jeffrey Timberlake of the University of Cincinnati and Rhys Williams of Loyola University Chicago who surveyed 2,100 Ohioans to gauge the overall public perception of immigrants. The results indicated that Asians were uniformly ranked first in the wealth, intelligence, and self-sufficiency categories relative to Europeans, Middle Easterners, and Latinos. On average, Asian Americans when compared to any other ethnic group in the United States attain more education and have a higher proportion (45%) concentrated in managerial and professional specialty occupations, relative to 34% of the total population. The U.S. Census Bureau (2004b) stated that in 2000, 44% of Asian Americans aged 25 and older had a college or professional degree, compared to only 28% of the White population and 24% of the total population that had achieved that level of education. The census data in 1997 revealed that 58% of Americans who descended from natives of the Indian subcontinent had undergraduate, graduate, or professional degrees (U.S. Department of Health and Human Services, 2001). Asian Americans are much more likely to earn a bachelor's degree (51% compared to 32% of non-Hispanic Whites), and the U.S. Census Bureau (2003) reported that in 2002, 87% of the 7.9 million Asian Americans aged 25 and older have earned at least a high school diploma. The average family income for Asian Americans tends to be higher than the national average. The median income of Asian families was over $9,000 higher than the median income for all families ($59,000 compared to $50,000) (U.S. Census Bureau, 2004b). Asian Indian and Japanese families' median income were more than $10,000 higher than that of all Asian families, with Cambodian, Hmong, Korean, Laotian, Pakistanis, Thai, and Vietnamese family incomes substantially lower than the median for all Asian families. However, some subgroups of Asian Americans, namely, Hawaiian and other Pacific Islanders, Cambodian, Hmong, and Laotians, did not have high educational attainment, and the poverty rates for Asians is similar to those of total population, with Hmong having the highest individual poverty rates, followed by Cambodians (U.S. Census Bureau, 2004b). Therefore, as we look behind the success myth, there exists a wide variation in the economic attainment of Asian Americans as a group (Takaki, 1989; U.S. Department of Health and Human Services, 2001). This is a prime example of the danger of stereotyping, because 17% of Asian and Pacific Islander families had incomes of less than $25,000 compared to 15% of non-Hispanic Whites families, which in turn means that Asian and Pacific Islanders are more likely to live in poverty than non-Hispanic Whites.

Immigration Experience

Counselors working with Asian immigrants need to be mindful that individual Asian immigrants may have different migration experiences. Chung, Bemak, Ortiz, and Sandoval-Perez (2008) stated that the immigration process itself is filled with a series of complex stressors that affect the mental health and quality of life of immigrant populations. Not all immigrants migrate voluntarily. The factors affecting their migration experiences may range from escaping the tyranny of a brutal regime for social and political security to seeking more freedom and economic and educational opportunities in the United States. The immigrants' experiences of coming to the United States can also be diverse. They range from immigrants having suffered a complete loss of all their possessions or a loss of close family members, to having to risk their life and witness their fellow refugees die in their attempts to escape oppressive regimes, to dealing with other horrific events. The traumatic journey can take its toll on the immigrants and their families, especially those without a social network of support. Regardless of their migration circumstances, they must adapt to survive and prosper in the new land. This adaptation process is often gradual and slow, and it forces the immigrants to cope with a set of different beliefs and behaviors in every facet of their lives such as child rearing, family structure, gender roles, religious practices, and others. These beliefs, behaviors, and lifestyles are often in sharp contrast with their familiar cultural beliefs and behaviors. The adaptation process requires the immigrants to learn, understand, and internalize the new culture to the extent that it becomes familiar, controllable, and supportive.

Migrating from one country to another and learning how to adapt to the new place is much like being on a continuum with two extremes: enculturation and acculturation. Enculturation is a process of retaining one's indigenous cultural values, behaviors, knowledge, and identity. Thus, those who are closer to this end of the continuum, that is, enculturation, are perceived to adhere more to Asian cultural values such as collectivism, conformity to the norms, deference to authority figures, emotional restraint, filial piety, hierarchical family structure, and humility (Chung et al., 2008; Kim, Atkinson, & Yang, 1999; Sue & Sue 2008). The opposite or contrasting end of the spectrum is acculturation, which is a process of adaptation to the dominant U.S. cultural norms. Thus, we see some Asian immigrants who completely identify with mainstream American culture, whereas others may develop adaptive bicultural identification that enables them to feel comfortable and functional within mainstream American culture as well as their culture of origin. Still there are those who continue to feel uncomfortable with life in the United States and instead choose to live and work exclusively within the confines of an ethnic enclave (Hong & Domokos-Cheng Ham, 2001; Sue & Sue, 2008). For the immigrant families, this transgenerational process takes each successive generation one step further toward acculturation, with the second generation usually being more acculturated than the first, and the third generation one step more acculturated than the previous two (Chung et al., 2008; Hong & Domokos-Cheng Ham, 2001). Kim and Omizo (2003) suggested that Asian Americans who strongly adhere to Asian cultural values tend to have less positive attitudes about seeking help and are less willing to see a counselor relative to those who do not adhere strongly to Asian cultural values. Kim, Ng, and Ahn (2009), however, concluded in their study of 61 Asian American clients at a counseling center at a large university on the West Coast that client adherence to Asian cultural values was not a significant predictor of counseling session outcome.

The Family

Generally, a dominant Asian cultural milieu is that of collectivism as opposed to individualism, a dominant cultural milieu in the United States. Collectivism emphasizes close family ties, hierarchy, and order as opposed to independence and autonomy of the individual. Asians' concept of family and how they define family may differ from that of counselors coming from mainstream American culture. The family relationships are often closer than those in mainstream American families. For instance, the concepts of being overly close or enmeshed or lacking boundaries may be interpreted differently by counselors from mainstream American culture than by their Asian immigrant families who come from an Asian cultural background. These two different frames of reference are what make it more challenging to counsel Asian immigrant families. For example, clients from Asian culture, especially those adhering very closely to Asian values, may exhibit interpersonal reliance and dependency. Although these may be considered healthy cultural norms in Asian culture, the same cannot be said in mainstream American culture. Counselors with a mainstream American cultural background who are not sufficiently knowledgeable of these cultural norms can easily and inadvertently diagnose Asian immigrants as having a dependent personality disorder (Chung et al., 2008). Another example of cultural norms is that first cousins are often viewed and presented as if they are siblings by Asian immigrants. It is a common experience or practice for cousins to grow up and be raised in the same household, typically cared for by the grandmother or eldest uncle or aunt. For some who are from a Muslim culture, the fact that two infants were breast-fed by the same woman makes them siblings for their entire lives. Thus, the worldview of Asian immigrants in terms of family relationships and whom they consider as members of their family may differ relative to mainstream Americans.

Asian immigrant families tend to be more hierarchical and patriarchal than mainstream American families (Hong & Domokos-Cheng Ham, 2001; Sue & Sue, 2008). Asian Americans are more likely to live in households that are composed exclusively of family members. In 2004, 76% of Asian Americans live in this family household arrangement compared to 67% of non-Hispanic White and African American households (U.S. Census Bureau, 2004a). They place more emphasis on the authority of parents over children and of the older sibling over younger siblings. Other than the fact that communication flows downward, the tradition dictates deference to the elders. For instance, a married son's primary allegiance (family loyalty) remains with his parents, as opposed to the circumstances in contemporary mainstream American culture. Sue and Sue (2008) also pointed to the roles of the mother in a family system among Asian Americans, among which is to serve and mediate communication within the unit. Troubled Asian Americans typically rely on their mothers to transmit messages to their fathers. Within this context, it is common to see adult Asian immigrants asking for and valuing the opinions of their parents or older siblings and relatives who are still overseas when making important decisions here in the United States.

Taking into account how culture shapes or influences the expression and recognition of various psychological distress, counselors take into account the family's worldview and level of acculturation. The case in point is a common dilemma Asian immigrants and their families are facing during family counseling sessions. Because of their hierarchical culture, Asian immigrants may feel uneasy about disclosing their issues in the presence of their children, and the children may feel it is improper to expose their parents' problems in their presence (Hong & Domokos-Cheng Ham, 2001). Sue and Sue (2008) pointed out that public display of strong emotions are considered to be signs of weakness in terms of maturity or a lack of personal control. Thus, the father may appear peripheral to mainstream American counselors, whereas within the context of Asian cultural milieu, he is properly maintaining his role and position within the unit by remaining authoritative and distant and not appearing to be emotionally demonstrative or involved with his children. Sue and Sue (2008) cautioned counselors working with Asian Americans to be careful in using counseling microskills that focus directly on emotions, as it may be uncomfortable and a shame- producing event for traditional Asian Americans. Those emotions can be addressed but in an indirect manner. For example, rather than placing emphasis on the client by saying, "You look troubled," a more face-saving statement about the generality or the event instead of the person is preferable, such as "This predicament would make anyone troubled."

Often, the children of Asian immigrants who are raised and educated in the United States are more proficient in and become more identified with mainstream American culture relative to their parents, who tend to have stronger memories and emotional ties to their Asian cultural roots. At the same time, the children are being bombarded with messages from peers, schools, and the mass media championing that Western standards are superior and better than their own. How they adapt to the majority culture and at the same time retain their connection to their culture of origin can produce enough stress within the individual and the family. Okubo, Yeh, Lin, Fujita, and Shea (2007) quoted a scenario in which Asian youths behave in their negotiation and balance their bicultural living by being more "American" outside of their home and being more "Chinese" or "Indian" at home. This dual living can be stressful and exhausting and becomes more important when making critical choices such as future career plans, dating, and marriage (Okubo et al., 2007). Often during counseling sessions, these intergenerational mixed with acculturation conflicts play themselves when immigrant youths accuse their parents of being old-fashioned or controlling, and the parents complain that their children are rebellious or corrupted by the host American culture. This cultural gap creates friction that can be intense enough to lead to family conflicts. These parent–child conflicts are the most common presenting problems for Asian American college students seeking counseling (Lee, Su, & Yoshida, 2005; Sue & Sue, 2008). In their study of 8 Chinese American youths with a median age of 16.8 years (SD = 1.36) in New York City with the number of years in the United States ranging from 1 to 16, Okubo et al. (2007) found that other than cultural values and cultural expectation, Asian youths do consider their individual interests and familial expectations when making career-related decisions. The youths also factored in issues such as maintaining the family reputation, saving face, caring for parents, and respecting elders' wishes as well as their own goals in their chosen profession.

Asian American children often face greater pressure to succeed academically, and they have more fear of academic failures when compared to their European American counterparts (Sue & Sue, 2008). Schools in Asia are much more structured and regimented with stricter rules and regulations relative to the public schools in the United States. In Asian countries, students are typically required to wear school uniforms. In the classroom, students may stay quiet and listen to teachers. The open discussion format, flexibility, and egalitarian and participatory atmosphere in American public schools could be a source of confusion for Asian American immigrants. Asian American students tend to spend twice as much time each week on academic work compared to non–Asian American students, but they also report feeling isolated, depressed, anxious, and that they receive little or no praise for their accomplishment (Kao, 1995; Sue & Sue, 2008). Asian American parents may have specific career goals in mind for their children, usually in technical fields or hard sciences (Okubo et al., 2007; Sue & Sue, 2008). Often this is merely a reflection on the part of the parents about their expectations and insistence and that they appear to be oblivious to the individual child's talent or interest. Hong and Domokos-Cheng Ham (2001) pointed out an often-occurring misunderstanding between Asian immigrant parents and public school teachers centered on the parents' complaints of their children not having enough homework assigned to them, whereas the teachers advised them not to put too much academic pressure on their children. Asian Americans place high value on education, and the successful performance of their children is viewed as an affirmation and validation of their good parenting skills along with an expectation of moving toward achieving higher social status within the community. Thus parents often have high expectations for their children to achieve academically, and from an Asian collectivistic perspective, education of children is also an investment in a family's future (Hong & Domokos-Cheng Ham, 2001; Sue & Sue, 2008).

Counseling Issues

Asian collectivist tradition does not distinguish the mind and body. It places a premium of maintaining social and familial harmony. Often, the route Asian Americans take toward that end is by discouraging their open display of emotions and avoiding exposure of personal weakness. Asians Americans are taught to deny the experience and expression of emotions. It is more acceptable to express psychological distress through the body. This cultural attribute contributes to a large amount of expression of somatic symptoms among Asian Americans when compared to White Americans (U.S. Department of Health and Human Services, 2001). In other words, Asian Americans do not necessarily suppress or repress affective symptoms, but rather it is the context in which what is being presented and how it is presented. For example, a Chinese client may display somatic symptom such as aches and pains or fatigue to a clinician but show depressive symptoms to others. The U.S. Department of Health and Human Services (2001) acknowledged that our present knowledge of the counseling needs of Asian Americans is very limited and that Asian Americans have the lowest rates of utilization of mental health services among ethnic group populations. In a study of 242 Asian American college students at a large mid-Atlantic university and a large university in Hawaii, Kim and Omizo (2003) showed an inverse relationship between adherence to Asian cultural values and attitudes toward seeking professional psychological help. The study also showed the same inverse relationship between adherence to Asian cultural values and willingness to see a counselor. The study by Gloria, Castellanos, Park, and Kim (2008) supported this contention that decreased adherence to cultural values was predictive of increased help-seeking attitudes among second-generation Korean American undergraduates.

Migration experience and adjustment challenge the very structure and organization of the family as a unit. Asian immigrant families may find that their traditional Asian family structure is no longer sustainable in this new adopted land. For example, Asian immigrant children, influenced by the values of mainstream American society, may demand greater autonomy and treatment along a continuum ranging from less than hierarchical to egalitarian than culturally permitted in traditional Asia settings. On the other hand, the first-generation Asian immigrants are struggling in their negotiations to balance the past and all those cultural backgrounds and attachments with the pragmatic present. Remember, when the newer generation is asking the older generation to redefine themselves, it touches the core of the individual's self-identity and hence the presence of a robust energy within each of the holon of the entire system, a dynamic that counselors have to grapple with when providing counseling services.

For immigrant couples who have to leave their parents behind in Asia, their inability to care for aging parents may create constant feelings of guilt, especially when they have no other siblings there to assume the responsibility. Some may choose to sponsor their aging parents to immigrate and live with them in the United States. At their advanced age, the older parents often find it difficult to adjust to the new lifestyle and culture in the United States, and for the couple, the entry of their parents into the nuclear family will change their life patterns. Asian immigrants are not immune to universal issues such as in-laws and generation conflict. Thus, the solution about caring for older parents can be stressful for both the couple and their older parents.

There are family rituals that Asian immigrants are accustomed to, and they face an agonizing dilemma surrounding developmental issues such as births, weddings, and deaths. The rituals as practiced in mainstream American cultures may seem insufficient and inadequate for some Asian Americans, and they are left feeling guilty and despondent over their inability to carry out the full gamut of rituals as they experienced in their native land. They often travel to their home countries to continue and follow up with a more elaborate and "corrected version" of the rituals. Rituals such as welcoming a newborn or planning a wedding can be postponed, but a funeral has a special urgency and meaning, hence its profound effects on the immigrants. (Hong & Domokos-Cheng Ham, 2001)

Issues for Counselors

Engaging Asian immigrants in counseling poses a unique challenge for counselors. Counselors need to become more responsive to a culturally adapted counseling approach when counseling Asian immigrants who tend to retain strong cultural values (Kim et al., 2009; Portland, 2009; Sue & Sue, 2008). The structural approach in counseling Asian immigrants, with its emphasis less on insights but more on behavioral changes and the interventions that focus on a family's organization and its communication in the present, seems closer to the Asian cultural milieu. Hammond and Nichols (2008) recommended that counselors use a collaborative partnership approach, although seemingly known for its forceful directive interventions, in their attempts to make their interventions effective. To be effective when working with immigrant families, counselors must develop self-awareness of their own feelings, attitudes, and beliefs about immigrants and working with them (Portland, 2009). Counselors need to be flexible and practical to provide effective interventions that are focused and clear and to learn about their clients and the particulars of the family's culture in terms of roles, rules, values, and relationships (Portland, 2009; Poulsen, 2009). The goal of the intervention is for the clients to develop new perspectives that will lead them to adopt new actions, not by pushing clients to change but by understanding and affirming them via reaching and motivating them to accept responsibilities for changing their behaviors (Hammond & Nichols, 2008). The prerequisite, according to Hammond and Nichols (2008), is for the counselors to make active efforts to elicit and acknowledge what their clients think and feel and, at the same time, work as respectful collaborative partners before embarking on the tasks of challenging them to change. As helping professionals, counselors are working in a constant state of mediating the influences of cultural forces within self, clients, and others, and within this context, they must be proactive in responding to the needed knowledge, awareness, and skills necessary to be of service to their clients (Portman, 2009).

From the outset, when a counselor forms an alliance with his or her clients, the goals have always been to free the identified patient of the symptoms, to reduce conflict and stress for the family, and for the family to learn new ways of coping (Minuchin & Fishman, 1981). Counselors must consider the behaviors, values, and priorities relating to other developmental landmarks such as dating practices, marriage, and gender roles in the context of cultural backgrounds of their Asian American clients (Madathil & Sandhu, 2008). At the same time, this subtle process enables the counselor to gather data about the family's existing hierarchies, values, and norms while affirming and acknowledging each member of the family. In a roundabout way, the joining process is conducive to the Asian cultural milieu, taking into account the Asian immigrant clients' cultural expectations such as the counselor is a professional with expert knowledge and that he or she respects the hierarchical structure of common patriarchal Asian families. The counselor is letting the clients know that he or she understands them and is working with and for them. Generally, these attempts by the counselor to gain acceptance and admission to the family are viewed as congruent with what typical Asian immigrants expect from counseling.

Asian immigrants tend to define their presenting problems in concrete terms, and they expect the counselor, being an expert, to provide them with solutions. Coming for counseling treatment may be viewed as bringing shame to the family. Mental and emotional disorders carry a stigma within the community. Guilt and shame within the context of Asian "loss of face" carry a big stick that implies that the entire family is losing respect and status within the community when one of them is shamed. That identified patient is then positioned in an untenable place and is under heavy pressure to keep the harmony and order within the unit by minimizing any conflicts and problems that could shame and bring guilt to the family (Chung et al., 2008; Ho, 1990; Kim et al., 1999; Sue & Sue, 2008). Thus, a counselor needs to carefully balance his or her attempts to identify the problem while appearing to respect the client's cultural background in a congruent manner. Often, the client's initial description of the presenting problems may appear to the counselor as one in which the client externalizes the root causes and spends a lot of time complaining and blaming. It is not uncommon to hear a client who lost his job to attribute such loss to his wife's inability to execute household chores and duties or to attribute their child's poor school performances on the wife's spoiling and babying the child too much.

In the context of Asian immigrants' cultural milieu, the counselor can use the techniques of relabeling, reframing, and therapeutic paradox in his or her attempt to interrupt the sequences of problem-generating behaviors of family members. This attempt is congruent with the concept of "saving face" but is deemed more important in the context of collectivistic, hierarchical family structure of Asian immigrants in which no one in the family is blamed for the sequences of problematic behavior, but instead the expert, in the person of counselor, continues to honor and respect each member of the family by affirming their roles and place in the unit. Counselors need to relabel or reframe the behavioral sequence of the presenting problems to make solutions of the presenting problems appear doable and within the capability and competence of the family. Once the family buys this, it is easier to move gradually to other issues beyond the presenting problems. The counselor, being accepted as an expert by the clients, can easily encourage the members to interact with each other and with the counselor. The counselor can observe the process through which the presenting problems often emerge. On occasion, the counselor will be called to intensify the current transactions to gauge the family's understanding and acceptance of challenges and the ways they perceive reality. The counselor regulates the transactions in terms of affect, repetition, and duration. Observing interactions within the session is the hallmark of the systemic approach of counseling. Counselors adopting this approach may attempt to shape the competence of the family members in taking care of themselves (without the presenting problem) from the very moment when they meet the family and begin the counseling relationship (Nichols & Schwartz, 2006).

Often, an ability to converse in English can place the family unit in a hierarchical inversion situation, especially when the parents are unable to speak or master the language (e.g., English), and they have to rely on their children to translate, a dynamic that often inverses the traditional hierarchical structure of the family. The parents will find themselves more isolated from mainstream institutions and have to rely on and become dependent on their children to connect to the outside world. This hierarchical inversion can have a destructive effect on the family. Just as it is an awesome task for each of the family members to adjust to the new environment, it is also an equally challenging task for the counselor to formulate effective intervention strategies acceptable to the family members. It can either make or break the counseling relationship with this family.

Counselors also need to be careful when asking each family member to describe what he or she perceives of the family patterns. Often the response is very much influenced by factors such as whether a family member was born and raised in Asia or born in the United States. Hong and Domokos-Cheng Ham (2001) illustrated such instances in which the parents, born and raised in Asia, may identify a family pattern of responsibility and sacrifice and hence the discipline ("I did that for your own good," "It hurts me more than you ever know when I punish you"), a theme consistent with Asian cultural values, whereas the children, born and raised in the United States, may identify the same values by relabeling them as stifling restriction, authoritarian, and perhaps downright abusive.

The transactions within the family may reveal the fact that the children, exposed to the egalitarian concept in the mainstream culture, expected to be asked instead of being told, and the parents may perceive such a request as akin to reducing their position within the familial hierarchy or downgrading their status or perhaps perceive it as an act of teenage rebelliousness, defiance, or downright disrespectfulness. In their attempts to reestablish and maintain such traditional hierarchical structure, and not reduce their stature as parents by acquiescing to the demands of the teenage children, they will continue with the same old family patterns to maintain control, hence perpetuating the homeostasis. A keen counselor can detect such scenarios when the observed member starts using the words "demand" or "telling" as opposed to "let's see" or "asking." It is incumbent on the counselor to be conscientious in tracking all of these family patterns and in formulating culturally appropriate treatment plans and goals.

When working with recent Asian American families, counselors need to be aware of the within-group diversity and how they relate to the counseling process. Acculturation issues remain a focus that counselors must assess throughout the counseling sessions.

References

Chung, R. C., Bemak, F., Ortiz, D. P., & Sandoval-Perez, P. (2008). Promoting the mental health of immigrants: A multicultural/social justice perspective. *Journal of Counseling and Development, 86,* 310–317.

Gloria, A. M., Castellanos, J., Park, Y. S., & Kim, D. (2008). Adherence to Asian cultural values and cultural fit in Korean American undergraduates' help-seeking attitudes. *Journal of Counseling and Development, 86,* 419–428.

Hammond, R. T., & Nichols, M. P. (2008). How collaborative is structural family therapy? *The Family Journal: Counseling and Therapy for Couples and Families, 16,* 118–124.

Ho, C. K. (1990). An analysis of domestic violence in Asian American communities: A multicultural approach to counseling. *Women and Therapy, 9,* 129–150.

Hong, G. K. & Domokos-Cheng Ham, M. (2001). *Psychotherapy and counseling with Asian American clients: A practical guide.* Pacific Grove, CA: Sage.

Kao, G. (1995). Asian American as model minorities? A look at their academic perfor-mance. *American Journal of Education, 103*, 121–159.

Kim, B. S. K., Atkinson, D. R., & Yang, P. H. (1999). The Asian values scale: Development, factor analysis, validation, and reliability. *Journal of Counseling Psychology, 46*, 342–352.

Kim, B. S. K., Ng, G. F., & Ahn, A. J. (2009). Client adherence to Asian cultural val-ues, common factors in counseling, and session outcome with Asian American cli-ents at a university counseling center. *Journal of Counseling and Development, 87*, 131–142.

Kim, B. S. K. & Omizo, M. M. (2003). Asian cultural values, attitudes toward seeking professional psychological help, and willingness to see a counselor. *The Counseling Psychologist, 31*, 343–361.

Kim, B. S. K., Yang, P. H., Atkinson, D. R., Wolfe, M. M., & Hong, S. (2001). Cultural value similarities and differences among Asian American ethnic groups. *Cultural Diversity and Ethnic Minority Psychology, 7*, 343–361.

Kluger, J. (2009, August 12). Stereotypes persist even where immigrants don't. *Time*. Retrieved August 12, 2009, from: http://www.time.com/time/health/arti-cle/0,8599,1915768,00.html

Lee, R. M., Su, J., & Yoshida, E. (2005). Coping with intergenerational family con-flict among Asian American college students. *Journal of Counseling Psychology, 47*, 211–222.

Liu, L. W. (2009, July 22). California apologizes to Chinese Americans. *Time*. Retrieved August 12, 2009, from http://www.time.com/time/nation/article/0,8599,1911981,00.html

Madathil, J. & Sandhu, D. S. (2008). Infidelity in Asian Indian marriages: Implications for counseling and psychotherapy. *The Family Journal: Counseling and Therapy for Couples and Families, 16*, 338–343.

Minuchin, S. & Fishman, H. C. (1981). *Family therapy techniques.* Cambridge, MA: Harvard University Press.

Nichols, M. P. & Schwartz, R. C. (2006). *Family counseling: Concepts and methods* (7th ed.). Boston, MA: Allyn and Bacon.

Okubo, Y., Yeh, C. J., Lin, P. Y., Fujita, K., & Shea, J. M. (2007). The career decision-making process of Chinese American youth. *Journal of Counseling and Development, 85*, 440–449.

Portman, T. A. A. (2009). Faces of the future: School counselors as cultural mediators. *Journal of Counseling and Development, 87*, 21–27.

Poulsen, S. S. (2009). East Indian families raising ABCD adolescents: Cultural and gen-erational challenges. *The Family Journal: Counseling and Therapy for Couples and Families, 17*, 168–174.

Takaki, R. (1989). *Strangers from a different shore: A history of Asian Americans.* New York: Little, Brown.

Sue, D. W. & Sue, D. (2008). *Counseling the culturally diverse: Theory and practice* (5th ed.). Hoboken, NJ: John Wiley & Sons.

U.S. Census Bureau. (2003, May). *The Asian and Pacific Islander population in the United States: March 2002; Population characteristics.* Retrieved October 14, 2009, from http://www.census.gov/prod/2003pubs/p20-540.pdf

U.S. Census Bureau. (2004a, March). *Current population survey, annual social and economic supplement, 2004, racial statistics branch, population division.* Retrieved October 14, 2009, from http://www.census.gov/population/socdemo/race/api/ppl-184/tab3.pdf

U.S. Census Bureau. (2004b, December). *We the People: Asian in the United States* [Census 2000 Special Reports]. Retrieved October 14, 2009, from http://www.census.gov/prod/2004pubs/censr-17.pdf

U.S. Department of Health and Human Services, Office of the Surgeon General, SAMHSA. (2001). Culture, race and ethnicity: A supplement to mental health. In *Mental care for Asian Americans and Pacific Islanders* (pp. 107–126). Rockville, MD: Author. Retrieved October 14, 2009, from http://www.surgeongeneral.gov/library/mentalhealth/cre/sma-01-3613.pdf

Chapter 8

Working With Asian Immigrant Families, Part II: South Asia

Mala Madathil

Contents

Shahid is a 42-year-old engineer living in the Northwest. He immigrated to the United States 20 years ago from India. Shahid and his wife, Mina, have been married for 17 years and have three children. They have no other relatives in the United States. Theirs was an arranged marriage. Mina is a stay-at-home mother. Shahid was promoted to a managerial position three years ago, and this position comes with many perks. It also requires for him to travel out of state and out of the country several times a year. Mina is the primary caregiver for the children. The children are 15, 13, and 9 years old. This family has been having some problems lately. Mina has not been feeling well overall in the past several years, and she has been feeling even sicker in the past year or so. She complains of several body aches and pains and states that overall she is not feeling "good." Her physician has not yet been able to diagnose her symptoms accurately. The oldest daughter, Maya, who is 15, has taken on more of the caregiving responsibilities of the younger siblings. The youngest son, Amir, who is 9, has been having problems in the school recently. The teacher reported that Amir has been lying about his homework and grades. He is also stealing things from other children in the class. Amir's teacher contacted Shahid and Mina and recommended that they get him some help. Mina turned to her family physician for help. The family physician suggested that they contact a counselor and gave the name of a counselor to Mina. Although Shahid was very reluctant at first, he now believes that it might be helpful for the family to talk to someone. He hopes that it will help Mina feel better and that the counselor can also help them with Amir's behavioral problems. The family is apprehensive of talking to a counselor. The family members are worried that the counselor will not understand their cultural norms and child-rearing practices. They are also worried that the counselor will not understand the context of arranged marriages.

What would a counselor planning to work with this family need to be aware of? What multicultural competencies might be needed? What unique cultural and social experiences might this family have that might be different from those of the counselor? How can a counselor from a different culture help this family?

The purpose of this chapter is to focus on the experiences of individuals such as Shahid, Mina, and their children. It provides an overview of the Asian cultures and the unique experiences of the Asian American families in the United States. This chapter also includes information on ways in which counselors can become culturally competent in working with Asian immigrant families in the United States. Although it is important for counselors to be aware of the different cultural norms and expectations, it is also equally important that the counselor not use this information to stereotype Asian immigrant families and individuals. Therefore, it is a delicate balance of having information to help Asian immigrant families while at the same time not using this information about the culture to label and stereotype the family's experiences or concerns.

Asian American Families: Who Are They?

Who are Asians as a group? What are the similarities between the different Asian immigrant groups? These questions are addressed in the following section. Asian immigrants compose a very diverse group consisting of different ethnic backgrounds. These groups are significantly different in their traditions, customs, norms, language, religion, and immigration history. According to the

U.S. Census Bureau (2004) estimate, there are over 33 million immigrants in the United States. Although more than half of the population originates from Latin America, a considerable number of these individuals come from various Asian countries (Sue & Sue, 2008). Asians composed 30% of the total population of U.S. immigrants in 2000 (U.S. Department of Commerce, 2000). More than half of the Asian population in the United States are first-generation immigrants from various Asian countries, and 66% of the population speaks no or limited English (Barnes & Bennett, 2002).

Reasons Often Associated With Why Residents Migrate to Other Countries

Increased immigration to the United States can be attributed to two main events: (a) passing of the Immigration Act of 1965 and (b) ending of war in Southeast Asia in 1975. Although easing of legal restrictions started after World War II, immigration rates remained low until the changes to immigration laws, which allowed a larger number of immigrants. In 1965, Congress abolished the national origins quota system, which had favored Northwestern Europeans, limited Eastern Europeans, and those from Mediterranean countries and virtually excluded Asians. Entry to the United States was determined no longer by race but by the potential skills of what they could bring to the United States (Prathikanti, 1997). As a result, a large percentage of immigrants were highly educated professionals. Another demographic shift happened in the 1980s, as Asian Americans started sponsoring their families through the Family Reunification Act. Many of these immigrants were less educated and less fluent in English (Sandhu & Malik, 2001).

The Asian American population consists of East Asians (Chinese, Korean, Japanese), Southeast Asians (region between Vietnam and Pakistan), and South Asians (Indians, Pakistanis, Sri Lankans). The Asian American population is one of the fastest growing groups in the United States. As of 2005, there were over 10 million Asian Americans (U.S. Census Bureau, 2005). The Asian American population is composed of at least 40 different subgroups that differ in language, religion, and values, and there may be between-group differences within the Asian American group that may be considerably large (Sandhu, 1997). It is important to keep in mind that even as a group, South Asians are considered as being significantly different from the East and Southeast Asians. As a result of these differences, it is difficult to define the Asian culture. This is important information for a counselor preparing to work with Asian immigrant families in the United States.

In addition to the between-group differences, there are considerable within-group differences. Individuals and families may vary on migration and relocation experiences, degree of assimilation and acculturation, and religious beliefs (Sue & Sue, 2008). There is great diversity within this population with regard to religious affiliations, language abilities, immigration history, socioeconomic status, education, and acculturation levels (Inman & Tewari, 2003). In addition, these individuals and families may also be different in their length of residence in the United States. Kim, Atkinson, and Umemoto (2001) stated that Asian Americans who immigrated many years earlier or perhaps even generations ago might be more likely than those who immigrated recently to follow the mainstream American cultural norms. It would be more appropriate to consider Asian Americans as a group representing very different cultural and religious groups rather than define the Asian culture. Cultural differences, degree of assimilation, socioeconomic background, educational experiences, and family experiences influence each individual differently (Sue & Sue, 2008).

Traditional Asian Cultural Values, Immigration-Related Experiences, and Counseling Implications

Kim, Atkinson, and Yang (1999) identified 14 value dimensions of Asian Americans: avoidance of family shame, collectivism, conformity to family and social norms and expectations, deference to authority figures, filial piety, importance of family, maintenance of interpersonal harmony, placing others' needs ahead of one's own, reciprocity, respect for elders and ancestors, self-control and restraint, self-effacement, educational and occupational achievement, and ability to resolve psychological problems. It is important to keep in mind that there may be significant between-group and within-group differences on the level of adherence to these values. However, these may be some of the characteristics and values that may set the Asian groups apart from other major ethnic groups.

In 2000, one in five Americans either was born in another country or had at least one parent who was (Lollock, 2001). Over two thirds of Asian Americans are born overseas. English may not be the first language of many of the immigrants in the United States. A majority of Americans, including immigrants, support the recognition of English as a national language of the United States, and the English-only stance taken by agencies and organizations may cause immigrants to feel excluded because of language (Sue & Sue, 2008). Many Asian immigrant family members are less than proficient in English. Therefore, language barriers and limitations due to the limited proficiency of English may be something that these immigrant families experience. They may experience discrimination based on this difference alone. The individual family members may be experiencing feelings of shame and frustration associated with the language barrier. This language barrier may also limit their opportunities in the employment market. It might be helpful for the counselor working with Asian immigrants to address these topics. It is important to keep in mind that these topics would need to be addressed in a culturally sensitive and respectful manner clarifying the counselor's intention to help. It is also possible that within the same family there may be some members who are more proficient in the English language than the others. How does this influence the family dynamics? Does this English-language proficiency influence an individual family member's role and position within the family system? How might this language barrier influence the counseling process? There may be communication difficulties between the counselor and the immigrant family members because of the language barriers. These are some dynamics that the counselor working with Asian immigrant families might need to be aware of.

Sometimes, immigrants are viewed as taking jobs away from natives, and this sentiment may lead to negative feelings toward the immigrants. Asian Americans have been exposed to discrimination and racism throughout history and continue to face anti-Asian sentiments (Sue & Sue, 2008). Most Asians have distinct physiological features that make it easy to identify their Asian origin. These physiological distinctions may also make them stand out in groups and sometimes make them victims to discrimination. Many of these immigrants and their children may also have names that sound different from the common names, making them stand out or be easy targets for discrimination as well. Asian American immigrants are grouped as people of color because by appearance, they cannot assimilate into the dominant U.S. culture (Kim & Park, 2008). The Asian family members who have been discriminated against based on their looks or names may carry feelings of shame, anger, or frustration. They may also have unique experiences of their children being treated differently in school and other education and social settings for these reasons. Since the terrorist attacks in 2001, Arab immigrants and other Asian immigrants are viewed with suspicion because of their physical characteristics or skin color. Several incidents of hate crimes toward Asian immigrants in the recent past have been tied to this erroneous perception. Some of these experiences are tied to Asian immigrants' physical appearances and accents. These could be sources of stress for Asian immigrant family members. These are also factors that are out of their control. It is possible that as a result, the adults and the children in these families experience fear, humiliation, and anger. Experiences of individual and institutional acts of racism may lead to low self-esteem and depression among Asian immigrants. It might be helpful for counselors to be aware of the experiences of Asian immigrant families as they prepare to work with them.

Asian immigrant families experience a wide variety of psychological stressors relating to the acculturation process as they attempt to adapt to the cultural norms, values, and political, social, and economic systems of the United States. These stressors may include culture shock, experiences of prejudice, changes in ethnic identity, shifting gender roles, family conflict, sense of inferiority, communication problems, sense of uncertainty, loss of support systems, nostalgia or homesickness, and feelings of guilt (Sandhu & Madathil, 2007). Kim and Park (2008) identified "marginalization—where the individuals abide neither by the norms of their original culture nor that of the dominant culture" as the most problematic acculturation status for Asian Americans. Integration or bicultural status on the other hand has been identified as the healthiest status for these individuals (LaFromboise, Coleman, & Gerton, 1993). It is very likely that Asian immigrant families vary on their level of acculturation levels. It is also important for counselor to keep in mind that even within the same family system, there may be individuals who are on different levels of the acculturation process. These acculturation differences might be a source of stress or conflict for the family members. It is important not to assume that all of the family members are at the same level of the acculturation process and therefore have similar views or values. It is important to keep in mind that acculturation conflicts between Asian immigrants and their children are common. It is necessary to assess the particular family member's level of acculturation as well as the person's racial/ethnic identity development process during the psychological assessment process and while choosing the counseling direction and interventions.

Immigrant families face several challenges as they begin the process of adjusting and settling down in the new host country. These include adjusting and adapting to a society different from their own, dealing with and understanding a new set of cultural norms and expectations, and experiencing the loss or modification of identity experienced in the country of origin. They may experience culture shock and may not have the familial or social support needed. Social and cultural norms may be considerably different from those of their native countries. These immigrants may experience feelings of isolation, loneliness, helplessness, anxiety, and depression (Sue & Sue, 2008). The process of adaptation to the cultural norms, behaviors, and values of the dominant group generally causes psychological distress for the immigrants (Sandhu, Portes, & McPhee, 1996).

It is necessary to explore further the development of the specific family system. The entire family may or may not have immigrated to the United States together. Many times, one or two family members immigrate first, and the rest of the family joins them later. This is influenced by many factors, including the circumstances at their home countries, immigration process, length of time required for the immigration approval in the United States, and relationship between the immigrant who is sponsoring the relative from the native country.

Asians are often viewed as the model minority. This stereotype suggests that Asian Americans are examples of the "American success stories." It also implies that they are doing well and are immune from cultural conflicts and discrimination (Kim & Park, 2008). Kim et al. (1999) argued that Asian cultural values such as frugality, emphasis on educational and occupational achievement, ability to hide psychological problems, and maintenance of face reinforce the stereotype. It is important to keep in mind that although there are several highly visible successful Asian immigrants, the model minority stereotype does not apply to all Asian immigrants. The model minority stereotype may add to the mental health difficulties for these clients. This stereotype may also create problems for individuals, families, and groups that may be experiencing difficulties and may need help. This stereotype in itself could be a hindrance to the Asian immigrant family seeking mental-health-related help. Many times these families believe that they have to live up to the model minority image, and this results in their not addressing the concerns or problems of the individual family members. Numbers indicate that at least 10% of Asian Americans, or 1.3 million, live in poverty (Reeves & Bennett, 2003). The model minority stereotype may also cause rifts between Asian Americans and other ethnic minority groups (Kim & Park, 2008). Children from Asian immigrant families are often under great pressure to succeed academically and to have successful careers. These expectations can also cause conflict among family members.

Asian immigrant individuals and families may not trust counselors, worrying that the information they share might be conveyed to the immigration department or other federal agencies. Even documented immigrants may sometimes have relatives and friends who may not have all the required documentation. It is possible that to protect these individuals, clients may not want to share certain information to the counselors or other helpers whom they view as representing the "system." For these reasons, it might be extremely important for the therapist to discuss confidentiality and limits of confidentiality, including situation-specific examples for the immigrants. This might be needed to build trust with Asian immigrant clients. Mental health professionals working with Asian immigrants would need to pay attention to these factors.

Asian immigrant women are consistently overrepresented in intimate-partner femicide (Asian and Pacific Islander Institute on Domestic Violence, 2005), which indicates a higher risk of partner violence and partner abuse for these women. However, very little is known about the extent and nature of victimization of Asian immigrant women (Lee & Hadeed, 2009).

Asian cultures emphasize collectivist orientation, patriarchy, social hierarchy, obedience, gender roles, gender norms, and gendered division of labor (Lee & Hadeed, 2009). The cultural values and expectations may prevent Asian immigrants, particularly Asian women, from discussing family problems with the outside world.

During the settlement period after immigration, changes in socioeconomic status combined with financial instability may result in an increased number of Asian immigrant women entering the workforce, resulting in greater power because of their economic contribution to the family. This may challenge the traditional male dominance and control, which may leave the families vulnerable to conflict and marital violence (Lee & Hadeed, 2009). Traditional gender norms and patriarchy may increase Asian immigrant women's vulnerability to forced sex or sexual assault within marriage (Dasgupta, 2000). Lee and Hadeed also argued that somatization might be more prevalent in Asian immigrants because of the pressure to suppress or internalize conflict.

Asian Americans do not often seek psychological services. They also tend to prematurely terminate professional help. Studies have shown that Asian Americans seek help from family and friends and that they would seek professional help only as a last resort. Several factors may limit the use of counseling services by Asian American immigrants. These individuals may perceive the counselors as lacking cultural sensitivity. Asian immigrants who are not acculturated to the mainstream culture may believe that the mental health services are foreign to their culture, and they may even find these concepts threatening (Sue & Sue, 2008). On the basis of a culturally sensitive psychological assessment, counselors may combine talk therapy with culturally sensitive and relevant interventions. It is important to keep in mind that counseling therapy may be foreign concepts to Asian immigrants. Counselors may need to explain the process and expectation to these individuals.

Asian immigrant family members may also feel ashamed about having mental health problems and may find it inappropriate to share their concerns with anyone outside of their family. Major values of Asian immigrants often include formality in interpersonal relationships, inhibition of strong feelings, obedience to authority of elders, primary allegiance to family, and deep respect for religion (Atkinson, Morten, and Sue, 1998). It is important for counselors to keep in mind that some of these values may be in conflict with the expectations of the majority culture, where independence, individualism, and autonomy are valued. Counselors would need to be aware of these differences to avoid labeling the client's behavior as dysfunctional or inappropriate (Sandhu & Madathil, 2007). These values also influence the manifestation of psychological problems, the expression of emotions, and help-seeking behaviors (Sue & Sue, 2008). Public emotional displays are considered to be signs of immaturity. Therefore, a counselor working with Asian immigrant families would need to be aware of the differences in expressing emotions so as not to mislabel interpersonal emotional behaviors between the family members as well as the family members' behaviors toward the counselor. A counselor working with an Asian immigrant family may not want to overly focus on expression of emotions, as this may be uncomfortable for the family members. It may be much more appropriate and helpful to focus on the behaviors rather than on the expression of emotions with these family members.

Asian immigrant family members may prefer counselors who are ethnically similar. They may value the counselor's cultural knowledge (seen as more credible), may expect solutions and strategies from the counselor, and may respond more favorably to a rational, directive, and authoritative style of counseling (Sue & Sue, 2008). Counselors may be seen as the experts, and clients may look up to them to solve their problems. While working with Asian immigrant families, counselors may safely assume that the counseling process might be most effective if the process includes several different components: The counselor may take on the role of the educator, advocate, ally, and sometimes even cultural ambassador in addition to being a mental health counselor. In addition to needing mental health counseling, Asian immigrants may need help in finding employment and information on improving one's skills (such as information on courses offered through community colleges, local universities, etc.). They may also need help in navigating the educational system for their children. It is possible that a counselor who is perceptive to the cultural dynamics of interaction between family members might be more accurate in conceptualizing the concerns of the family as well as in cocreating goals. The counseling process and interventions would need to factor in the unique cultural characteristics, values, and traditions of the Asian family (such as factoring in the mate selection process and marital expectation and satisfaction, as in the case of the scenario described at the beginning of this chapter). It would be helpful to assess what the family's needs are and to use an approach that is time limited and focused on concrete resolution of problems. The family could also benefit from a collectivistic perspective on the problem resolution (as opposed to the individualistic approach often used in the Eurocentric approaches).

Communication pattern is a factor to keep in mind while working with Asian immigrants. Asian Americans tend to use a high-context style of communication where the listener is expected to infer the meaning based on the context of the communication and the person's knowledge of the person sharing the information (Kim & Park, 2008). This pattern of communication is something to be mindful of while working with Asian immigrant families. The clients may expect that the counselor understands the cultural nuances of their verbal and nonverbal communication. Clients may find it inappropriate to have to verbally state all of their thoughts or emotions. The counselor may need to be aware of the cultural component of the verbal and nonverbal interaction between the family members, especially between the adults and the children. Counselors also would need to be aware that Asian immigrants may not express their emotional feelings openly and that in most Asian cultures emotional displays are considered inappropriate.

Asian cultures also tend to be patriarchal whereby men and older family members hold a higher status. Asian American parents tend to be more directive and authoritarian with their children. It might be necessary to explore the dynamics between parents and children in a culturally sensitive manner so that the clients do not feel criticized for this value difference.

It is recommended that depending on the particular acculturation level, the counselor may consider integrating native (indigenous) healing methods (such as tai chi) while providing counseling services to Asian immigrant families. It is also recommended that counselors combine the conventional counseling approaches and traditional cultural values while working with Asian American families (Kim & Park, 2008). Asian cultures consider the mind and body to be inseparable. Physical complaints are a common and culturally accepted way of expressing psychological concerns (Sue & Sue, 2008). A counselor working with Asian immigrant families may need to consider the somatic complaints as part of the presenting problems. Certain approaches that focus on the person's emotional expression or in-depth self-exploration may not be appropriate for Asian immigrant clients whose cultural values may place emphasis on the family and group rather than on the individual. It may also be helpful for these counselors to be perceived as having an understanding of the experience of immigration. It might be helpful if these counselors are involved with various communities and are familiar with the resources available within the immigrants' ethnic community as well. Counselors may be expected to play an active role in the sessions. These clients may expect specific suggestions and recommendations from their counselor. A counselor may be seen as an authority figure and therefore considered as an expert. It would be necessary for the helper to keep in mind the cultural differences that exist between the counselor and the Asian immigrant client. In the case of Shahid and Mina (described at the beginning of the chapter), it might be helpful to start with their son's behavioral problems at school and then address the relationship dynamics between Shahid and Mina. The counselor may also consider recommending yoga or meditation to help Mina feel calmer.

As stated earlier, the Asian American clients may seek counseling only as a last resort. It is widely known that Asian American individuals and families underutilize counseling and other mental health services (Sue & Sue, 2008). There may be some amount of shame and embarrassment when seeking counseling. Counselors must be aware of the culture-related concerns and apprehensiveness of these clients. Asian cultures typically value a collectivistic orientation. It is necessary for the counselor to consider this cultural factor in working with Asian immigrant families. Effective counseling of Asian American families would require an understanding of the diverse cultural systems of Asian immigrants. It is possible that the entire family may not ever be present for a counseling session.

The family members manifesting behavioral concerns may be brought to the counselor. On the other hand, it is also possible that family members who may not be considered as part of the nuclear family may be present for a counseling session. Both of these circumstances would need to be viewed from the Asian cultural perspective.

Mental health professionals must keep in mind the important roles religion, spirituality, and spiritual leaders play in the lives of Asian immigrants by providing social support (Jeung, 2004). Asian Americans tend to have high rates of religious affiliation. In addition to access to a place of worship, these immigrants may receive a range of formal and informal social services such as food and employment through these affiliations (Lee, 2007).

Summary

It is important to remember that there could be considerable differences between the various Asian American groups and between the first-generation immigrants and the second- or third-generation Asian Americans. It is important for mental health professionals working with Asian immigrants to look beyond the success myth of Asian immigrants and focus on understanding the experiences of the particular family member. Counselors and mental health professionals may also have to modify their approaches and interventions to be culturally sensitive to the needs of Asian immigrant families. It is important not to overgeneralize group characteristics. Counselors must focus on the needs of the individual clients and families. Cultural information and knowledge can be helpful tools for counselors working with Asian immigrants. It is also important to remember that values and behavior patterns may change over time (Sue & Sue, 2008).

Counselors must be aware of their own assumptions and biases. Helpers must also recognize the myths and mistaken beliefs about this group. The counselor may be expected to take an active role. It would be helpful to assess the client's level of acculturation as part of assessment and discuss interventions accordingly. In couples and marriage and family therapy situations, it would be important to keep in mind that some of these individuals might be in arranged marriages, and the counselor would need to be culturally aware and sensitive about dealing with the family dynamics. A counselor who is aware of his or her own assumptions and biases and is willing to be open and learn might be able to build rapport with these couples and families. A counselor may need to step out of the traditional therapist role and provide case management services as well in situations where the immigrant might need help in understanding how the system works.

In spite of having several mental health concerns, Asian immigrant families hesitate to seek mental health services. It is important that mental health service providers consider this factor to provide culturally sensitive counseling services to these individuals and families. Counselors are strongly encouraged to assess the client's acculturation level to provide interventions that are appropriate for the particular client. Counselors are also encouraged to integrate conventional counseling strategies and indigenous methods when ethical and appropriate.

References

Asian and Pacific Islander Institute on Domestic Violence. (2005). *Domestic violence in Asian communities: Factsheet—July 2005*. San Francisco: Author.

Atkinson, D.R., Morten, G., & Sue, D.W. (1998). Counseling American minorities: A cross cultural perspective (5th ed.). New York, NY: McGraw-Hill

Barnes, J. & Bennett, C. E. (2002). *The Asian population: 2000*. Washington, DC: U.S. Census Bureau.

Dasgupta, S. D. (2000). Changing the course: An overview of domestic violence in the South Asian community in the United States. *Journal of Social Distress and the Homeless, 9*, 173–185.

Inman, A. G. & Tewari, N. (2003). The power of context: Counseling South Asians within a family context. In G. Roysircar, D. S. Sandhu, & V. E. Bibbins, Sr. (Eds.), *A guidebook: Practices of multicultural competencies* (pp. 97–107). Alexandria, VA: Association for Multicultural Counseling and Development.

Jeung, R. (2004). *Faithful generations: Race and new Asian American churches*. New Brunswick, NJ: Rutgers University Press.

Kim, B. S. K., Atkinson, D. R., & Yang, P. H. (1999). The Asian values scale: Development, factor analysis, validation, and reliability. *Journal of Counseling Psychology, 46*, 342–352.

Kim, B.S., Atkinson, D.R., & Umemoto, D. (2001). Asian cultural values and the counseling process: current knowledge and directions for future research. *The Counseling Psychologist, 29*, 570–603.

Kim, B. S. K. & Park, Y. S. (2008). East and Southeast Asian Americans. In G. McAuliffe & associates (Eds.), *Culturally alert counseling: A comprehensive introduction* (pp. 188–219). Thousand Oaks, CA: Sage.

LaFromboise, T., Coleman, H. L. K., & Gerton, J. (1993). Psychological impact of biculturalism: Evidence and theory. *Psychological Bulletin, 114*, 395–412.

Lee, E. (2007). Domestic violence and risk factors among Korean immigrant women in the United States. *Journal of Family Violence, 22*, 141–149.

Lee, Y. S. & Hadeed, L. (2009). Intimate partner violence among Asian immigrant communities: Health/mental health consequences, help seeking behaviors and service utilization. *Trauma, Violence and Abuse, 10*(2), 143–170.

Lollock, L. (2001). *The foreign-born population in the United States: March 2000*. Washington, DC: U.S. Census Bureau.

Prathikanti, S. (1997). East Indian American families. In E. Lee (Ed.), *Working with Asian Americans: A guide for clinicians.* (pp. 79–100). New York: The Guilford Press.

Reeves, T. & Bennett, C. (2003). *The Asian and Pacific Islander population in the United States: March 2002.* Retrieved September 20, 2009, from http://www.census.gov/prod/2003pubs/p20-540.pdf

Sandhu, D. S., Portes, P. R. & McPhee, S. A. (1996). Assessing cultural adaptation: Psychometric properties of the Cultural Adaptation Pain Scale. *Journal of Multicultural Counseling and Development, 24*, 15–25.

Sandhu, D. S. (1997). Psychocultural profiles of Asian and Pacific Islander Americans: Implications for counseling and psychotherapy. *Journal of Multicultural Counseling and Development, 25*, 7–22.

Sandhu, D. S. & Malik, R. (2001). Ethnocultural background and substance abuse treatment of Asian Indian Americans. In S. L. A. Straussner (Ed.), *Ethnocultural factors in substance abuse treatment* (pp.368–392). New York: Guilford Press.

Sandhu, D. S. & Madathil, J. (2007). South Asian Americans. In G. McAuliffe (Ed.), *Culturally-alert Counseling: A Comprehensive Introduction* (pp. 353–388). Thousand Oaks, CA: Sage.

Schmid, C. (2003). Immigration and Asian and Hispanic minorities in the new south: An exploration of history, attitudes and demographic trends. *Sociological Spectrum, 23*, 129–157.

Sue, D. W. & Sue, D. (2008). *Counseling the culturally diverse: Theory and practice* (5th ed.). Hoboken, NJ: John Wiley & Sons.

U.S. Department of Commerce, Bureau of Census (2000). Census. Washington, D.C: U.S. Government Printing Office.

U.S. Census Bureau. (2004). *The foreign-born population in the United States: 2003.* Washington, DC: U.S. Government Printing Office.

U.S. Census Bureau. (2005). *We the people: Pacific Islanders in the United States.* Washington, DC: U.S. Government Printing Office.

Chapter 9

Working With Middle Eastern Immigrant Families

Naji Abi-Hashem

Contents

People from Middle Eastern and Arabic backgrounds are migrating to every region of the world. They venture either alone or with their families. Some travel for business, training, consultation, trade, education, treatment, or exchange programs; others travel for leisure, vacation, adventure, and exploration; yet still, others travel to join their established family members, spouse-to-be, or lifelong close friends from back home. To understand their unique characteristics, backgrounds, mind-sets, emotional needs, lifestyles, values, challenges, and variety of subcultures, one would need, as a general way of introduction, to learn more about their many countries of origin and about the Near East region as a whole.

The Middle East is a vast region known for its rich history, ancient heritage, and wide variety of cultures. It has been called the birthplace of many civilizations and the meeting ground of many world powers and empires. The Arabic-speaking countries range from the East Mediterranean gate, also called the Levant or Crescent, and extend east to the Gulf Peninsula and west through all North Africa. However, besides the classical Arabic language (in written or in highly spoken forms), several basic cultural norms and religious faiths and practices, and a collective memory of their place and role in history, there is actually not much in common among these countries, people, and societies. Of course, the other common denominator for some is their share of the beautiful geographic environment around the Mediterranean Sea. Each community seems to have its own subculture, mentality, way of life, spoken accent, dress code, level of ethnopolitical integration, and version of social customs, habits, traditions, and values. Each corner of that vast region converses with a distinct accent of colloquial Arabic with the existence of a few distinct and separate dialects in the area. Neighboring communities and countries understand each other well; however, the further one travels, the more difficult it becomes to fully comprehend or meaningfully relate to others, as the spoken language and social norms considerably vary (e.g., the intricate dynamics and communication style facing someone from Kuwait or upstate Iraq when visiting, teaching, or doing business with someone from Cairo, Egypt, or Rabat, Morocco).

Officially, there are 22 Arabic-speaking nations, which are active members of the League of Arab States (also known as the Arab League), a voluntary association of countries whose people are mainly from Arabic ancestry. Many have a local national language and French or English as a second official language next to Arabic, not counting several communal and tribal dialects that are prominent in rural areas of North Africa and the Arabic-Persian Gulf region. The 22 nations are (alphabetically listed) Algeria, Bahrain, Comoros, Djibouti, Egypt, Iraq, Jordan, Kuwait, Lebanon, Libya, Mauritania, Morocco, Oman, Palestine, Qatar, Saudi Arabia, Somalia, Sudan, Syria, Tunisia, United Arab Emirates, and Yemen. Other related or concerned nations are observant, and a few are pending for membership (League of Arab States, 2006). Geographically, they are distributed into regions: The Maghrib—from Morocco to Libya; Northeastern Africa—Egypt, Sudan, and so on; the East Mediterranean known as the Levant—Lebanon, Syria, Jordan, Iraq, and so on; the Arabian Peninsula—Saudi Arabia, Yemen, and so on; and the Arabic-Persian Gulf—Bahrain, Kuwait, Qatar, United Arab Emirates (Nydell, 2006).

It has been said that America is so diverse in its population and geographical landscape. Yet, in comparison, the Arabic Middle Eastern world is much more varied and diverse, because of its long history, stretched territories, combined heritage, traditional faiths, integrated ethnicity, multifaceted customs, and sociopolitical dynamics. Those variations are good examples of how fluid and mosaic is *culture*, as a concept, entity, and dynamic. Through the ages, many observers have noticed that cultures and social traditions are a function of religion, and religious values and traditions, as broad phenomena, are an expression of and an extension of culture itself. Tillich (1959) once concluded that culture can be seen as a form of religion, and religion can be seen as the substance of culture.

In conclusion, the Middle East can be described as a region where ancient civilizations, world religions, established traditions, and modern lifestyles all meet together. It is a strategic place that serves as the gateway to three major continents. Its people are still rooted in the land and deeply cherish their heritage and cultures. Most urban people operate well within the modern and complex lifestyles without losing their social customs, religious identity, or communal uniqueness. Depending on the region, life in the Middle East is constantly shaped by local traditions, surrounding events, socioeconomic developments, religious faiths, and psychopolitical dynamics, both on the local-regional level and on the global level (cf. Abi-Hashem, 2004, 2007; Barakat, 1993; Hourani, 1991; Nydell, 2006).

Migration, Survival, and Coping

Presently, people from the Middle East and Arabic countries, of all ages and backgrounds, are traveling across the world and settling down in many hosting countries, near and far. They seek business deals, further education, new opportunities, a refuge place, or an alternative country of residence. Some are simply motivated by the love of adventure, and they like to explore new horizons. Others are escaping social stagnation, economic hardship, religious persecution, or political turmoil. Yet others are seeking asylum as refugees for various reasons, as they have been under pressure, mistreated, displaced, or victimized because of extended instabilities, ethnopolitical conflicts, regional wars, and psychoemotional traumas (Abi-Hashem, 1999a, 2006). They lost their homes, work, status, professions, and land. They probably were harassed, oppressed, or persecuted and therefore have no other place to dwell. Many are migrating as individuals or couples, whereas others are migrating as families and groups with the hope of joining friends and relatives or just seeking safety, stability, and a fresh beginning.

The first six months of any new settlement or relocation for any foreigners (students, workers, immigrants, refugees, etc.) are usually crucial, as they determine the pattern of coping and survival. Any move or transition has its toll on the mind, psyche, function, and relationship of individuals and groups alike. Always there are benefits to reap and prices to pay with every cross-cultural move. Thus, the question becomes, in which areas are immigrants gaining, and in which areas are they suffering? How are they coping with the impact of being uprooted from one environment and transplanted into another? Migration seems to either strengthen the longing to one's homeland, family, friends, relatives, and so on or weaken those ties as the person merges with the hosting society and detaches from the previous world. This is a similar phenomenon to transplants and mobile people who move within the United States, like when young people leave home or when families uproot and relocate to another far away state.

Caregivers need to find out how people from Arabic and Middle Eastern backgrounds are coping, adjusting, and surviving! What are they missing the most about their home countries, and how are they functioning right now in their host societies? What connections have they built (any new and meaningful relationships); what resources do they use (including ethnic or local communities and worship centers); to what peer groups do they belong (school, work, clubs); who have they befriended (healthy or unhealthy peers); and what attitudes have they recently developed toward both their homeland and their newfound land (critical, grateful, cynical, apathetic)? In other words, it is essential to find out what are the unresolved issues they are bringing with them from their country of origin, what is the level of satisfaction versus dissatisfaction they are experiencing right now, and what are the current stressors, tensions, and challenges they are facing (both internally and externally). Knowing these factors and dynamics will help both the provider and the immigrant work together more effectively toward better resolution, healthy adaptation, reasonable restoration, and sound and balanced acculturation (cf. Abi-Hashem, 2006, 2007; Ajrouch, 2007; Amer & Hovey, 2005; Barry, 2005; Faragalla, Schumm, & Webb, 1997).

History and Demography

In terms of the history of Arabic Middle Easterners in the United States, there were basically two large waves of immigration. The first was at the end of the 19th century (around 1880), mainly from the Christian communities of the greater region of modern-day Lebanon and Syria. The second wave was after the end of World War II. However, immigration increased dramatically in the late 1960s and continued steadily until recently (cf. El-Badry, 2009). Middle Easterners and Arabic-speaking people come to the West from virtually all backgrounds, heritages, nationalities, social classes, settings (urban, rural, or mixed), traditions, and religious faiths. They are spreading across the United State and Canada in large numbers, mixing within the larger society or creating unique neighborhoods and vibrant communities on their own. Interestingly, the majority of the Middle Eastern Arabic people who are living, studying, or working in the United States are of Lebanese descent.

There are currently about eight million people with a Muslim background in the United States and only about four million people considered as Arab Americans, that is, from Arabic-speaking countries with roots in the Middle East and North Africa (cf. Abi-Hashem, 2007; Arab American Institute, 2009; Brittingham & de la Cruz, 2005).

Hendricks (2005) noted, "People of Arab descent are a small but growing slice of the multiethnic American pie and, with higher-than-average levels of education and income, they are succeeding in the United States, according to findings in a new report from the U.S. Census Bureau" (p. A-7). Similarly, Oberman (2005) affirmed that Arabs and Muslims, in general, integrate into the American mainstream better than they do in most European countries.

However, like other minorities or immigrant groups, some Arabs and Muslims remain uninvolved and nonintegrated. They struggle to learn the social system and language, settle down emotionally and culturally, and make an acceptable, productive living. Some of them merge quickly within the hosting culture and begin to identify themselves primarily with the Western or American society. Others struggle to maintain their cultural integrity and unique background while, at the same time, they try to draw a clear line between integration and cultural separation. In the process they consciously or unconsciously resist full absorption and assimilation.

Several agencies attempt to monitor and advocate the affairs of Arabic-speaking individuals, families, and communities in the United States. Among these are the Arab American Institute (AAI) and the American-Arab Anti-Discrimination Committee (AAADC). Besides, there are local Arab American associations in almost every region. Subdivisions also exist and are formed according to the needs of a certain minority and established community. An example would be the Lebanese American Association, based in San Francisco, California.

According to Al-Krenawi & Graham (2000), although Arabic Middle Eastern societies share many attributes in common, the variety of cultural facets of immigrants who settled in Western nations have manifested different rates of acculturation, which in turn has influenced considerably the differential patterns of how these subcultures were then transferred, expressed, and experienced in the new hosting country.

Ethnic Arab societies are highly diverse and consist of heterogeneous systems of social differentiation based on ethnic, linguistic, sectarian, familial, tribal, regional, socioeconomic, and national identities. On one level, therefore, Arab peoples may be perceived as having deep social and class distinctions and as being disunited and politically fragmented, transnationally and within national borders. Ethnic Arab peoples likewise follow more than one faith tradition. Also, Western cultural norms have penetrated much of the Arab world, but their effect has been experienced differently in communities and across societies. (Al-Krenawi & Graham 2000, para. 6)

Counseling and Psychotherapy in the Middle East and Arabic Countries

Besides the availability of modern health care programs and medial facilities in Middle Eastern and Arabic-speaking countries, there is also a long and established history of folk remedies and ancient medicine that tends to combine traditional, herb, and ointment treatments with spirituality and ritual beliefs all in one approach.

Western and modern-day counseling practitioners will encounter talks and references about such rituals, beliefs, and practices, especially from those coming from traditional communities and the older generations. It is important not to dismiss these matters upfront but to listen to the underlying concerns, fears, and anxieties as well as to the faith and hope for healing. These matters have been attached to the historical background of people and have been popular for generations. They include some practices, views, and approaches that are based on suspicion and spiritualism (e.g., black-eye belief).

Psychotherapy and counseling are not common in the Middle East in general, and, when available, they are mainly attached to medical hospitals and health clinics rather than freestanding on their own. Educational institutions and religious agencies are offering their own versions of counseling, family guidance, and community social work. On the other hand, psychiatry is a more established profession, usually offered in conjunction with other medical specialties, like neurology. However, some references to psychological conditions or emotional treatment are still correlated with mental illnesses and psychiatric hospitals, which are a stigma in the mind of most people in the Middle East. New awareness and acceptance of guidance and counseling are spreading fast among the new generation and educated classes (through media and other programs) who are living and working in large cosmopolitan cities. Most universities have a psychology major, but it is within the department of humanities and social studies. Recently, specialized graduate training in some form of family guidance and personal counseling now exists in several capitals of the Middle East.

People of ethnic Arab origin tend to be suspicious of counseling or have a negative view of psychology and mental health in general. They tend to seek help from elders, teachers, close friends, family health care providers (nurse, midwife, physician), clergy (pastor, priest, sheikh, imam), ritual healers, mentors, and so on. They tend to underuse psychological help when it is available or mistrust it all together, especially when counselors and mental health professionals disregard (or diagnose) other peoples' traditional views, habits, beliefs, and values. Although there are exceptions on both sides of the caregivers–care receivers equation, it can be safely assumed that many Arabic Middle Eastern people still view psychological services in a negative light. This is compounded by their apprehension of being labeled crazy or fear of being subjected to mind control. They do not possess the language or terminology to describe all emotional labels, operations, and professional roles, that is, *counseling, coaching, psychotherapy, mental health clinics*, and so on, or to distinguish among psychiatrists, psychologists, social workers, and other specialists (cf. Abi-Hashem, 1998, 2007; Al-Krenawi & Graham, 2000).

Therefore, it is essential for the Western-minded practitioner to respect the traditional background of the ethnically and religiously different people, tone down his or her technical language and detailed office procedures (including paperwork), and explain necessary steps needed for the creation of such a special relationship. All should be done without intimidating these newcomers. In addition, all efforts should be made to welcome them, encourage their trust, and appreciate their heritage, social values, and religious practices, which, for many of them, are a genuine source of solace, comfort, and healing.

Major Religions and Social Meanings

The Middle East is known for being the birthplace of many great world religions—Judaism, Christianity, and Islam—and the convergence of many philosophies, faith traditions, and worldviews. Each of them is well established and active, with long-standing centers for learning and practicing. Thus, it is essential to defuse any misconceptions and narrow classification of the people in the Middle East and Arabic countries. Although the majority of the population in the region call themselves Muslims (Sunnis or Shiites), not all Arabs are in fact Muslims. Christian communities, of all types and variations—from the ancient liturgical churches to the modern free evangelical congregations—are an integral part of the whole Middle East composition. They are deeply rooted in the land and culture, as their historical presence traces back to the very first century. Judaism is also very ancient and well established. Jewish communities were flourishing in all corners of the Arabic Middle East and were blended nicely with the local communities. The Druze and Alawites are smaller in number but active, well-known, and recognized as well. Other minorities and branches of the main faiths have existed side by side for centuries. Religion is only one aspect of people's social identity and cultural heritage. Like its landscape, the Middle Eastern and North African people, especially those on the East Mediterranean side, are like a mosaic piece of art and a colorful tapestry of mixed cultures. They have lived with each other, traded with each other, shared the same resources, married each other, and been good friends and neighbors—until an invader or political power came along and divided their loyalty, which resulted in ethnic, racial, religious, and cultural tensions; sociopolitical conflicts; and hard feelings of animosity.

Another misconception is that all Middle Easterners are Arabs. That is not true either! Many Middle Eastern nations and communities do not speak Arabic as their main language (e.g., Turkey, Iran, and Cyprus). Languages like Syriac-Aramaic, Hebrew, Armenian, Greek, Turkish, Persian, and so on are common and an integral part of the region yet are not Arabic. Also, not all Muslims are Arabs! Large Muslim communities are well established in many places around the world, in different shapes, forms, and degrees—the Far East, Africa, Southeast Asia, Latin America, and now Europe and North America, with the largest Muslim population found in Indonesia.

Finally, not all Arabs are Middle Easterners! The countries of North Africa are Arabic-speaking nations yet are not a part of the Middle East or do not qualify to be called so. Actually, North African people, depending on their location, may feel closer to other sub-Saharan communities, on one hand, and to southern Europe, on the other hand. Many, like the Tunisians, Algerians, and Moroccans, migrate back and forth and use French as their second official language, along with several other local and regional dialects like Berber, Sudanese, Bedawi, Maghrebi, and so on.

Religious identity is an important ingredient in the social fabric of the Middle East and Arabic-speaking people. Families' religious branch or affiliation, such as Sunni, Shiite, Eastern Orthodox, Maronite, Latin, Greek Catholic, Jewish, Druze, and so on, is normally listed on their personal identification cards. In most Arabic Islamic nations, religion is virtually inseparable from culture and the social contexts. Therefore, it is common to hear references to spirituality and faith or the mention of God and deity in casual conversations or in formal settings—in private or in public, in business, media, education, medical facilities, or politics (Abi-Hashem, 2007). People recognize and respect each other's customs, faiths, and particulars, yet they share the common value and broad spiritual worldview. When they are struggling with a hardship or crisis or having a joyful celebration, they normally expect to hear from their peers something about God that is relevant to their occasion, either an encouragement to rational surrender or a call to be reasonably grateful. Recognizing God and relying on faith in troubled times can be essential at times for survival. "People are typically quite open to receiving spiritual encouragement, even in generic sense, offered as a part of social support and expressions of solidarity with them. For some, even blaming God and their fate in life can be a common dynamic in their personal coping and emotional expressiveness" (Abi-Hashem, 2007, p. 121). Therefore, counselors, educators, and caregivers need to expect such repertoire of language and mode of thoughts from their Middle Eastern, Arabic, and Muslim clients.

Tenets of Faith and Modes of Religious Practice

Because most Westerners and North Americans are not familiar with the Islamic faiths, scriptures, and writings (Koran, Hadeeth, Law, Shariaah—mostly spelled Shari'a); Islamic history and philosophy; or the major Islamic branches and derivations, it would be beneficial to briefly review some of these elements here (cf. Akbar, 1999; Dwairy, 1999, 2006; Kobeisy, 2004; Nydell, 2006; World History, 2006).

There are variations among those who call themselves Muslims, whether individuals, communities, denominations, or nations. Similar to other religions and affiliations (Christians, Jews, Hindus, agnostics, etc.) or other national, racial, and ethnic identities (Russian, African, American, Asian, etc.), there are many differences in the mind-set, norms, traditions, and life applications of Muslims. Some lead a parallel life, balancing between their faith and their profession. Others lead a more integrated life with a tangible observance and application of their religious essentials and doctrinal faiths. Yet others lead a disconnected life marked by separation and compartmentalization (nominal Muslim). That is true of large groups of people and governments as well. Although some tend to be only culturally Muslims, keeping some distance between mosque and state, others tend to be literally Muslim, heeding to the sacred teachings of all Islam and applying the detailed Shariaah to all aspects of their civil life. According to Mozaffari (1996, as quoted in Storey & Utter, 2002), the nationalistic and fundamental Muslims, unlike the moderate liberal Muslims, believe in the absolute indivisibility of all dimensions of existence, namely, the three Ds: Deen—the core of religion, doctrine, and spirituality; Dunya—the present world and our life on earth; and Dawla—the governing state and rules of law. In other words, Islam is considered as the glue that holds the fabric of society together.

Contemporary Islam has been described as having many faces, forces, and frames yet with constantly evolving dynamics. The degree of internal harmony versus disharmony in the Islamic mind-set varies among locations. The two major polarities appear on the religious spectrum—reformation and revolution (cf. Esposito, 1997). Many traditional Arab-Muslim societies are gradually incorporating the trends of modern life and globalization. Although some of the new integrative approaches are slow and cautious, others are more rapid and liberal. Radical groups, on the other hand, are trying to combine medieval theology and rigid ideology with modern socioeconomics and global politics. They have rejected Western values, broke off with pan-Arabism, and began active movements on their own to promote pure faith and preserve pure tradition (Sivan, 1985).

Thus, Muslim immigrants may come from a variety of Islamic societies (cf. Abi-Hashem, 2004, 2007): (a) folk-traditional type, (b) cultural-nominal type, (c) national-sociopolitical type, (d) moderate-rational type, (e) literal-fundamental type, and so on.

Generational Gaps, Cultural Trends, and Counseling Considerations

In working with people from Arabic Middle Eastern descent, counselors will find it imperative to learn whether they are first, second, or third generation in the hosting society; whether they come from an urban, cosmopolitan setting (e.g., Beirut, Cairo, Amman, Damascus, Athens) or from a rural, traditional area (e.g., small villages, countrysides, mountain areas); whether they are highly educated and fluent in several languages or have limited skills, exposure, and professional experience; and whether they are nominally religious or practicing believers who are intimately devoted to their faith, that is, social affiliation versus close observance of doctrines and rituals, a deep connection to their faith and community, and their belief systems that inform every aspect of their lives. Also, it is important to find out what is the purpose and circumstances of their travel, relocation, or migration! Are they coming from a stable, accomplished, and affluent background (e.g., large cities, rich Gulf countries) or from a poor suburb or a struggling community? Or are they coming from a restricted, unstable, troubled, and war-torn area (e.g., parts of Iraq, Israel, Palestine, Iran, etc.)?

As the case has been with other immigrants, travelers, settlers, refugees, and transplants, some eventually feel shy, intimidated, misfit, or negative about their experience and presence in the new environment, regardless of how hard they try. For them, the barriers are too many to overcome. Therefore, they try to maintain a low profile. They miss home terribly and face tremendous limitations and restrictions in the new society. Some may feel quite unwelcomed because of their lack of language skills, social maneuvers, or just being different in their shape, form, skin tone, or general outfit. Others obviously feel very positive, comfortable, well accepted, and rather highly motivated. They look forward to the new adventures and opportunities and feel quickly at home. They merge well into the hosting society and its subcultures and make the most of their experience. Yet others, though a tiny minority, may feel proud and entitled to all new-found benefits and freedoms, demanding more rights and privileges (seemingly arrogant at times), expecting the hosting country to adapt to them in a one-way accommodation, and even tending to impose their practices, lifestyles, habits, beliefs, dress codes, languages, worship styles, and so forth on the hosting society and place of their settlement.

Born and Raised in North America

People from Middle Eastern heritage and Arabic-speaking countries or from predominately Muslim, non-Arabic nations, have been living and working in North America for generations. Some of them are professionals, academicians, and entrepreneurs and are making significant contributions to the American life and society. They are frequently known and referred to as Arab Americans or Muslim Americans. However, these connotations cause potential for generalization or unhealthy projections, as if all Arabs, all Muslims, and all Middle Easterners are the same brand of people, have the same social characteristics, or fit into one image and psychological profile. Actually, besides the background diversity and sociocultural variations, there are many other factors that distinguish them from each other, like national origin, social status, age, gender, educational level, economic rank, religious faith, ethnic background, psychopolitical affiliation, and generational differences.

Middle Easterners in the West present themselves in a variety of social categories: single adults, newlywed couples, young families with children, and extended families including older people. Children and adolescents are the most adaptable of all generations. Non-English-speaking adults and seniors struggle the most and suffer from loneliness and severe homesickness, even if they are connected to others of similar background. Another category that counselors and helping professionals may encounter is that of mixed marriages, which present a host of new psychoemotional and sociocultural dynamics and require careful blending and negotiation of the two separate backgrounds.

Gender roles have different connotations and meanings in different regions around the world. They even vary within one local community and extended family. They are influenced by many psycho, social, religious, and cultural factors and manifest themselves in multiple forms across the life span. In working with ethnically Arabic Middle Easterners, one may encounter gender roles that are either well set and traditional, highly rigid and fixed, occasionally negotiated and maneuvered, or totally mixed, unclear, and confused. Moving and migrating usually do upset previous roles. Transition into a new cultural settlement can either reinforce old patterns and views or correct them and stretch them beyond people's comfort zone, in both private and public life, both inside and outside the family home. Providers and counselors need to check on gender roles at some point in the process. They can be instrumental in helping immigrants, internationals, or minority families calmly and realistically reevaluate, redefine, and renegotiate their relationships, inwardly and outwardly, without stirring in them any fear, defensiveness, or intimidation. It is important to emphasize what they might benefit or gain from such an exercise and to encourage them to give a voice and respect to every member, especially those undershadowed, underrepresented, and underpowered.

An interesting phenomenon happens among children of immigrants. They pick up the language and lifestyle so quickly that they alter the equilibrium of the family as they gain a significant cultural advantage over their parents. At times, the parents depend on their children to translate and guide them in public. When tension arises within the family, children may refuse to help their parents and thus enter into a power struggle with them by indirectly controlling or punishing them. Another sensitive dynamic occurs around authority and discipline. Parents find themselves, all of a sudden, unable to practice all their routines and methods of parenting that have been familiar to them because of the fear of being too harsh or abusive. Ironically, children at times threaten their parents to call the police, something that is intimidating and totally unheard of in their homeland. Although school-aged children become Westernized or Americanized fairly quickly, teenagers, on the other hand, struggle to reconcile both worlds and subcultures. Many find it easier to compartmentalize by being the good son or daughter and speaking their native language and living their traditional culture at home while acting like their Western American peers outside the home. Therefore, caregivers need to work through these dynamics and sensitive matters very wisely and carefully!

Multi-Identity or Multiple Identity

Like most immigrants and internationals, the majority of people from Arab or Middle Eastern descent are multiethnic, multiracial, multilingual, multigenerational, multinational, or a combination of the above. Therefore, they present themselves with a multilayer self and cultural disposition.

Refugees, on the other hand, equally vary. Some are well accomplished and come from well-established places in their original homeland, but for certain socio-economic, political, or religious reasons they could not safely remain in their communities anymore, or they were pressured to leave their countries. These minorities have been seeking asylum in open and freer societies for generations, either next door or across the oceans. Yet others, who perhaps constitute the majority of the refugees, are escaping armed fighting, ethnopolitical turmoil, and various types of persecution in their war-torn regions (Sudanese, Iraqis, Palestinians, etc.).

Thus, for such a diverse-background population, working with a monocultural provider (in a Western or American sense) is a challenge for them as well as for the counselor. Clients who seek consultation on their own or who are referred to counseling by the school, social agency, or court, normally face the difficult task of trying to explain themselves to the provider and make sense of their experiences. All the while, the practitioner is trying hard to understand and build an accurate framework of their clients' mental and emotional condition and sociocultural situation. Conceptualizing cultural cases with little or no international exposure, insight, or experience can be really hard and challenging, if not confusing and misleading—not to mention dissatisfying and unrewarding! One remedy is for counselors to work through a competent multicultural and multilinguistic translator until they can gain deeper experience and wider perspective and consequently acquire better helping skills.

Because of the significant diversity of the people from the Middle East and Arabic-speaking countries, it is wise not to classify them in one category or group. Although the label *Arab Americans* is often used in the media and literature to describe these populations, it nevertheless can be misunderstood, too broad, and frequently misleading. According to Erickson and Al-Timimi (2001),

> Arab Americans are one of the most diverse ethnic groups in the United States in their cultural and linguistic backgrounds, political and religious beliefs, family structures and values, and acculturation to Western society (Abraham, 1995; Abudabbeh & Nydell, 1993; Jackson, 1997). Originating from many different countries with tremendous regional and national differences in language, politics, religion, and culture (Abraham, 1995), in many ways Arab Americans are only a loosely connected ethnic group. Because of this, there are a number of important national differences among Arab Americans that must be considered. (p. 310)

In addition, the openness and receptivity of the so-called Arab Americans to the counseling experience depend on the interaction of several factors, including country of origin, educational level, time since leaving their homeland, current community involvement, and their perception of the Western societies and lifestyles in general and of the United States in particular (cf. Jackson, 1995, 1997). "Essentially, this complex equation of factors constitutes the context of assimilation.... This self-identification of heritage can play out in terms of counseling issues... and may affect how an Arab American client perceives a non-Arab therapist or other mental health professional" (Nassar-McMillan & Hakim-Larson, 2003, p. 157). Such an interactive and emerging identity becomes a function of the actual overlap and combination of many identifications, affiliations, and identities—Middle Eastern, Arabic, Western, American, and so on—and the outcome of that process is different for every individual, couple, family, or associated group.

The Concept of Cultural Self

Caregivers and practitioners who are involved in cross-cultural counseling, multicultural service, and international humanitarian work must first consider the contours of their cultural identification and carefully discover the nature of their cultural self, who they are culturally, and what is their psychosocial makeup, global mind-set, and current disposition. Then, they will be able to better understand and relate to others, especially immigrants, refugees, and minorities. Furthermore, they will be able to help mobile populations discover their own *cultural* constitution, *cultural* function, and *cultural* progression. Remarkably, both the providers (normally part of the majority group or representing the hosting culture) and the recipients (normally part of the minority group as settlers or guests within that culture) are equally affected by globalization, acculturation, secularization, industrialization, modernization, materialization, radicalization, and internationalization. Yet each human being, family unit, or small group is affected differently and distinctively. Thus, we all experience different levels of tension, struggle, and disorientation as well as different levels of accomplishment, richness, and satisfaction.

The concept of *cultural self* is something I have been personally thinking and contemplating about, and further stretching and developing, based on my travels, readings, observations, and international experiences. Apparently, there is a part of us that is larger than our psychoemotional intrapsychic self and our socionational identity. It is connected to and influenced by the global trends and what is happening in our world today. Therefore, *cultural self* can be conceptualized as the accumulation of global exposures and transnational identities and the building up of the collective worldviews and ethnosocial habits, customs, and heritages. It is a fluid entity, constantly shaping and forming, that is broader than our local personal identity, psychosocial self, or mere nationality. It is the result of the overlapping interaction of the local and universal forces and the dynamics of cultural exposures and mixtures. As the world is changing so is our view of ourselves and of each other. That is true of individuals, families, communities, and countries alike.

Much has been written in the literature about identity formation, acquisition, development, and definition. Yet presently these processes are compounded by the forces of internationalization, the changing forms and norms of human relationships, the overload of the news media and the technical age of information, the increased discrepancies in society and the world, the uncertainties of future plans and programs, and the constant mixing of subcultures, religions, politics, and mentalities.

Many immigrants, refugees, and foreigners are struggling to define themselves and to sort out the many layers of their identity. Caregivers, providers, and practitioners are equally impacted by the changing forces of globalization and are similarly in need to discover their multiple identities and who they are becoming globally and culturally (cf. Abi-Hashem, in press; Arrow & Sundberg, 2004; Giddens, 2000; Kellner, 2002).

Naturally, we all belong to more than one culture and subculture. Most people are able to function well within many spheres, granted they have enough time for cultural transition, emotional adjustment, and schema reorientation. This phenomenon is similar to switching languages and mind-sets simultaneously or even to mixing languages, perspectives, and worldviews at once—like bridging the Eastern and Western mentalities together or combining Arabic, English, and French in one sentence or paragraph (e.g., in Beirut, many people, especially the educated and young generation, express themselves using the three main languages). Thus, unlike the monocultural person who is limited to the repertoire of one-dimensional schema and experiential language, the multicultural person is usually able to function within a few ethnosocial modes and move in and out of many spheres, normative habits, linguistic perspectives, and global mind-sets rather easily and effectively.

Obviously, we are more comfortable (and less anxious) relating to or dealing and working with people who are similar to us, in terms of worldview, education, social class, skin color, nationality, belief system, and lifestyle. However, that is not the reality of our world anymore. In fact, every encounter is becoming, to some degree, a *cross-cultural encounter*. According to Dwairy (2006), "Practitioners who work with clients of Arab/Muslim descent in the West should expect to encounter some emotional, cognitive, and behavioral styles that are not typical to Western clients" (p. 147). Judging these styles against rigid Western theories or quickly classifying them by one diagnosis or boxed criterion can lead to misperception, clinical mistakes, and personal misunderstanding and misrepresentation on the part of the provider and, at the same time, can lead to discouragement and distancing on the part of the clients. Dwairy added, "Of course, not all Arab/Muslim clients are alike, but rather they are spread along a continuum from traditionalism to Westernization. In fact, the personality of most Arab/Muslim clients has a traditional portion and a Western portion. The differing proportion of the two portions makes the cultural differences between the clients. The more traditional a client, the more his [and her] identity is collective" (p. 147).

Suggested List of Proper Etiquette and "Do's & Don'ts" Behavior

This is a sample list of practical tips, poignant hints, and codes of conduct to enhance your relationship with people from an Arabic, Muslim, or Middle Eastern background. Observing etiquette and proper manners is essential for safe encounters, better connections, favorable cross-cultural communication, and relational and therapeutic outcome (cf. Abi-Hashem, 2007; Boulby & Laroche, 2000; Cross-Cultural Communication, n.d.; International Business Center, 2007; Kobeisy, 2004; Nation Master, 2005; Nydell, 2006; TRADOC DCSINT Handbook, 2006).

- Remember the names of the people you are working with, because names reflect personalities and always have special meanings. It is always a compliment to say, "That is a beautiful name!" Then follow up with a smile and ask, "And what does your name really mean?" People of all ages are glad to answer and share the history and meaning of their given names.
- When talking with them, sitting or standing, do not back away to keep your distance or resort to a comfortable personal space. Sit and stand rather straight to imply attention and project respect of your company. Most Arabs and Middle Easterners sit, stand, talk, and walk in close proximity. That is especially true within the same gender. Backing away too far will be perceived by them that you do not like them and find them distasteful or you are a cold, impersonal, and unengaging person.
- Using your left hand to greet others or handle precious items is considered poor manner and disrespectful.
- When sitting, it is better to keep both of your feet on the floor, especially during serious or intense meetings. Crossing your legs with your shoes facing your clients is offensive. The sole of the shoe is considered as the lowest and dirtiest part of the human outfit or clothes where the person makes contact with the dust of the earth. The human face is considered the most precious part of the body where the eyes and the countenance are beheld as the windows to the inner soul and the channels of human pride and

dignity. It also reflects the honor and confidence of the person. Therefore, *losing face* is one of the most devastating experiences people can endure, and *saving face* is one of the most coping strategies people utilize to avoid public shame, appear decent at any cost, and preserve their dignity, social approval, family status, and public image.

■ Dress appropriately with businesslike attire when having formal meetings or counseling sessions. That shows respect to the clients and their families and generates more trust and confidence. Too casual dress (e.g., T-shirt, jeans, tennis shoes) does not reflect the sense of professionalism needed for such a huge step and serious undertaking on their part, especially for those who heard about counseling but never had the experience.

■ Body language and hand gestures are important. They have different meaning in different societies. Some common Western American gestures can be confusing, misunderstood, or considered impolite. For example, pointing one finger toward someone else in a meeting can be considered belittling or accusing. Rather use the full open palm as a sign of respect and invitation for them to join. Also, avoid the *thumbs up*, which can also have inappropriate or offensive meaning.

■ Most Middle Eastern mature adults and older people ought to be addressed using a label, title, or surname but never by their first name alone. If there is no clear label or connotation, like sheikh, uncle, elder, reverend, master, grandpa, or grandma, use *Umm* (mother of…) or *Abou* (father of…) and so on. Generic titles are always safe to use as well, like Mr., Mrs., Miss, and so on, exactly as Westerners would like to be called when they are overseas. It is common to call Middle Easterners with a title and their first name as well, which reflects the due respect with the personal endearment.

■ Discussing the women with men separately, especially during early encounters, is not appropriate. Inquiring about the personal life of female members of the family is considered an internal matter. When you are not sure, ask for guidance and permission from them.

■ Be careful about touching or hugging women prematurely. Some traditional or dedicated Muslim ladies would not like to be touched by or would not shake hands with a man unrelated to them. Wait until a woman extends her hand first before you reach out to her. Otherwise, she will let you know! Then you respond by nodding your head in greetings. Best to not stare or linger your eye contacts with adult women.

■ With men, the greeting is usually different. Hand shakes last a long time. Touching on the shoulder or locking arm into arm while walking down the hall or to a meeting room is common. Kissing on the cheek is a very warm form of greeting and showing affection. Do not jump if someone initiates such gestures with you. Being in close proximity, touching, and holding arms with those of the same gender have totally different meaning in most parts of the world than in Western American societies.

■ Do not expect rigid formalities or undivided focus when dealing with Arab Middle Easterners, especially in large settings, like training sessions, family therapy, classrooms, home gatherings, and so on. More than one person might speak at the same time. Some talk to each other, whereas others appear to compete for your attention. At times, people are silent, shy, reluctant, and intimidated by the process. So try to be patient, model verbal expression, and feed them practical sentences and terminology.

■ Practice the names you learn. Mispronouncing names or making fun of them because they are long or different is disrespectful. As already emphasized, in most parts of the world, names have precise meaning. They reflect the character of people and carry rich family stories.

■ When visiting a cultural center or religious congregation or interacting among conservative Arabic, Muslim, or Middle Eastern groups, try to abide by the local standards of behavior and dress code, act with modesty and openness, and respect their customs and tradition.

■ Practicing Muslims do not eat pork, drink alcohol, or discuss the female members of their group or clan in public. Others do comfortably. Thus, kindly ask before offering questionable items.

■ Most Muslims observe the mandate of fasting during the month of Ramadan, which is their special season of prayer, alms giving, and purification. Thus, refrain from eating or drinking in front of Muslims during the month of Ramadan. Business hours are usually shortened during Ramadan to facilitate religious preparations, social activities, and family gatherings.

■ Never interrupt devout Muslims during their prayer rituals even if they are practicing them in public. Five times a day is required of each believer. Do not be offended if they have to stop whatever they are doing and seek a quiet place to recite their daily rituals. They are trying to be faithful to their belief system.

■ Westerners, both men and women, should always wear modest clothing when entering traditional Arab Muslim homes, communities, or countries. This is not an issue with the new generation or in large cosmopolitan cities.

■ If you are a dog person, having your pet in the room, talking about dogs in personal endearing terms (as a part of the family), or using a dog illustration to make a human behavioral or relational point can be not only distractive but also very disrespectful and usually a turnoff to immigrants and non-Westerners alike. To most international people, dogs and cats are *it* and not *he* or *she*. Animals, especially dogs, can be loosely part of a household, mostly outdoor pets, or protectors but never considered as children, given intimate affection and full indoor privileges, or even treated like humans. In some cultures, calling someone a *dog* is a curse and a strong demeaning act of disgrace. So be careful about this matter, and do not assume that everybody you encounter adores dogs the same way most Westerners do.

■ Learn a few words and expressions in Arabic, and use them periodically. Surprise the people with whom you are working by occasionally saying *Marhaba* (Hello), *Keef Halkom* (How are you? [plural]), and so on. They will be absolutely delighted and will immediately feel closer to you.

■ People of Arab, Muslim, and Middle Eastern background would welcome you in their home freely and repeatedly. They will prepare all the entertainments and meals. So make sure to eat whatever food is presented without too much questioning or hesitation. Be polite and kind as you decline the many seconds they will keep putting on your plate. Also, during the first visit or two, you may hear a lot of repeated welcome phrases, mainly the classical one, *Ahlan Wa Sahlan* (You are most welcome). Hospitality is imbedded in their psyche and heritage. They will express joy and satisfaction for having you and feel honored by your presence, therefore, they will try to esteem you even though they might be poor. At times, they will give you gifts. Cordially accept the gift and show gratitude. Do not worry that such an act would manipulate or contaminate the relationship. Not at all! Actually, exchanging gifts (psychological or tangible) enhances any relationship. Refusing the gift can cause more harm and serious feelings of rejection.

Integration Versus Alienation

The goals of coaching, counseling, guiding, educating, and caregiving with any minority group in general and with people from Middle Eastern Arabic descent in particular is to help them adjust reasonably well, constructively reconcile their inner and outer tensions, and smoothly navigate within the new society or hosting culture. The early process of acculturation may not always end up with favorable outcomes. Therefore, caregivers and therapists need to watch for signs of splitting or alienation and challenge people to reverse the unhealthy reactions or coping styles so they can eventually reach a sound level of inner–outer harmony and integration.

Unfavorable acculturation outcomes can be evident by the following characteristics: cultural splitting; increased inter- and intrapsychic conflicts; heritage switching; interpersonal, intercommunal, and intercultural tensions; mental and functional shifting; socioemotional avoiding; ethnotraditional skipping; identity altering; new trait and role pretending; and so on, which all can lead to a splitting (*either–or*) mode of operating, loyalty dividing, core fragmenting, and worldview compartmentalizing.

On the other hand, favorable and healthy acculturation outcomes can be manifested by the ability to harmonize tensions, integrate polarities, expand identities, adjust to sociocultural stresses, reconcile national differences, broaden horizons, operate from a *with–and* mode, explain oneself with multiheritage terms, and add to the already existing worldview(s). Such desired acculturating processes and results will obviously lead to minimizing dissonance, social awkwardness, and psychoemotional alienation and will enhance a cohesive sense of self, a balanced inner–outer coexistence, a sound assimilation–accommodation process, and a smooth navigation among all the social road blocks and cultural nuances facing such minorities.

Therapeutic Modalities and Orientations

Theory and therapy approaches depend mainly on the immediate needs of the Arabic Middle Eastern person, family, or group and on their accumulated cultural history, level of exposure, coping styles, and degree of adaptation-assimilation. Because no one theoretical approach or therapeutic modality has all the answers or claims total effectiveness, especially when dealing with minorities and internationals, it is essential for the helping professionals to incorporate interdisciplinary and transtheoretical approaches. Using one's personal flexibility, creativity, and integrative ability is necessary for good counseling results. This proves to be a much better skillful practice than operating solely by the book or being limited strictly to one single theory, therapy, technique, or modality.

Most traditional people expect the mentor or the guide to be instructive, interactive, and directive without being controlling. They look up to the helping professional with respect and sense of authority and will respond better to a more structured, active, and experiential environment.

Working with a large immigrant or refugee family, the caregiver at times finds himself or herself facing four distinct generations—older individuals, adults, adolescents, and children. Each age group normally has a different cultural experience, presents with a different level of anxieties and tensions, and exhibits a unique version of dreams and aspirations. Caregivers and therapists must learn how to maneuver among these levels and generations and consequently to help the family draw from the strength of each one rather than feed into the inter–intra tension and cultural–generational friction.

Again, the best counseling strategies are the ones where the therapist is verbally interactive, physically active, experientially creative, and therapeutically integrative while, at the same time, keeps the *sociocultural* perspective at the background, as the constant reference point and guiding principle to the helping relationship and counseling process (Abi-Hashem, 2008, in press).

Regarding evaluation and assessment forms, it is essential to custom tailor them to be suitable to the people's sociocultural background and level of apprehension, especially those born and raised overseas. It is wise to avoid complicated forms and tools purely designed for the North American average population. In addition, counselors and providers should include a separate box on the intake sheet, another option for people to check when asking about their ethnic/racial background, called *Middle Easterner.*

> When psychological testing is involved or is necessary, it is recommended to use mostly projective instruments especially with first generation and low educated immigrants. With the younger generations, who were born and raised in North America, are fluent in English, and are fairly acquainted with the American mentality and lifestyle, it is safer to administer more technical tests (intelligence, personality, etc.). It is essential to remember that these tests were originally designed and standardized in the West in general and for North America audience in particular. They reflect the psycho-emotional structure and cognitive-mental views of this group. They have serious limitations and do not apply to all populations of the world. Some researchers and clinicians in the Arab World have translated English tests with little or no modifications. Some have developed their own but without proper standardization and validation. They tend to borrow concepts and theories from the Western literature without cultural screening or appropriation (cf. Khaleefa, 1999). (Abi-Hashem, 2007, p. 147)

Insights and Guidelines for Counseling and Caregiving Among the Culturally and Religiously Diverse Middle Eastern and Arab American Populations

Providing care and conducting counseling and psychotherapy with people from Arabic or Middle Eastern decent is a unique and specialized endeavor that is both challenging and rewarding. Whether these activities are in the form of education, cross-cultural communication, interviews and inventories, supportive counseling, or in-depth psychotherapy, "they must be culturally sensitive, clinically accurate, socially appropriate, and humanly respectful" (Abi-Hashem, 2007, p. 164). The following guidelines, suggestions, insights, and recommendations are designed for general practitioners and helping professionals to take into consideration and incorporate into their transcultural, transgenerational, and transnational work, as they provide care, support, and therapeutic service to several minorities who are locally born and raised or new immigrants and transplants and who virtually represent the new globalized citizens of this 21st century (cf. Abi-Hashem, 1999a, 1999b, 1999c, 2007, 2008, in press; Al-Krenawi & Graham 2000; American Psychological Association, 2002; Chaleby & Racy, 1999; Dwairy, 1999, 2006; Erickson & Al-Timimi, 2001; Gerstein, Heppner, Ægisdóttir, Leung, & Norsworthy, 2009; Hall, 2001; Jackson, 1997; Kobeisy, 2004; Meichenbaum, 2009; Nassar-McMillan & Hakim-Larson, 2003; Nobles & Sciarra, 2000; Pedersen, Draguns, Lonner, & Trimble, 2008; SAMHSA National Mental Health Information Center, n.d.; Sue, Arredondo, & McDavis, 1992; Trimble, 2003).

1. Be gentle and sensitive as you inquire about the values, norms, heritage, mentalities, faiths, lifestyles, and traditions of the people from Arabic, Muslim, and Middle Eastern backgrounds.
2. Realize that not all immigrant or refugee families or individuals (adult or children) are the same, that is, have the same struggles or achieve the same degree of adjustment.
3. Make sure to always be friendly, welcoming, open, and warm, especially early in the encounters and at the beginning of each meeting.
4. Look for commonalities and shared grounds and attempt to quickly build bridges with them. That will help you earn their trust, respect, and confidence as a good caregiver, not only in their view but also in the view of their family and community.
5. Inquire about their level of education, international exposure, and familiarity with Western thoughts and North American societies.
6. Find out whether they are "fresh from the boat" as a recent immigrant or they are second or third generation. Ask them what do they enjoy most and what do they dread the most in the present time of their journey.
7. Learn about the various societies, main cultures, and spiritual traditions existing in the world today, especially those emerging in your own area of work and residence.
8. Recognize that the world is getting smaller and closer in many ways yet, at the same time, is growing apart and becoming alienated in many other ways.
9. Avoid the questioning-interrogative mode of gathering information or personal data. That style comes across as mechanical and impersonal and will put extreme pressure on the ethnocultural people you are trying to

help, especially those who lack language proficiency or intricate knowledge of the cultural nuances and communication styles of your hosting
society.

10. Delay the identification of the presenting problem or distressing matter as
you get to know each other better, and do not rush into classifying them
within one diagnostic label or criterion.

11. Constantly increase your ethnocultural, cross-national, and cross-theo-
retical knowledge, awareness, and skills. When appropriate, acknowledge
the obvious differences between you and them, and ask if they have any
concern(s) about working with you.

12. Expect your internal anxiety to rise when you begin working with people
who are different from you in background, lifestyle, language, beliefs, or
global mentality. Your anxiety will subside as they gradually bond and feel
closer to you. The therapeutic relationship then begins to be enjoyable and
more rewarding.

13. Because it is fairly easy to fall into unhealthy biases and misconceptions or unconsciously adopt generalized impressions from the news
media (or other sources), it is essential that helping professionals check
their worldviews and expectations and be aware of any misunderstand-
ings, negative views, or stereotypes. Avoid *debating* sensitive topics
with your clients (regional politics, religious doctrines, validity of certain cultural traditions, etc.). Such debates can be very divisive and
counterproductive.

14. Repeatedly extend warm welcomes to them, and show appreciation for
their heritage. Offer to support, help, guide, challenge, and serve them.
They will respond by adopting you as the mentor of their family.

15. Expect that some Arabic-speaking Middle Eastern people will use idioms
and metaphors to describe their experiences, feelings, events, relationships,
and so on. The Arabic language (formal or colloquial) is very colorful and
poetic. You need to probe further and ask them to describe the point,
symptom, or situation in different words, terms, and expressions until you
get the core meaning. Be open to and comfortable with working through
an interpreter as well, which will add another dimension to the helping
process and cross-cultural communication.

16. Acknowledge the fact that they may, occasionally or frequently, face
misunderstanding, hardship, or marginalization. Some who speak with
an accent or broken English dread the many automatic questions other
people ask each time they open their mouth (e.g., Where are you from?
How long you have been here? Do you have family and relatives, or do
you live by yourself? How often do you go back home? Are you or your
family Muslim?).

17. Discover any emotional residues carried over from their homeland, which would be compounded by additional challenges caused by the move and the merge into a new hosting society and its subcultures. That is true for transplants and migrants and those displaced even within their own country or continent.

18. Find out the degree of their grief, level of traumatic stress, and type of unresolved bereavement. Help them identify their psychosocial struggles, and list their losses (major and minor ones) and missed opportunities. This process may take time and patience, but it is worth the effort.

19. Introduce appropriate grief and bereavement counseling and apply critical incident debriefing, crisis management techniques, and basic trauma mastery and post-traumatic stress disorder treatment approaches as needed and depending on the intensity of their agony and condition. Most of the time, a combination of all of the above or simultaneous alternation between them is crucial and most effective, especially for those who have been exposed to so much for so long. Many immigrants carry with them the scars of multiple crises, civil unrest, significant losses, war disasters, and horrifying acts of violence.

20. Do not interpret excessive politeness, slow disclosure, repetition, indirectness, agreeability, silence, or minimum eye contact as unhealthy appeasing, emotional disturbance, or psychological defensiveness. Make an effort to be relevant in your comments, feedback, and interpretations, without using much technical or psycholinguistic terminology, especially at first and when counseling unfamiliar, inexperienced people. Always be very clear and precise with your instructions and recommendations. Constantly check with them to see whether your analysis and suggestions make clear sense to them.

21. Avoid labeling minorities or generalizing Arab Middle Easterners! Never classify any people you are working with as one group, for example, "You Arab people...," "You Asian people...," "All Blacks are [or have] the same...," "Native Middle Easterners behave in an uncivilized way...," "All Muslims are fanatic...," "Your society is very male dominated...," "Women in the Muslim Arab world are oppressed...," "In your *third world* country...," or "Certain cultures are primitive and backward...." Such comments are harmful and will greatly damage your cross-cultural relationships. (Avoid using the term *third world country*, as it implies there are first- and second-class countries on the top of the list while the rest are at the bottom. Better use terms like *developed, developing, economically unfortunate country*, and so on.)

22. Help them reflect on their multiple identities and the basic constitution or makeup of their *cultural self.* How many international trends and exposures

have they been through? With how many nationalities, languages, and races or ethnicities do they intimately identify, and to how many political ideologies, spiritual religiosities, and ethical moralities do they personally belong? And what is the level of cultural stress and social polarization they currently experience? Help them to reconcile these various layers and tensions (inner, inter, intra, etc.) and to reach a balanced harmony of global characteristics and national identities.

23. Create a good balance between listening and guiding, attending and probing, and waiting and initiating. Your timing and agenda may be totally different from theirs. They will learn from your modeling and encouraging. So, most Middle Eastern Arabic people appreciate a warm mentor to bond with and a structured authority to respect and follow.

24. Again, inquire gently! Allow enough time for processing, and show appreciation for the positive aspects you discover in them along the way. Most minorities and immigrants feel inadequate or unblended and do not have the vocabulary to describe their feelings and deep thoughts. They need assurance and positive regards that they are still valuable and have rich heritage and something worthwhile to offer the hosting culture.

25. Listen to their verbal and nonverbal cues, their common signals and phrases, and their gestures and common styles. Beware not to impose on them your solutions, values, or personal preferences. Present your ideas and analysis only as options and recommendations.

26. Involve them in practical steps and exercises. An integral part of any helping endeavor, counseling, or therapy relationship should be assignments and homework, especially with immigrants and cultural minorities. However, make sure that you both clearly agree on every assignment, exercise, or piece of homework as a combined project and team effort.

27. Watch for any hint, sign, symptom, or tendency that may indicate a potential for fundamentalism, fanaticism, or radicalism. Certainly, this is a delicate matter and appears to be a subjective measure of value and personal judgment. However, the need in our globalized and polarized age is to be open and alert to any serious attitudes and behaviors that if not attended to and contained can flourish to become abnormally skewed and fanatic. It is essential to pay attention to any repeated statements or obvious patterns that may sound extreme or radical in nature, as with any other emotional instability, mental disturbance, or behavioral problem. When these are detected early, the chances of adjustment, reversal, and recovery are greater (e.g., suicide ideation, antisocial revelation, gang involvement, or destructive ritual participation). Seek to understand the source, meaning, background, and intention of these sentiments and statements. Some of them may be due to the individual's prior experiences of injustice and trauma.

Others may be the result of the individual being exposed to legalistic literature, joining an extreme group, or, worse, being indoctrinated under the teaching of radicals. Engage in slow exploration of the root causes, and gradually present other points of view, sentiments, and examples to counter the skewed and most extreme ones. Assigning various readings and introducing the person to local groups for social mixing and better exposure to alternative mind-sets and worldviews are essential. The process of reversing the gradual rapprochement toward extremism and the process of *deradicalization* are both equally important in helping the seeker or vulnerable prospect who may be easily recruited for advanced levels of fundamentalism. Intervention should also include mobilizing a variety of people and resources and referring the person(s) in question to influential leaders like clergy, teachers, and mentors and healthy programs like volunteer centers, public lectures, social action groups, and so on, all of which are available in the community at large.

28. Be faithful to all that you learn from them, as they expect you to remember names, history, landmarks, and private information they already shared with you. Ally yourself with them by using terms like *we, together, us, let's,* and so on for solidarity with them rather opposition to them. Avoid using *me* versus *you* as a professional barrier. That will give them comfort and assurance. It will break the class divide that often exists between the expert doctor and the ill patient.

29. Show respect and acceptance in your words by welcoming them and avoiding superficial joking in your deeds by displaying an appropriate smile and appropriate touching (or lack of with the opposite sex) and in your body posture and dress, all of which can result in appreciation and further bonding. A mechanical approach, a detachment style, social biases, a sense of superiority, or emotional indifference will result only in discomfort, mistrust, resentment, and separation.

30. Asking individuals to introduce themselves is uncommon, inappropriate, and impolite. Introducing oneself can be considered as boasting or promoting the self rather than practicing a decent practical measure. Either you learn enough about them ahead of time or you just ask someone else who knows them well to do the introduction.

31. Learn to differentiate between what is *cultural* and what is *pathological* and between what is *normal* (natural) and what is *abnormal* (clinical). Realize that what is heavily diagnosed in one culture is totally tolerated in another.

32. Be flexible, creative, and nonconventional in your work. For example, you do not have to meet with them only in your office or behind closed doors. That can be quite restricting and limiting to many, especially those unfamiliar with counseling. Most non-Westerners and those from developing

countries prefer less formal, less rigid types of consultation, like meeting around coffee or a meal or going for a walk. Remember spontaneity and friendliness could produce better results.

33. Notice yet another influencing factor, present in many cultures, that people, especially older people, avoid being negative or appearing ungrateful, which is considered bad manners and a disgraceful attitude. They try to avoid *shame* at any cost, which can be a driving force behind many social behaviors and values.

34. Have a list of community resources ready that you can suggest to the Middle Eastern Arabic people with whom you are working. It should include professionals, volunteer agencies, mainstream religious centers, law enforcement officers, moderate political groups, specialized pastors and clergy leaders, physicians, nurses, psychiatrists, crisis and hotline centers, free English as a second language classes, public libraries, and so on.

35. Capitalize on the human goodness, high tolerance to pain, and resiliency in the face of adversity you find in them. Eventually their new positive outlook on life and their spirit of survival and gratefulness are a great asset to healing and restoration. They will appreciate any help or investment of yourself and will accordingly respond in a graceful and grateful manner.

36. Finally, become a peace builder and a cultural mediator (or cultural broker) who promotes understanding and enhances healthy worldviews. In this way, you can make a needed contribution toward a better local community and, eventually, toward a better world.

References

Abi-Hashem, N. (1998). Returning to the fountains. *American Psychologist, 53*(1), 63–64.

Abi-Hashem, N. (1999a). Ethnopolitical conflicts: A Lebanese perspective. *International Psychology Reporter: APA Division 52 Newsletter, 3*(2–3), 29–31.

Abi-Hashem, N. (1999b). Grief, loss, and bereavement: An overview. *Journal of Psychology and Christianity, 18*(4), 309–329.

Abi-Hashem, N. (1999c). Trauma. In D. G. Benner & P. C. Hill (Eds.), *Baker encyclopedia of psychology and counseling* (2nd ed., pp. 1229–1230). Grand Rapids, MI: Baker.

Abi-Hashem, N. (2004). Peace and war in the Middle East: A psychopolitical and sociocultural perspective. In F. M. Moghaddam & A. J. Marsella (Eds.), *Understanding terrorism: Psychosocial roots, consequences, and interventions* (pp. 69–89). Washington, DC: American Psychological Association Press.

Abi-Hashem, N. (2006). The agony, silent grief, and deep frustration of many communities in the Middle East: Challenges for coping and survival. In P. T. P. Wong & L. C. J. Wong (Eds.), *Handbook of multicultural perspectives on stress and coping* (pp. 457–486). New York: Springer.

Abi-Hashem, N. (2007). Arab Americans: Understanding their challenges, needs, and struggles. In A. Marsella, P. Watson, F. Norris, J. Johnson, & J. Gryczynski (Eds.), *Ethnocultural perspectives on disasters and trauma: Foundations, issues, and applications* (pp. 115–173). New York: Springer.

Abi-Hashem, N. (2008). *Working with Arab Americans* [DVD]. Washington, DC: American Psychological Association. Available from http://www.apa.org/videos/4310843.html

Abi-Hashem, N. (in press). Caregiving and counseling in an age of globalization, secularization, and radicalization. *Pastoral Psychology.*

Ajrouch, K. J. (2007). Resources and well-being among Arab-American elders. *Journal of Cross-Cultural Gerontology, 22*(2), 167–182.

Akbar, S. A. (1999). *Islam today: A short introduction to the Muslim world.* New York: St. Martin's.

Al-Krenawi, A. & Graham, J. R. (2000). Culturally sensitive social work practice with Arab clients in mental health settings [Electronic version]. *Health and Social Work, 25*(1), 9–22. Retrieved from http://www.socialworkers.org/pressroom/events/911/alkrenawi.asp

Amer, M. M. & Hovey, J. D. (2005, Winter). Examination of the impact of acculturation, stress, and religiosity on mental health variables for second-generation Arab-Americans. *Ethnicity and Disease, 15,* 111–112.

American Psychological Association. (2002). *Guidelines on multicultural education, training, research, practice, and organizational change for psychologists.* Retrieved October 6, 2009, from http://www.apa.org/pi/multiculturalguidelines.pdf

Arab American Institute. (2009). Arab Americans: Demographics. Retrieved February 15, 2010, from http://www.aaiusa.org/arab-americans/22/demographics

Arrow, H. & Sundberg, N. (2004). *International identity: Definitions, development, and some implications for global conflict and peace.* Retrieved February 20, 2010, from http://ebooks.iaccp.org/ongoing_themes/chapters/arrow/arrow.php?file=arrow&output=screen

Barakat, H. (1993). *The Arab world: Society, culture, and states.* Los Angeles: University of California Press.

Barry, D. T. (2005). Measuring acculturation among male Arab immigrants in the United States: An exploratory study. *Journal of Immigrant Health, 7*(3), 179–184.

Boulby, M. & Laroche, L. (2000, April). Doing business in the Arab world [Electronic version]. *Canadian Chemical News.* Retrieved from http://www.allbusiness.com/north-america/canada/563027–1.html

Brittingham, A. & de la Cruz, G. P. (2005). *We the people of Arab ancestry in the United States* [Census 2000 special reports]. Washington, DC: U.S. Department of Commerce, Economics, and Statistics Administration, U.S. Census Bureau.

Chaleby, K. S. & Racy, J. (1999). *Psychotherapy with the Arab patient.* Tuscon, AZ: Kutaiba Chaleby & John Racy.

Cross-Cultural Communication. (n.d.). *Egypt.* Retrieved January 26, 2010, from http://www.cba.uni.edu/buscomm/InternationalBusComm/world/africa/egypt/egypt.html

Dwairy, M. (1999). Toward psycho-cultural approach in Middle Eastern societies. *Clinical Psychology Review, 8,* 909–915.

Dwairy, M. (2006). *Counseling and psychotherapy with Arabs and Muslims: A culturally sensitive approach.* New York: Teachers College Press.

El-Badry, S. (2009). *Arab-Americans, well-educated, diverse, affluent, highly entrepreneurial.* Retrieved February 15, 2010, from http://www.allied-media.com/Arab-American/arab%20american%20demographics.htm

Erickson, C. D. & Al-Timimi, N. R. (2001, November). Providing mental health services to Arab Americans: Recommendations and considerations. *Cultural Diversity and Ethnic Minority Psychology, 7*(4), 308–327.

Esposito, J. L. (Ed.). (1997). *Political Islam: Revolution, radicalism, or reformation?* Boulder, CO: Lynne Rienner.

Faragalla, M. H., Schumm, W. R., & Webb, F. J. (1997). Acculturation of Arab-American immigrants: An exploratory study. *Journal of Comparative Family Studies, 28,* 182–203.

Gerstein, L. H., Heppner, P. P., Ægisdóttir, S., Leung, S.-M. A., & Norsworthy, K. L. (2009). *International handbook of cross-cultural counseling: Cultural assumptions and practices worldwide.* Thousand Oaks, CA: Sage.

Giddens, A. (2000). *Runaway world: How globalization is reshaping our lives.* New York: Routledge.

Hall, G. C. N. (2001). Psychotherapy research with ethnic minorities: Empirical, ethical, and conceptual issues [Electronic version]. *Journal of Consulting and Clinical Psychology, 69*(3), 502–510.

Hendricks, T. (2005, March 9). Data show U.S. Arab population growing: Census report says education, income are above average. *San Francisco Chronicles,* p. A-7. Retrieved from http://www.sfgate.com/cgi-bin/article.cgi?f=/c/a/2005/03/09/MNGHLBMJCN1.DTL

Hourani, A. (1991). *A history of the Arab peoples.* New York: Warner Books.

International Business Center. (2007). *United Arab Emirates.* Retrieved January 25, 2010, from http://www.cyborlink.com/besite/uae.htm

Jackson, M. L. (1995). Counseling youth of Arab ancestry. In C. C. Lee (Ed.), *Counseling for diversity* (pp. 41–60). Needham Heights, MA: Allyn & Bacon.

Jackson, M. L. (1997). Counseling Arab Americans. In C. Lee (Ed.), *Multicultural issues in counseling: New approaches to diversity* (2nd ed., pp. 333–349). Alexandria, VA: American Counseling Association.

Kellner, D. (2002, November). Theorizing globalization. *Sociological Theory, 20*(3), 285–306.

Kobeisy, A. N. (2004). *Counseling American Muslims: Understanding the faith and helping the people.* Westport, CT: Praeger.

League of Arab States. (2006). Covenant and by-laws (Arabic). Retrieved January 28, 2010, from http://www.arableagueonline.org/las/picture_gallery/covenant2009.pdf

Meichenbaum, D. (2009, May). *Psycho-cultural assessment and interventions: The need for a case conceptualization model.* Paper presented at the 13th annual meeting of the Melissa Institute, Miami, Florida.

Nassar-McMillan, S. & Hakim-Larson, J. (2003). Counseling considerations among Arab Americans. *Journal of Counseling and Development, 81*(2), 150–159.

Nation Master. (2005). *Etiquette in the Middle East.* Retrieved January 26, 2010, from http://www.statemaster.com/encyclopedia/Etiquette-in-the-Middle-East

Nobles, A. Y., & Sciarra, D. T. (2000). Cultural determinants in the treatment of Arab Americans: A primer for mainstream therapists. *American Journal of Orthopsychiatry, 70*(2), 182–191.

Nydell, M. K. (2006). *Understanding Arabs: A guide for Westerners* (4th ed.). Yarmouth, ME: Intercultural Press.

Oberman, M. (2005). *Arabs, Muslims more integrated in US than in France.* Retrieved February 17, 2010, from http://www.middle-east-online.com/english/?id=14971

Pedersen, P. B., Draguns, J. G., Lonner, W. J., & Trimble, J. E. (Eds.). (2008). *Counseling across cultures* (6th ed.). Thousand Oaks, CA: Sage.

SAMHSA National Mental Health Information Center. (n.d.). *Developing cultural competence in disaster mental health programs: Guiding principles and recommendations.* Retrieved October 6, 2009, from http://mentalhealth.samhsa.gov/publications/all-pubs/sma03-3828/sectiontwo.asp

Sivan, E. (1985). *Radical Islam: Medieval theology and modern politics.* New Haven, CT: Yale University Press.

Storey, J. W. & Utter, G. H. (2002). *Religion and politics: A reference handbook.* Santa Barbara, CA: ABC Clio.

Sue, D. W., Arredondo, P., & McDavis, R. J. (1992). Multicultural competencies and standards: A call to the profession. *Journal of Counseling and Development, 70,* 477–486.

Tillich, P. (1959). *Theology of culture.* New York: Oxford University Press.

TRADOC DCSINT Handbook. (2006). *Arab cultural awareness: 58 factsheets.* Retrieved January 26, 2010, from http://www.fas.org/irp/agency/army/arabculture.pdf

Trimble, J. E. (2003). Cultural competence and cultural sensitivity. In M. Prinstein & M. Patterson (Eds.), *The portable mentor: Expert guide to a successful career in psychology* (pp. 13–32). New York: Kluwer Academic/Plenum.

World History. (2006). *Islam.* Retrieved January 23, 2010, from http://history-world.org/islam3.htm

Chapter 10

Working With Australian Families: Invisible Immigrants

Sally Hunter

Contents

A Personal Story

As a migrant from England to Australia in 1986, I was delighted to write this chapter. My experiences of immigration are similar in kind, but not in detail, to those of many immigrants who move to the United States from Australia.

I have used the term *invisible immigrant* (Hammerton & Thomson, 2005) to describe the experience of migration between countries with developed market economies, such as from Australia to the United States or from Great Britain to Australia (United Nations, 2002). This term was used to describe the 1.5 million Britons who migrated to Australia in the 25 years after World War II on an assisted-passage scheme (Hammerton & Thomson, 2005). They traveled to Australia for 10 pounds each, and when they arrived, they had the temerity to complain about the flies, the snakes, the sharks, the mosquitoes, and the food. It had previously been assumed that they "would easily assimilate and thus 'disappear' into such a familiar society" (Hammerton & Thomson, 2005, p. 9), thereby becoming invisible. In fact, large numbers returned home to Great Britain as soon as they were able.

Like many other migrants before me, I did not find it particularly easy to assimilate into society when I first arrived in Australia. I had to go through a slow and, at times, painful process of acculturation. I felt desperately homesick for the first five years and unable to speak about this publicly for fear of being labeled a "whinging Pom" (Hammerton & Thomson, 2005). As a result of my personal experience, I feel for other invisible immigrants who are often ill prepared for the shock of migration and have false expectations about fitting in easily. Like me, they may feel guilty when they ask for help because they believe that the needs of many refugees and other, more visible, immigrants far outweigh their own.

My husband and I decided to move from England to Australia because he was offered a promotion within the same organization. For him, the move was an exciting opportunity to further his career and yet to remain connected to his peers within the company. For me, a mother with one small child at the time, it seemed like a good idea, but turned out to be much harder than I had ever imagined. Without really realizing the implications of our choice, we left our families, our friends, and our entire support network behind in England.

I arrived in Sydney in 1986 knowing only one other person there. I struggled to make friends and to settle into a new culture that seemed, on the face of it, to be very similar to the culture that I had grown up in. In so many ways, I was invisible. It was not obvious that I was from a different culture. I did not stand out. It was not obvious that I was unhappy or in need of friends. I spoke roughly the same language, looked like an Australian of European background, and blended into the culture well at a superficial level.

However, there were many subtle differences in language, meaning, expectations, and customs, as I was soon to realize. As a newcomer to Australia, I felt out of place, like a fish on a bicycle. I did not automatically know what to wear, how to behave, or what to say. I did not realize when I was unintentionally giving offense. I could not understand much of the conversation going on around me because I did not know the names of popular local TV shows, companies, or shops. I knew very little about local politics, history, geography, culture, or the law. I felt very lonely and became depressed.

As a result of the difficulties that I was experiencing, I eventually decided to seek out therapy. What I needed from my therapist was help with the grieving process and the readjustment process and encouragement to maintain contact with my family and friends in England. My husband and I attended couples therapy and confronted the difficulties in the relationship that had arisen following our decision to emigrate. Having come to a mutual decision to remain in Australia, I gradually made new friends, learned the local culture, and found my way in my new country. I now have Australian nationality and two adult children who identify as Australian. This is our permanent home.

Reasons for Migration from Australia

The United States is among the top three destinations for emigrants from Australia. In 2006–2007, it was the third most popular destination for Australian-born residents who migrated permanently after New Zealand and the United Kingdom, with 10% of Australian emigrants moving to the United States (Australian Bureau of Statistics, 2008). More people emigrate from the United States to Australia than the other way round. For example, in 2006–2007, there were 10,270 arrivals from the United States and 5,040 departures from Australia to the United States. These immigrants to the United States were predominantly in their 20s and 30s (Australian Bureau of Statistics, 2008) and were regular, as opposed to "irregular" or illegal, immigrants (McMilan, 2008). They would be considered as voluntary migrants, not as refugees.

Hence, emigration from Australia to the United States is relatively small and is often related to work opportunities for the main earner within the family. For example, many engineers, scientists, and researchers move to the United States to further their careers (Giles, Ski, & Vrdoljak, 2009). They describe their main reasons for emigrating as a lack of job security in Australia, a lack of organizational support, and better career opportunities overseas. They also believe that they would receive better remuneration in the United States and be more able to achieve a work–life balance (Giles et al., 2009). Such families often move to the United States on temporary work visas and later decide to emigrate.

Most immigrants arrive in their new country accompanied by a partner or family, and the selection process tries to determine which families will make a smooth transition. However, most of the studies of immigration have focused on the individual migrant, leaving many questions unanswered about the ability of families and children to assimilate and settle in their host country (Cobb-Clark, Connolly, & Worswick, 2005). Many immigrant couples experience a gender struggle, particularly when they have left a country in which male dominance was an acceptable part of the culture (Maciel, van Putten, & Knudson-Martin, 2009). Even in Australian society, there is a tendency for traditional gender roles to dictate which partner invests in formal education in the new country (Cobb-Clark et al., 2005).

Immigration is not conducted in isolation but has a context. It is a life event that often occurs in the context of other life events such as starting a new job, moving house, and buying and selling property. It may occur simultaneously with other life span developmental changes such as getting married or becoming a parent for the first time. As a result, the migration process can disrupt the gender balance between partners. A recent study examined the impact of childbirth and family migration on women's earnings in the United States and the United Kingdom. The woman's capacity to earn was reduced by both childbirth and migration, with childbirth having significantly more impact than migration. However, given that migration significantly increased the male's earning capacity, the difference between the couple's earning capacity increased, leaving the woman more dependent on her male partner than prior to migration (Cooke, Boyle, Couch, & Feijten, 2009).

Economic reasons are often important drivers in the immigration process (Arah, Ogbu, & Okeke, 2008; Giles et al., 2009). There is often one person within the family who is keen to emigrate, and other family members may either embrace the prospect or remain unhappy about it for many years. There is often intergenerational conflict over immigration, with one adult believing that he or she is making the right decision for the whole family. Other family members, particularly adolescent children, may be reluctant to leave their peer group and start afresh in another culture. Sometimes a gulf opens up between parents and children, because each generation has such different expectations and experiences of the new culture (Piedra & Engstrom, 2009). Given that Australian immigrants to the United States are able to return to their homeland with relative ease, this remains a possibility or dream that may resurface for many years.

Counseling and Psychotherapy in Australia

Attending individual counseling or psychotherapy is a reasonably well-accepted practice in Australia. Many people go to see a counselor when they experience difficulties in their personal lives, at work, or in their interpersonal relationships. Client-directed, outcome-focused therapy and strength-based approaches have been influential in Australia (Miller, Mee-Lee, Plum, & Hubble, 2005), along with narrative therapy, which encourages the discussion of cultural issues

(White, 2003). Australians expect counselors to be empathic, to offer them emotional support, and to help them to overcome personal difficulties.

Under the *National Action Plan on Mental Health (2006–2011)* (Council of Australian Governments, 2006) in Australia, psychiatrists, GPs, psychologists, and mental health nurses can provide affordable services through a government rebate scheme (Resnick, 2009). Counselors and psychotherapists have not been included in this scheme or in the Mental Health Professions Network in Australia, which also includes social workers and occupational therapists (Resnick, 2009). In my experience, Australians find it difficult to differentiate between the roles taken by psychologists and psychiatrists, as opposed to counselors and psychotherapists.

Women are relatively comfortable attending therapy, unlike their male partners. As in the United States, Australian men are socialized to be "stoical, resistant to feelings, and laconic, resistant to the expression of feelings and emotions in language, behavior or culture" (Tacey, 1995, p. 50). Masculinity in both cultures is associated with negative attitudes toward psychological help-seeking behavior (Mahalik, Good, & Englar-Carlson, 2003). This gender socialization process means that men are more reluctant than women to attend therapy and tend to believe that they should be capable of solving their own problems. They often have difficulty recognizing that they have emotional problems due to their restricted emotionality and the emphasis that they place on being in control emotionally and on being self-reliant (Englar-Carlson, 2006). This makes it hard, though not impossible, to engage a couple or family in therapy.

Narrative therapy is a popular modality in Australia, partly as a result of the work of Michael and Cheryl White (White, 2003). Narrative therapy is also popular for working with Aboriginal people and has been used for working with issues around immigration, given the importance it places on cultural sensitivity (Akinyela, 2002). Working in a culturally competent way is very important when working with immigrant families. White's concepts of the landscape of action and the landscape of identity are particularly relevant to the issue of emigration, because immigrants often struggle with issues of cultural identity (Sawrikar & Hunt, 2005).

The Invisible Acculturation Issues Facing Australian Immigrants to the United States

A great deal is known about the challenging acculturation process that refugees from war-torn countries face. For example, Sudanese adolescent refugees in Australia face acculturation stress related to poor English-language proficiency, issues of parental control, and conflicting cultural rules. Often these young immigrants tend to go through a process known as "culture-shedding: some aspects of culture lose their value in the current context when individuals learn about the new host culture" (Poppitt & Frey, 2007, p. 162). Many experience ongoing stress as they struggle to straddle two cultures. They experience the need to develop a new cultural identity by balancing their native culture with the host culture (Sawrikar & Hunt, 2005). Some immigrant groups, such as Greeks in Australia, live in close proximity to each other to maintain their native cultural identity (Tamis, 2005).

Some refugees remain fearful of reprisals from members of their own ethic group, even after migrating to a safer environment. For example, many Salvadorian refugees living in Australia continue to live in fear. In addition to their employment and residential needs, cultural and linguistic needs, and the need for social support, "their past trauma still lingers on" (Santos & Webber, 2009, p. 38). This can lead to a form of "personal and family mutism" (Apfelbaum, 2000, p. 1011) when immigrants choose to remain silent about their previous experiences, partly to protect their children but partly because there is no forum in which it is safe for them to speak out.

The acculturation difficulties facing Australians immigrants to the United States are not nearly as severe as those facing most refugees, and far less is known about the invisible acculturation process faced by people moving from one English-speaking country to another. The literature suggested, "Good mental health, and hope for the individual's future, stem from an optimal combination of retaining traditional cultural elements together with learning those of the host society" (Kabir & Rickards, 2006, p. 18). This bicultural or balanced acculturation is perhaps more easily achieved by this group of immigrants.

Australian immigrants recognize that they do not face the same level of challenge that people do when emigrating from significantly different cultures, whose stories are full of "heroism, endurance and adaptation" (Jordens, 2008, p. 7). They also know that they will not face the same racism that migrants to Australia faced during the "white Australia" era (Jayasuriya, Walker, & Gothard, 2003). Even though the adjustment process may still be challenging for them, they are less visible to counseling organizations that support immigrants, as they are less likely to seek help.

Like the "10 pound Poms" that migrated to Australia from Britain in the postwar period, Australians expect to be able to fit in easily in a culture that they perceive to be similar to their own (Hammerton & Thomson, 2005). The reality is, of course, somewhat different. Many English writers, including George Bernard Shaw, Sir Winston Churchill, and Oscar Wilde, have been attributed with saying that England and the United States are two countries divided by a common language. Russell (1944, p. 57) wrote, "It is a misfortune for Anglo-American friendship that the two countries are supposed to have a common language." Australian immigrants to the United States often find themselves struggling to adjust to a similar, but different, language and culture.

It is hard to determine whether migrants suffer from mental health disorders as a result of migration. Given that they are obliged to pass a medical examination, they may be healthier than the local population in many regards (Kirmayer et al., 2007). Meta-analyses show that suicide rates among migrants correlate with rates in their country of birth rather than the country of destination (Voracek & Loibl, 2008), suggesting that a vulnerability to suicide may be a genetic risk factor. By contrast, a personal or family history of migration is an important risk factor for developing schizophrenia (Cantor-Graae & Selten, 2005). Recent migration is certainly considered to result in higher levels of stress for both migrants and refugees (Yakushko, Watson, & Thompson, 2008).

Stress levels would be higher among Indigenous than non-Indigenous Australians migrants. Indigenous Australians represent only 2.6% of the population (Australian Bureau of Statistics, 2009). As a people, they have suffered under past government policies, such as the removal of Aboriginal children from their families, known as The Stolen Generations (Bird, 1998). As a result of historical oppression and living in poverty, Indigenous people overall have poorer housing, have higher levels of incarceration, and suffer more mental health problems than non-Indigenous Australians. They have experienced systemic racism, poverty, higher levels of unemployment, poor schooling, and poor health outcomes (Davis, 2006; Department of Health and Community Services, 2005). There are many language groups and cultures within Indigenous Australia, and it is very hard to generalize without stereotyping. Culturally, most Indigenous Australians would probably identify most closely with Native American Indians or First Nations Canadians.

The motivations for Indigenous Australians choosing to migrate to the United States would be very different from those for mainstream Australians, and, hence, they would have very different needs in relation to counseling in the United States (Vicary & Andrews, 2001). The difficulties that they would face would be closer to those of many refugees worldwide, who have to contend with "discrimination, lack of knowledge and familiarity with community support systems, absence of culture specific services, racism, and cultural insensitivity in mainstream programs" (Paine & Hansen, 2002, p. 275). Indeed, many Indigenous Australians would have already faced these issues in their own country.

How Therapists Can Help

Given that Australian immigration to the United States is relatively small, it is not surprising that there is very little literature that refers to the specific therapeutic needs of this population. From what we know of the process of migration in general, we can assume that Australian immigrants need supportive counseling to help them adjust to their new surroundings. Given that most Australian immigrants have not experienced traumatic events before arriving in the United States, they are unlikely to be suffering from post-traumatic stress disorder or to need specialized long-term psychotherapy or specific trauma therapy (Briere & Scott, 2006; Nieves-Grafals, 2001; Rothschild, 2000; Shamai & Levin-Megged, 2006). However, they still need to go through an acculturation process and will experience the normal stressors related to making a major life change. The "acculturative stress" (Poppitt & Frey, 2007, p. 160) relates initially to language difficulties and to conflicting cultural rules, and the ongoing stress relates to experiences of loss and of being between cultures. Given that migrants can now remain connected more easily and economically (via the Internet) to family members back home, this can lead to "the ambiguities of living with two hearts instead of a broken heart" (Falicov, 2007, p. 158).

What Australian immigrant families experience may be a form of disenfranchised grief (Apfelbaum, 2000). They believe that they should be coping better than other immigrants, because they share a common language and many cultural similarities with the host country. They may feel "culturally orphaned" (Apfelbaum, 2000, p. 1009) but also feel a lack of entitlement to grieve, because they believe that they should not need support. As a result, they may struggle to acculturate and grieve silently, all the while believing that they should be focusing on the future rather than grieving for the past. They may lack the hopefulness that can be protective against depressive symptoms and other mental health problems (Stark & Boswell, 2001).

It is likely that Australians immigrants would prefer to seek out therapists who have some knowledge of Australian culture. It is obviously important for therapists working with immigrants to be aware of the importance of the concept of a "homeland" and to have some knowledge of the difficulties faced by immigrants from any culture (Parris, 2008). Therapists also need to have a willingness to engage in a conversation about race and culture (Cardemil & Battle, 2003). It is important for the therapist not to minimize the distress of Australian immigrants or to dismiss their immigration experiences as trivial compared to the atrocities faced by many refugees.

Therapists need to explore the meaning to immigrants of family, community, and culture. It would be useful for therapists to adopt a family therapy model that focuses on these three levels in relation to migration: (a) relational stresses within the family, (b) difficulties building new communities and social networks, and (c) acculturation difficulties (Falicov, 2007). Relational stresses within the family are the inevitable result of the stresses placed on each individual during the immigration process. These relational difficulties may be a result of the changing power dynamics within the family or new intergenerational stresses between parents and children. It is also difficult to build new communities and social networks at the same time as adjusting to a new culture. There is often a juggling act between maintaining a social identity as an Australian (Turner, 1999) and becoming bicultural (Kadir & Rickards, 2006).

When using this model (Falicov, 2007), therapists also need to take into account the needs of different family members, as these can differ widely. For example, it is likely that the (often female) partner of the main person within the family who is driving the immigration process may be experiencing changes to the gender balance in the relationship or discrimination in the workforce based on gender (Cobb-Clark et al., 2005). Unlike immigrants from countries that accept male dominance, where women often experience an increase in awareness of women's rights on arriving in the United States (Maciel et al., 2009), Australian women may experience the reverse. They may be feeling disempowered, particularly if they are unable to find work that they consider to be suitable.

Inevitably gender stress produces relational stress. According to Falicov (2007, p. 160), "Relational stress is a nearly inevitable, and often transient, aspect of the family strains imposed by migration" as partners adjust to their new environment. When relational stress continues, it may be advisable to see the couple together for couple therapy. The bond between the couple may have been damaged by the empathic failures that occur in stressful situations and may be in need of repair in "the transitional space between the partners" (Crawley & Grant 2008, p. 36). An attachment injury is seen to have happened when one partner fails to comfort the other in the expected manner at a time of great danger, vulnerability, or distress (Johnson, Makinen, & Millikin 2001). Johnson (2002) conceptualized emotionally focused couples therapy in three stages: stabilizing the relationship and creating a secure base, restructuring the bond between partners, and integrating changes into the relationship and both partners' sense of self. Therapy would be used to stabilize the couple relationship and to repair any damage caused during the immigration process, determine new ways in which the couple wanted to operate within the host country, and integrate the experiences of immigration into the couple's sense of the relationship. In this way, the couple becomes more able to comfort one another and to experience a stronger sense of attachment within the couple relationship.

Relationship difficulties may also be compounded by intergenerational stresses (Falicov, 2007). Children will face issues different from those of their parents and may experience particular difficulties adjusting to a new school culture. A significant gap may open up between their experiences and those of their parents (Piedra & Engstrom, 2009). Their peers may operate in families with family rules that are significantly different from their own. Intergenerational stress often leads to relationship stresses, both between spouses and between parents and their children. Narrative therapy may be a useful approach to use with immigrant families, given that it is a systemic approach and it involves a "heightened sensitivity to cultural and intergenerational contexts" (Lieb & Kanofsky, 2003, p. 187). By externalizing the problem as "immigration," individuals within the family can take a position on the issue individually and collectively, and the therapist can build empathy between family members (Payne, 2000).

Various forms of art therapy are recommended for children who have gone through traumatic experiences or who are considered at risk (Camilleri, 2007; Karkou & Sanderson, 2006; Levine, 2005; St. Thomas & Johnson, 2007). These are usually divided into art therapy, music therapy, drama therapy, and dance movement therapy (Karkou & Sanderson, 2006). There is an emphasis on the process rather than the outcome and on meaning-making and healing through the freedom of creative expression (Levine, 2005). There are many approaches that can be adopted, using a wide variety of expressive arts, and many of these approaches could be suitable for use with children in immigrant families. For example, combining the creation of sculpture with journal writing has been shown to help people externalize their problems and to feel an increased sense of empowerment as a result (Keeling & Bermudez, 2006).

Discussion and Recommendations

It is difficult for U.S. therapists to help Australian immigrants when they themselves barely recognize the legitimacy of their own needs. These are the invisible immigrants who believe that they should be able to adapt to a culture relatively similar to their own and to fit in well in their host country. They come from a country with a policy of multiculturalism, designed to encourage immigrants to maintain their own cultural heritage (Jupp, 2002). Therapists need to approach each immigrant on an individual basis and not make assumptions based on similarities between cultures but rather explore the impact of subtle cultural differences on the functioning of both individuals and families.

A family systems approach is recommended that takes into account the importance of family, community, and culture to all immigrants (Falicov, 2007). This approach entails reducing relational stresses within the family, building new communities and social networks, and helping with the acculturation process. The acculturation process inevitably involves a sense of loss, as well as excitement and hope for the future. For many Australian immigrants, this sense of loss is complicated by a lack of entitlement to grieve. A poststructural approach, such as narrative therapy, enables the wider cultural context to be considered, including this sense of disenfranchised grief. It also enables the problem of immigration to be externalized and an examination of both the landscape of action and the landscape of identity, as influenced by the immigration process, to occur in therapy (Payne, 2000). The therapeutic conversation can move from the actions taken over time, such as migrating to a new country and making new friends and experiencing a different culture, to the impact that these actions have on the identity of those involved, and vice versa.

Discussion Questions

1. How do the experiences of voluntary migrants from developed market economies differ from those of refugees or those migrating from war-torn countries?
2. How do the experiences of migrants moving from English-speaking countries differ from those from different language groups?
3. What are the difficulties faced by invisible immigrants that are not experienced by refugees?
4. How does the Internet help or hinder immigrants in terms of the acculturation process?
5. How can U.S. therapists best support immigrants from Australia to come to terms with feelings of disenfranchised grief?
6. What therapy modalities are best suited to working with Australian immigrants?

References

Akinyela, M. (2002). De-colonizing our lives: Divining a post-colonial therapy. *The International Journal of Narrative Therapy and Community Work, 1*(2), 32–43.

Apfelbaum, E. R. (2000). And now what, after such tribulations? *American Psychologist, 55*(9), 1008–1013.

Arah, O., Ogbu, U., & Okeke, C. (2008). Too poor to leave, too rich to stay: Developmental and global health correlates of physician migration to the United States, Canada, Australia, and the United Kingdom. *American Journal of Public Health, 98*(1), 148–154.

Australian Bureau of Statistics. (2008). *Migration, Australia.* Canberra: Author.

Australian Bureau of Statistics. (2009). *Experimental estimates of Aboriginal and Torres Strait Islander Australians, June 2006.* Canberra: Author.

Bird, C. (Ed.). (1998). *The stolen children: Their stories including extracts from the report of the national inquiry into the separation of Aboriginal and Torres Strait Islander children from their families.* Milsons Point, Australia: Random House.

Briere, J., & Scott, C. (2006). *Principles of trauma therapy: A guide to symptoms, evaluation, and treatment.* Thousand Oaks, CA: Sage.

Camilleri, V. A. (Ed.). (2007). *Healing the inner city child: Creative arts therapies with at-risk youth.* London: Jessica Kingsley.

Cantor-Graae, E., & Selten, J.-P. (2005). Schizophrenia and migration: A meta-analysis and review. *The American Journal of Psychiatry, 162*(1), 12–24.

Cardemil, E. V., & Battle, C. L. (2003). Guess who's coming to therapy? Getting comfortable with conversations about race and ethnicity in psychotherapy. *Professional Psychology: Research and Practice, 34*(3), 278–286.

Cobb-Clark, D., Connolly, M. D., & Worswick, C. (2005). Post-migration investments in education and job search: A family perspective. *Journal of Population Economics, 18*, 663–690.

Cooke, T. J., Boyle, P., Couch, K., & Feijten, P. (2009). A longitudinal analysis of family migration and the gender gap in earnings in the United States and Great Britain. *Demography, 46*(1), 147–167.

Council of Australian Governments. (2006). *National action plan on mental health (2006–2011).* Canberra: Author.

Crawley, J., & Grant, J. (2008). *Couple therapy: The self in relationship.* Basingstoke, UK: Palgrave Macmillan.

Davis, A. (2006). Who's minding the kids? Child protection in Queensland. *Indigenous Law Bulletin, 6*(23), 25–27.

Department of Health and Community Services. (2005). *Aboriginal health and families: A five year framework for action.* Darwin, Australia: Author.

Englar-Carlson, M. (2006). Masculine norms and the therapy process. In M. Englar-Carlson & M. A. Stevens (Eds.), *In the room with men: A casebook of therapeutic change* (pp. 13–47). Washington, DC: American Psychological Association.

Falicov, C. (2007). Working with transnational immigrants: Expanding meanings of family, community, and culture. *Family Process, 46*(20), 157–171.

Giles, M., Ski, C., & Vrdoljak, D. (2009). Career pathways of science, engineering and technology research postgraduates. *Australian Journal of Education, 53*(1), 69–86.

Hammerton, A. J., & Thomson, A. (2005). *Ten pound Poms: Australia's invisible migrants.* Manchester, UK: Manchester University Press.

Jayasuriya, L., Walker, D., & Gothard, J. (Eds.). (2003). *Legacies of White Australia: Race, culture and nation.* Crawley: University of Western Australia Press.

Johnson, S. (2002). *Emotionally focused couple therapy with trauma survivors: Strengthening attachment bonds.* New York: Guilford.

Johnson, S. M., Makinen, J. A., & Millikin, J. W. (2001). Attachment injuries in couple relationships: A new perspective on impasses in couples therapy. *Journal of Marital and Family Therapy, 27*(2), 145–155.

Jordens, A.-M. (2008, September). Refugee stories. *National Library of Australia News*, pp. 7–10.

Jupp, J. (2002). *From White Australia to Woomera: The story of Australian immigration.* Cambridge, UK: Cambridge University Press.

Kabir, N., & Rickards, T. (2006). Students at risk: Can connections make a difference? *Youth Studies Australia, 25*(4), 17–24.

Karkou, V., & Sanderson, P. (2006). *Arts therapies: A research based map of the field.* London: Elsevier.

Keeling, M. L., & Bermudez, M. (2006). Externalizing problems through art and writing: Experience of process and helpfulness. *Journal of Marital and Family Therapy, 32*(4), 405–419.

Kirmayer, L. J., Weinfeld, M., Burgos, G., Galbaud du Fort, G., Lasry, J.-C., & Young, A. (2007). Use of health care services for psychological distress by immigrants in an urban multicultural milieu. *Canadian Journal of Psychiatry, 52*(5), 295–304.

Levine, S. K. (2005). The philosophy of creative arts therapy: *Poiesis* as a response to the world. In P. J. Knill, E. G. Levine, & S. K. Levine (Eds.), *Principles and practice of expressive arts therapy: Towards a therapeutic aesthetics* (pp. 15–74). London: Jessica Kingsley.

Lieb, R. J., & Kanofsky, S. (2003). Toward a constructivist control mastery theory: An integration with narrative therapy. *Psychotherapy: Theory, Research, Practice, Training, 40*(3), 187–202.

Maciel, J. A., van Putten, Z., & Knudson-Martin, C. (2009). Gendered power in cultural contexts: Part 1: Immigrant couples. *Family Process, 48*(1), 9–23.

Mahalik, J. R., Good, G. E., & Englar-Carlson, M. (2003). Masculinity scripts, presenting concerns, and help seeking: Implications for practice and training. *Professional Psychology: Research and Practice, 34*, 123–131.

McMilan, K. (2008). Irregular migration: New Zealand's experience and response. *New Zealand International Review, 33*(4), 2–6.

Miller, S. D., Mee-Lee, D., Plum, B., & Hubble, M. A. (2005). Making treatment count: Client-directed, outcome-informed clinical work with problem drinkers. *Psychotherapy in Australia, 11*(4), 42–56.

Nieves-Grafals, S. (2001). Brief therapy of civil war-related trauma: A case study. *Cultural Diversity and Ethnic Minority Psychology, 7*(4), 387–398.

Paine, M. L., & Hansen, D. J. (2002). Factors influencing children to self-disclose sexual abuse. *Clinical Psychology Review, 22*, 271–295.

Parris, J. M. (2008). The mandala as a visual "third" space for work with trauma survivors. *Creative Approaches to Research, 1*(2), 71–86.

Payne, M. (2000). *Narrative therapy: Introduction for counsellors.* London: Sage.

Piedra, L. M., & Engstrom, D. W. (2009). Segmented assimilation theory and the life model: An integrated approach to understanding immigrants and their children. *Social Work, 54*(3), 270–277.

Poppitt, G., & Frey, R. (2007). Sudanese adolescent refugees: Acculturation and acculturative stress. *Australian Journal of Guidance and Counselling, 17*(2), 160–181.

Resnick, J. (2009). The mental health professionals network. *Psychotherapy in Australia, 15*(3), 47.

Rothschild, B. (2000). *The body remembers: The psychophysiology of trauma and trauma treatment.* New York: W. W. Norton.

Russell, B. (1944, June 3). Can Americans and Britons be friends? *Saturday Evening Post,* pp. 14–15, 57–59.

Santos, B., & Webber, R. (2009). Starting life anew: Resettlement challenges of Salvadorian refugees in Melbourne. *Just Policy, 50*, 30–39.

Sawrikar, P., & Hunt, C. J. (2005). The relationship between mental health, cultural identity and cultural values in non-English speaking background (NESB) Australian adolescents. *Behaviour Change*, *22*(2), 97–113.

Shamai, M., & Levin-Megged, O. (2006). The myth of creating an integrative story: The therapeutic experiences of Holocaust survivors. *Qualitative Health Research*, *16*(5), 692–712.

Stark, K., & Boswell, J. (2001). Discussion of the Penn optimism program. In J. E. Giliham (Ed.), *The science of optimism and hope*. Philadelphia: Templeton Foundation Press.

St. Thomas, B., & Johnson, P. (2007). *Empowering children through art and expression: Culturally sensitive ways of healing trauma and grief*. London: Jessica Kingsley.

Tacey, D. J. (1995). *Edge of the sacred: Transformation in Australia*. North Blackburn, Australia: HarperCollins.

Tamis, A. M. (2005). *The Greeks in Australia*. Port Melbourne, Australia: Cambridge University Press.

Turner, J. C. (1999). Some current issues in research on social identity and self-categorization theories. In N. Ellemers, R. Spears, & B. Doosje (Eds.), *Social identity* (pp. 6–34). Oxford, UK: Blackwell.

United Nations. (2002). *UNCTAD handbook of statistics*. Geneva: United Nations Conference on Trade and Development.

Vicary, D., & Andrews, H. B. (2001). A model of therapeutic intervention with Indigenous Australians. *Australian and New Zealand Journal of Public Health*, *25*(4), 349–351.

Voracek, M., & Loibl, L. M. (2008). Consistency of immigrant and country-of-birth suicide rates: A meta-analysis. *Acta Psychiatrica Scandinavica*, *118*, 259–271.

White, M. (2003). Narrative therapy and externalizing the problem. In M. Gergen & K. J. Gergen (Eds.), *Social construction: A reader* (pp. 163–168). London: Sage.

Yakushko, O., Watson, M., & Thompson, S. (2008). Stress and coping in the lives of recent immigrants and refugees: Considerations for counselling. *International Journal for the Advancement of Counselling*, *30*(3), 167–178.

Chapter 11

Immigrant Families From Regions With Emerging Research

Adam Zagelbaum

Contents

The specific countries mentioned in this chapter have within recent years, primarily the past decade, been profiled within some research studies and peer-reviewed articles regarding counseling and psychotherapeutic issues. This is not to say that research is not being conducted in various other parts of the world or that the particular countries featured in this chapter have never had any formidable research to speak of but rather to note that particular matters have surfaced within these featured countries of which counseling professionals would be wise to gain a perspective and awareness. Some of these regions have, according to some who have surveyed their cultures, started to reexamine what the concept of counseling means (Rollins, 2006). Rollins (2006) also constructed an excellent feature article within *Counseling Today* that speaks to the recent trends of counseling associated with many of these areas of the world, which readers are highly encouraged to consult because of the fascinating details that showcase how far reaching the effects of counseling practice can be. As a result, one can see that a greater perspective on how counseling professionals can serve many of these populations is becoming of greater importance as studies continue to emerge. Cohen (2009) further delineated culture by including religion, socioeconomic status, and region within a country in an effort to help psychologists understand how cultural variations can emerge when people look for new ways and research to uncover these variables. By no means is the research presented in this chapter meant to be completely exhaustive of all that is examinable within these regions. The use of research and investigative study is a process that continues to expand and evolve on a steady basis. Inappropriate comparisons regarding cross-cultural study are always possible, especially considering how often testing and assessment instruments and other counseling techniques are exported from culture to culture (Chen, 2008). There is never a completely clean translation from region to region, study to study, and person to person. The intent of this chapter, which is also far from perfection, is to lay an initial foundation on which some of these regions and their people can be further explored and investigated by counseling professionals who wish to be better prepared for working with clientele who originate from these or highly similar regions. Readers are also advised to compare and contrast the perspectives of this chapter with those of previous chapters to see the similarities and differences that best inform the practices when serving this clientele. Emerging research is often a sparse beginning to larger and greater efforts, and examining these emergences may be the starting point needed to gain such efforts.

Northern Mariana Islands

The Northern Mariana Islands, like Puerto Rico, is officially a commonwealth in current political union with the United States. Its composition totals 15 islands by Hawaii and the Philippines. The U.S. Census reported in 2000 that of the 69,221 official inhabitants of the Northern Mariana Islands, 56.3% were Asian, 36.3% were Pacific Islander, 4.8% were mixed, 1.8% were Caucasian, and 0.8% were other. One other interesting statistic is that the Northern Mariana Islands reportedly has the highest female-to-male ratio in the world, with 1.30 females per male (Schmidley, 2001).

The perception of counseling within this region and culture has traditionally been that of an information-sharing process (Rollins, 2006). Many clients often seek the services of a counselor regarding matters of career decisions and professional development guidance (Zagelbaum, 2006). It should be noted that the process of career counseling and guidance does not mean that personal matters and issues of emotional concern and well-being are not discussed, but the main theme of counseling does not in these cases center around the concept of mental illness (Gim, Atkinson, & Whitely, 1990; Kim, Sherman, & Taylor, 2008). The same principle appears to apply to many natives of the Northern Mariana Islands who seek counseling services; it is not usually the goal of the client to consider issues of personality when engaged in counseling. Certain increases in obesity (Bruss et al., 2005), mood disorders, and child abuse issues, however, suggest the emergence of more emotionally related counseling services is beginning to take place (Spencer & Le, 2006).

Although it may not necessarily be a sign of weakness or abnormality to seek counseling within this culture, many of the beliefs that people hold about the counseling process and role of the counselor significantly impact the approaches that counselors use when working with such a clientele. Many counselors tend to engage in highly structured interviews and assessment-based techniques to take more of a diagnostic and informational approach (Buki, Ma, Strom, & Strom, 2003). Such approaches are common to many Asian and Pacific Island families who seek counseling services. Also, because of beliefs that many of these clients have regarding how parental roles can significantly impact family matters, parent education often plays an important role in the counseling process (Xiong, Eliason, Detzner, & Cleveland, 2005). The collectivistic notion that all members of the family are significant contributors to client issues makes parent education a natural fit for such families who wish to take an active approach to improving family dynamics and growth. Finally, the use of medication, though not a direct service of the counselor, is often involved in dealing with certain counseling issues within this culture. Symptoms of depression, especially among older clients, can be prevalent, and because these symptoms are viewed as medical concerns, prescribed medications can often play a role in treatment (Lai, 2004). Youths and young adults can also be prescribed medication as a form of treatment (Spencer & Le, 2006), and it is up to the counselor to consult with members of the medical community to best synergize his or her services accordingly. The primary role of the counselor is certainly not to oversee medications, but the professional should be prepared to consult with medical practitioners who are likely to be involved with the treatment of these clients.

In terms of acculturation issues, more research will be needed to specifically delineate how clients from the Northern Mariana Islands experience adjustment to their host culture. However, taking from existing studies that examine populations of significant Asian composition, it can be inferred that many cases appear to extend from stressors related to financial concerns and shifting roles within the family (Falicov, 2007; Gim et al., 1990). Because many individuals within their native culture are often caring for extended and older family members as primary positions within their immediate homes, immigrating to a host culture such as the United States may result in many of these individuals needing to take on work outside the household in addition to the caretaking procedures to which they are accustomed. This is often what makes the acculturation process difficult for women (Bunting, 2005; Falicov, 2007; Maramba, 2008). Men within these families can often be placed in financial positions where they take on work positions that they are overqualified for, especially in terms of academic skill (Larsen, Kim-Goh, & Nguyen, 2008). In addition, stresses and strains that are placed on the relationships between children or adolescents and parents seem to occur because of this displacement of family role and family care.

Child abuse is believed to be one significant manifestation of how the stresses and strains between parent and child are handled. Research has indicated that many Asian immigrant and Pacific Island immigrant families prefer not to openly discuss family matters with strangers or professionals within the community, so it is difficult to place an exact rate or statistic on issues of abuse and neglect that occur within these households (Larsen et al., 2008). It should also be noted that the concept of child abuse within many Asian regions is not recognized the same way, if at all, as it would be in a host country such as the United States. Therefore, many adults may be responding to acculturative stress by engaging in acts that would not necessarily have the same abusive connotation if they were occurring in their native land. This may explain why some of these issues are on the rise and why some Asian and Pacific Island clients are not always apt to seek counseling services (Adams, 2007). The family system can also model and reinforce some of these practices, inadvertently or otherwise, and this often affects the children and adolescents.

Reports of mood disorders and youth violence are becoming more prevalent within families from regions such as the Northern Mariana Islands as well as other Asian nations (Else, Andrade, & Nahulu, 2007; Spencer & Le, 2006). These incidents are often linked to family stressors and acculturative issues of identity (No et al., 2008). Violent behaviors are sometimes used as rebellious acts to channel away feelings of discomfort that may exist within the family system and are thus displaced onto more neutral stimuli. Young adult clients have called it a feeling of ambivalence that results from an understanding that although their parents are trying to protect them from certain obstacles regarding their childhood development, the strictness associated with certain rules and boundaries can make the protection seem more like a form of restriction or oppression (Maramba, 2008). Another source of discomfort that appears to be emerging more within this culture involves the stress that older siblings experience as they become caretakers for younger siblings (Larsen et al., 2008). It is a parentification process that appears to mirror the stress and anxiety that some adults experience as they attempt to care for their extended family and elders as they adjust to the host culture. Whether intended or not, the effects of having to balance familial care and responsibility with work and/or school responsibility can often take a toll on children and adolescents within many Asian and Pacific Island households. Disclosing these stressful matters to counseling professionals can sometimes be confounded by the fact that the norms of keeping family matters within the family are often difficult for children and adolescents to oppose (Kim et al., 2008). It is for reasons such as this that counseling professionals should be mindful of certain approaches that appear to align well with such cultural and family norms.

Bearing in mind the theories and theoretical perspectives that have been previously articulated within this text, there are some specific strategies that counselors should consider when working with certain clients from this region. Though many clients are able to recognize how their emotions play significant roles in family issues, more cognitively oriented and behaviorally oriented styles are recommended during the early stages of family therapy. Even in cases of child abuse and sexual abuse, collectivistic cultures and collectivistic families tend to view these issues in a systemic fashion where these matters are viewed as problems that all members must develop an understanding about and strategy to share regarding their treatment (Larsen et al., 2008). Counseling professionals are recommended to start from an informational base that is designed to educate family members about the issues involved with parenting styles and behaviors that can be interpreted as endangerment and abuse. This can sound counterintuitive to some counselors, but if taken under the perspective that the family system is attempting to restore honor and dignity to its identity, family–counselor relationships can function in a dynamic and collaborative role that is more likely to yield a positive therapeutic outcome. Starting from an informational base that focuses on educating the system about how to collaborate toward addressing the problem(s) clients are facing is not only culturally sensitive but also more encouraging for clients to believe that a professional can understand and facilitate the strengths of the system to achieve a successful end goal. Assessments and instruments that scale the severity of issues are not uncommon foundational tools to employ in the initial counseling stages (Buki et al., 2003). Because families from this region are often found to be intellectually and academically strong within many research studies (Larsen et al., 2008; Maramba, 2008; Xiong et al., 2005), families who seek counseling services are often able to be receptive to educational and informative strategies that professionals are able to provide.

Another technique that appears to be emerging as a possible method of working with such clientele is to engage sibling therapy as a way of dealing with aggression and conflict (Gnaulati, 2002). Because the main principle behind this method is the belief that a socially skilled child, often the older one in a family, who has made significant strides to adjust and acculturate into the host culture can be an effective liaison between the larger community system and the family system's dynamics, it appears that such an approach may fit well into a collectivistic family seeking counseling services. The modeling skills employed by this form of therapy also manage to keep the family members focused more on matters of stress and conflict in a problem-solving fashion than on deep-rooted emotional exploration, which can often be difficult for clients from this region to openly communicate about outside of the family system. Regardless, some collectivistic families may not be amenable to having siblings exclusively engage in their own counseling work, so parents and extended members may need to serve in a participant–observer role at the very least so as not to create more disruption within the family system as the therapeutic process unfolds. Counselors should also be mindful that using such approaches means that it is the clients who are trying to learn the necessary skills and methods of change and pass them on to other members of the system. The counselor is simply an agent who helps locate the strengths and abilities that each client has so that the members can ultimately address their issues as a cohesive group that does not need to rely on an external professional to reach this goal. More research regarding sibling therapy is certainly needed to provide more specific information about how collectivistic families can benefit from this approach, but the emergence of this counseling approach suggests that there is plausibility for providing it.

The Asian immigrant population is one of the fastest growing populations within the United States, and Filipino(a) Americans and Pacific Island Americans compose one of its largest subgroups (Maramba, 2008). The Northern Mariana Islands appear to represent an emerging population that counseling professionals will be seeing more of as members continue to migrate to America. The family dynamics and collectivistic norms of families from this region are also becoming more amenable to counseling services (Rollins, 2006), so it is important for counseling professionals to be mindful of the unique opportunities that working with this population can provide.

Jamaica, Barbados, and Related Parts of the West Indies

The West Indies as a whole region comprises more than 7,000 islands and other natural land formations. Within these landmasses are 27 territories that are composed of many different people and cultures. Many of these individuals are descendents of French, English, Dutch, and Portuguese people. There are also people who have descended from Asian ancestors. However, the majority of

Caribbean citizens appear to be of African ancestry (Engerman, 2000; Rollins, 2006). With an estimated regional population of 37.5 million people in the year 2000 (Engerman, 2000), this region clearly encompasses much diversity and opportunity for studying this concept.

Jamaica is one of the largest Caribbean islands, and it is also largely inhabited by individuals primarily of African decent. Specifically, 90.9% of its population is identified as African, 7.3% as mixed identity, 1.3% as East Indian, 0.2% as Chinese, 0.2% as White, and 0.1% as other identity (U.S. Department of State, 2008c). Its people have experienced one of the most significant slave uprisings of all islands within the West Indies, and there have been many political issues that have encompassed Jamaica's history until its initial independence in the mid-1940s (Black, 1983). It is estimated that about 20,000 Jamaicans immigrate to the United States each year, whereas about 200,000 at least visit the country on an annual basis. Many of these individuals tend to immigrate to major metro-politan areas such as New York, Miami, and Fort Lauderdale (U.S. Department of State, 2008c); this may be because these areas have the greatest concentrations of Jamaican and West Indies immigrants, so it is not fully known what other U.S. cities serve as major destinations for these people.

When counseling becomes a destination, however, it is often Jamaican women more than Jamaican men who seek the services (Rollins, 2006). Expectations that counselors are there to provide person-centered support and emotional reflection seem to contribute to this matter. This is not to say that men never participate in counseling, but the understanding of what counseling is appears to be more focused on feelings-based and emotionally laden topics such as grief, death, and dying and issues of how to handle stress (Marshall & Sutherland, 2008). This also can make things slightly challenging for family counseling and therapy, being that systemic thinking is not something that appears to be heav-ily concentrated on by members of the family. Children and adolescents, for example, are often engaged in issues of violence and aggression, but because of perceived academic strength, these individuals are often encouraged to handle these matters independently (Geary, Wedderburn, McCarraher, Cuthbertson, & Pottinger, 2006). Clearly, this is not the case for all Jamaicans, but such attribu-tions of individualistic responsibility and success can often suggest that mem-bers in the family system may not actively align with one another during the course of counseling.

Barbados is similar to Jamaica in that it is also one of the most inhabited islands within the West Indies. It also has a predominantly African popula-tion (90%), followed by Asian and mixed identity populations (6%), and then a White population (4%) (U.S. Department of State, 2008a). One of its interest-ing contrasts with some other Caribbean islands, however, is that its economy has been relatively stable and viable for several years because of its prominence in the banking and construction industries (British Broadcasting Corporation, 2008). Recently, however, job shortages have set in, and as a result, many Bajans are emigrating to find work abroad and support families back home (British Broadcasting Corporation, 2008). The stress and concerns involved with economic matters appear to be some of the most significant issues facing this particular group of immigrants.

Though similar stressors often bring Barbados, or Bajan, residents to counseling, the service of counseling is largely conducted in an open and public manner within the region. What is also noteworthy is the fact that no legal or professional regulation of the service exists within Barbados (Rollins, 2006). It appears that counseling can have very broad boundaries within Barbados, and for this reason, working with this immigrant population can be both enticing and challenging for the professional counselor.

In terms of some emerging research, one of the more significant issues that motivate some clients from the Caribbean to seek counseling appears to be related to "Black Family Breakdown" (Barnes, Farrell, & Banerjee, 1994; Barrow, 2001). Because so many immigrants from this region are seeking work outside of their native lands to provide for family and loved ones, extended family members are being cared for in less prominent capacities as the nuclear family. Such role reversals from more traditional family units, which have in the past encompassed grandparents and other relatives in addition to children, are affecting some acculturation processes and placing strain within the family unit that is said to correlate issues of alcohol abuse (Barnes et al., 1994), physical and emotional abuse, teenage pregnancy, divorce, grief and bereavement concerns (Marshall & Sutherland, 2008), and other matters that have been increasing within some of these families (Barrow, 2001; Read & Emerson, 2005).

It should also be noted that spirituality and the church are also important aspects (Marshall & Sutherland, 2008) that impact the decision for many of these immigrant families to seek counseling services in some fashions that are similar to those of African Americans within the United States (Blank, Mahmood, Fox, & Guterbock, 2002). The use of empowerment and individual resolve appears to be a significant theme within each of these domains and can often be a source of strength that may aid the counseling process or at least provide an additional outlet for families who need to mediate stressors within their system. Similar strengths and aspirations appear to relate to why many Caribbean schoolchildren and college students have strong aspirations toward education and careers as well (Mitchell, 2005). There appears to be strong senses of resolve and resiliency within these families, and being direct and straightforward about many of these matters appears to aid the counseling process as a result (Whitley, Kirmayer, & Groleau, 2006).

It appears that education and information are main principles to be included in the family counseling process involving immigrants from the Caribbean (Levitt, Lane, & Levitt, 2005; Mitchell, 2005). Whether centered on ideas of parenting strategies, career development issues, or academic success and achievement, the use of structured family sessions that focus on the cognitive behavioral aspects of these matters allows the family to bond and work together (Carten & Goodman, 2005) in a manner that is goal oriented, objectively concrete, and indicative of progress, which adheres to the strong work ethic and motivational factors that often prompt many of these immigrants to leave their homeland in the first place. Though the aspect of collectivism may not be a salient feature of these families, the individual efforts of each family member can be used as effective modeling tools that help the system maintain stability and adjust to stresses and strains that may come about as the acculturation process unfolds.

Also, the use of visual aids can be helpful when working with some of these Caribbean families because it helps to concretely identify patterns and concepts within the system that may otherwise be too abstract for members to grasp through nonvisual communication. One such technique that can be used to engage the family is the "Creative Career Constellation" (Zagelbaum, 2006). To engage child and adolescent clients in an active exploration of academic and work-related opportunities that link to their personal interests, the counselor constructs a radial diagram during the course of the session(s) whereby school courses, work experiences, personal interests, and links between these variables are displayed in a fashion that resembles a genogram or family constellation. Parents who assist with the construction of this constellation help to show their children that ideas and goals can be cocreated and shared among members of the system who are thus reinforced for linking their ideas to the career and academic interests of the child displayed in the constellation. In cases where language and written skills may be lacking, the use of pictorial representations can be displayed in the constellation instead of words. An exercise like this is often recommended at the beginning stages of therapy because it can serve as an effective icebreaker for opening up discussions about short-term and long-term goals for each family member. As a result of this visual and verbal way of establishing rapport, other visual methods can later be used during the course of therapy to solicit deeper levels of discussion about other family issues. Family constellations, for example, provide members the chance to explore issues of their cultural and familial background in a manner that visually displays links and patterns that exist between members of the system, as well as the larger systems that surround the family such as school and religious institutions (Mitchell, 2005). Making these connections in both literal and figurative manners helps the family communicate in common terms and express things in a concrete manner that helps the system align and comprehend the cognitive, behavioral, and emotional concepts that allow for therapeutic goals to be achieved. It is believed that although techniques like these will benefit many immigrant families, those from Barbados and Jamaica will be particularly aided by counselors who use such approaches and guide many of their sessions with the use of cognitive behavioral frames. The emerging research on these families and these counseling techniques will continue to showcase how great these opportunities can be.

Cyprus and Turkey

Readers should note that although previous chapters provided background information about Cyprus and Turkey in a general fashion, some emerging research from these regions is worth specifically noting. There have been recent developments regarding sociopolitical climate and natural phenomena that have shifted the stability of these regions, which has resulted in a fair amount of citizens leaving these regions. Thus, the current state of Turkey and Cyprus will have some important bearings on how counseling professionals may wish to work with families from these regions.

Turkey has been an independent country since 1923 and currently boasts a population of 70.5 million people. Approximately 80% of the population is identified as Turkish, and 20% is identified as Kurdish, with some identified segments composed of other identities. The Asian and European sections of this country have long been sources of diversity but also conflict. Political and religious differences make for some of these conflicts, as well as economic matters that have occurred over the years regarding accession and globalization (U.S. Department of State, 2008d). These issues continue to serve as reasons for people to emigrate. There have been concerns expressed about rises in postnatal depression cases within the country, which are starting to become more publicly recognized (Danaci, Dinc, Deveci, Sen, & Icelli, 2002). However, these matters are largely viewed through medical study. Much attention from the counseling community has been focused on the ravages of two significantly large earthquakes in 1999 that killed over 25,000 people, from which many traumas and issues stemming from these events have also contributed to some people's desire to emigrate (Munir, Ergene, Tunaligil, & Erol, 2004).

The trauma associated with the earthquakes appeared to greatly affect youth culture within Turkey, because it represented the largest demographic at the time (Munir et al., 2004). Because counseling within the country has largely been focused on school-based counseling and social work roles, crisis and trauma were not necessarily issues that could be treated on such a grand scale (Rollins, 2006).

The role of the counselor has traditionally been viewed as an education-based (Brizic, 2006) and planning-oriented encourager who addresses matters of academic development and career exploration. Thus, it is reasonable to assume that many Turkish clients who seek counseling services within community and other mental health agencies outside of the school system are likely being referred to deal with emotional responses to trauma- or crisis-oriented issues that extend beyond information-giving services. Behavioral skills and social skills training can certainly be part of this process (McWhirter, 1983), but there may be a greater need to deal with deeper levels of emotion as therapy progresses.

Cyprus gained its independence in 1960 and currently boasts a population of 788,000 within its government-controlled area and 260,819 people within its area designated by Turkish Cypriots. The last available census data in 1960 indicated that 77% of the people were identified as Greek, 18% as Turkish, and 4% as Armenian and other (U.S. Department of State, 2008b). Cyprus is similar to Turkey in that political, social, and economic factors have been sources of strength and conflict and also provide significant motivation for some residents to emigrate (Phalet & Hagendoorn, 1996; Zagefka, Brown, Broquard, & Martin, 2007).

Like the Turkish, Cypriots appear to desire more community-based counseling services within only recent years (Rollins, 2006). In the more traditional past, counseling was largely conducted among members of the clergy and within religious institutions. Professional counselors often clashed with the system, and the services provided by these professionals were largely viewed through a negative lens within the country. Emerging data and reports appear to indicate that this stigma is not as prominent among Cypriots, but mental illness and issues of anxiety and depression appear to compose a significant proportion of this country's clientele (Danielidou & Horvath, 2006; Rollins, 2006). Reports have surfaced about interpersonal difficulties occurring in Cypriot immigrants with coronary heart disease (Sochos, Biskanaki, & Tassoulas, 2006), but many of these individuals are seeking treatment not necessarily for the psychological issues as much as for the medical concerns. Certainly, this does not imply that individuals see no value in counseling or mental health services, but the medical issues appear to be of greater significance because they are not as subjectively analyzed. Thus, clients themselves may hold negative biases about counseling services because seeking such services may imply that they are very sick or highly nonfunctioning people. Bearing this information in mind may aid counselors to prepare for some resistance on the part of these clients during the initial phases of therapy.

It appears that to start from an effective therapeutic base, the counselor should engage clients in an information-giving process whereby the role of the counselor and the goals for working in family therapy can be readily established. The rationale for this approach stems from the idea that many clients from Turkey and Cyprus are apt to keep personal information to themselves (Danielidou & Horvath, 2006; Dijker, 1987), so expecting disclosures to occur by using open-ended questions or reflecting feelings and emotions does not appear to be productive. This says not that emotions will play no role in the family counseling process but rather that establishing a climate of openness and trust among the family system comes from an initial sharing of insights and data that helps the system understand what typically aids the healing process. Also, because many Turkish and Cypriot clients are used to dialoging with professionals within educational and religious institutions, this information-based start to family therapy does not force these clients to make an abrupt shift away from helping relationships that they are otherwise accustomed to having (Brizic, 2006; Rollins, 2006). In much the same way that clients from Jamaica, Barbados, and the Northern Mariana Islands appear to connect with family members around career- and school-oriented goals, families from Turkey and Cyprus prefer to start from this base in a cognitive behavioral fashion. It appears that because these topics can be spoken about in a concrete manner, be addressed through the use of testing and assessment that does not involve personal disclosure about deep-rooted matters that families wish to keep silent about, and place the counselor in more of a guidance role as opposed to a more nondirective listener, family systems can trust the counseling process to locate strengths and engage family members in a forward-focused process whereby goals can be reassessed and revisited during each session to determine where progress has been made. The process of family counseling is aided by the progress of the system.

Conclusion

Considering that all of these regions have recently emerged with findings and information about how families immigrate and deal with acculturative stressors associated with this process, revisiting the approaches that family counselors and mental health professionals take with these clients may one day prove useful to future professionals and clients who may experience similar phenomena in different regions. It is never easy to predict when natural disasters, economic concerns, or wars will arise, but studying these emerging research findings may one day be quite significant as families continue to acculturate and seek the services of counseling professionals. It is hoped that each of the regions featured in this chapter can serve as templates or benchmarks for how the process of immigration, as well as the process of family counseling, can emerge as an effective journey that immigrant clients can be better off for taking advantage of in this ever-changing world.

Discussion Questions

1. What are the key trends or concerns that have emerged in the past few years that you have seen in your own country or region of the world? How do these trends appear to affect your family? Your community? Your approach to acclimating with these trends?
2. What emerging trends do you see happening within the field of family counseling and marriage and family therapy? How will these trends affect your work with domestic and immigrant families?
3. What parallels do you see between how present-day generations deal with family stressors and concerns and how ancestral generations have done the same? Would this information impact who would be included in family counseling and therapy if extended family members were part of the system? Why or why not?

References

Adams, K. (2007). The sexual abuse of children in contemporary Japanese families. *Journal of Psychohistory, 34*, 178–207.

Barnes, G., Farrell, M., & Banerjee, S. (1994). Family influences on alcohol abuse and other problem behaviors among Black and White adolescents in a general population sample. *Journal of Research on Adolescence, 2*, 183–201.

Barrow, C. (2001). Contesting the rhetoric of "Black Family Breakdown" from Barbados. *Journal of Contemporary Family Studies, 32*, 419–431.

Black, C. (1983). *The story of Jamaica*. London: Collins Educational.

Blank, M., Mahmood, M., Fox, J., & Guterbock, T. (2002). Alternative mental health services: The role of the Black church in the South. *American Journal of Public Health, 92*, 1668–1672.

British Broadcasting Corporation. (2008). *Country profile: Barbados*. Retrieved December 23, 2008, from http://news.bbc.co.uk/go/pr/fr/-/2/hi/americas/country_profiles/1154116.stm

Brizic, K. (2006). The secret life of languages: Origin-specific differences in L1/L2 acquisition by immigrant children. *International Journal of Applied Linguistics, 16*, 339–362.

Bruss, M., Morris, J., Dannison, L., Orbe, M., Quitugua, J., & Palacios, R. (2005). Food, culture, and family: Exploring the coordinated management of meaning regarding childhood obesity. *Health Communication, 18*, 155–175.

Buki, L., Ma, T., Strom, R., & Strom, S. (2003). Chinese immigrant mothers of adolescents: Self-perceptions of acculturation effects on parenting. *Cultural Diversity and Ethnic Minority Psychology, 9*, 127–140.

Bunting, M. (2005, October 24). Importing our careers amounts to emotional imperialism. *The Guardian*. www.guardian.co.uk/society/2005/oct/24/globalisation.immigrationasylumandrefugeas/

Carten, A., & Goodman, H. (2005). An educational model for child welfare practice with English-speaking Caribbean families. *Child Welfare, 84*, 771–789.

Chen, F. F. (2008). What happens if we compare chopsticks with forks? The impact of making inappropriate comparisons in cross-cultural research. *Journal of Personality and Social Psychology, 95*, 1005–1018.

Cohen, A. (2009). Many forms of culture. *American Psychologist, 64*, 194–204.

Danaci, A., Dinc, G., Deveci, A., Sen, F., & Icelli, I. (2002). Postnatal depression in Turkey: Epidemiological and cultural aspects. *Social Psychiatry and Psychiatric Epidemiology, 37*, 125–129.

Danielidou, L, & Horvath, P. (2006). Greek Cypriot attitudes toward Turkish Cypriots and Turkish immigrants. *Journal of Social Psychology, 146*, 405–421.

Dijker, A. (1987). Emotional reactions to ethnic minorities. *European Journal of Social Psychology, 17*, 305–325.

Else, I., Andrade, N., & Nahulu, L. (2007). Suicide and suicidal-related behaviors among indigenous Pacific Islanders in the United States. *Death Studies, 31*, 479–501.

Engerman, S. (2000). A population history of the Caribbean. In M. Haines & R. Steckel (Eds.), *A population history of North America*. Cambridge, UK: Cambridge University Press.

Falicov, C. (2007). Working with transnational immigrants: Expanding meanings of family, community and culture. *Family Process, 46*, 157–171.

Geary, C., Wedderburn, M., McCarraher, D., Cuthbertson, C., & Pottinger, A. (2006). Sexual violence and reproductive health among young people in three communities in Jamaica. *Journal of Interpersonal Violence, 21*, 1512–1533.

Gim, R., Atkinson, D., & Whitely, S. (1990). Asian-American acculturation, severity of concerns, and willingness to see a counselor. *Journal of Counseling Psychology, 37*, 281–285.

Gnaulati, E. (2002). Extending the uses of sibling therapy with children and adolescents. *Psychotherapy: Theory, Research, Practice, Training, 39*, 76–87.

Kim, H., Sherman, D., & Taylor, S. (2008). Culture and social support. *American Psychologist, 63*, 518–526.

Lai, D. (2004). Impact of culture on depressive symptoms of elderly Chinese immigrants. *Canadian Journal of Psychiatry, 49*, 820–827.

Larsen, S., Kim-Goh, M., & Nguyen, T. (2008). Asian American immigrant families and child abuse: Cultural considerations. *Journal of Systemic Therapies, 27*, 16–29.

Levitt, M., Lane, J., & Levitt, J. (2005). Immigration stress, social support, and adjustment in the first postmigration year: An intergenerational analysis. *Research in Human Development, 2*, 159–177.

Maramba, D. (2008). Immigrant families and the college experience: Perspectives of Filipina Americans. *Journal of College Student Development, 49*, 336–350.

Marshall, R., & Sutherland, P. (2008). The social relations of bereavement in the Caribbean. *Omega, 57*, 21–34.

McWhirter, J. (1983). Cultural factors in guidance and counseling in Turkey: The experience of a Fulbright family. *Personnel and Guidance Journal, 61*, 504–507.

Mitchell, N. (2005). Academic achievement among Caribbean immigrant adolescents: The impact of generational status on academic self-concept. *Professional School Counseling, 8*, 209–224.

Munir, K., Ergene, T., Tunaligil, V., & Erol, N. (2004). A window of opportunity for the transformation of national mental health policy in Turkey following two major earthquakes. *Harvard Review of Psychiatry, 12*, 238–251.

No, S., Hong, Y., Liao, H., Lee, K., Wood, D., & Chao, M. (2008). Lay theory of race affects and moderates Asian Americans' responses toward American culture. *Journal of Personality and Social Psychology, 95*, 991–1004.

Phalet, K., & Hagendoorn, L. (1996). Personal adjustment to acculturative transitions: The Turkish experience. *International Journal of Psychology, 31*, 131–144.

Read, J., & Emerson, M. (2005). Racial context, Black immigration, and the U.S. Black/White health disparity. *Social Forces, 84*, 181–199.

Rollins, J. (2006). Getting a global perspective: A glimpse of the counseling profession in 27 countries. *Counseling Today, 1*, 1–34.

Schmidley, D. (2001). Profile of the foreign-born population in the United States: 2000. In *Current population reports, P23–206* (pp. 1–70). Washington, DC: U.S. Census Bureau.

Sochos, A., Biskanaki, F., & Tassoulas, E. (2006). Attachment style and interpersonal difficulties in immigrants with coronary heart disease. *North American Journal of Psychology, 8*, 145–162.

Spencer, J., & Le, T. (2006). Parent refugee status, immigration stressors, and Southeast Asian youth violence. *Journal of Immigrant and Minority Health, 8*, 359–368.

U.S. Department of State. (2008a). *Background note: Barbados.* Retrieved December 27, 2008, from http://www.state.gov/r/pa/ei/bgn/26507.htm

U.S. Department of State. (2008b). *Background note: Cyprus.* Retrieved December 27, 2008, from http://www.state.gov/r/pa/ei/bgn/5376.htm

U.S. Department of State. (2008c). *Background note: Jamaica.* Retrieved December 27, 2008, from http://www.state.gov/r/pa/ei/bgn/2032.htm

U.S. Department of State. (2008d). *Background note: Turkey.* Retrieved December 27, 2008, from http://www.state.gov/r/pa/ei/bgn/3432.htm

Whitley, R., Kirmayer, L., & Groleau, D. (2006). Public pressure, private protest: Illness narratives of West Indian immigrants in Montreal with medically unexplained symptoms. *Anthropology and Medicine, 13*, 193–205.

Xiong, Z., Eliason, P., Detzner, D., & Cleveland, M. (2005). Southeast Asian immigrants' perceptions of good adolescents and good parents. *Journal of Psychology, 139*, 159–175.

Zagefka, H., Brown, R., Broquard, M., & Martin, S. (2007). Predictors and consequences of negative attitudes toward immigrants in Belgium and Turkey: The role of acculturation preferences and economic competition. *British Journal of Social Psychology, 46*, 153–169.

Zagelbaum, A. (2006). The Creative Career Constellation. In L. Hecker & C. Sori (Eds.), *The therapist's notebook: Volume II; More homework, handouts, and activities for use in psychotherapy.* New York: Haworth Press.

Chapter 12

Working With Intercultural Immigrant Families

Dolores D. Tarver and Joy K. Harden

Contents

According to the U.S. Bureau of Census (2004), in 1992, approximately 1,161 families identified as *interracial*, and by 2002, that number had increased to 1,674. Although research on this growing population is not new to the literature, there has been some increase in publications in this area over the past 10 years (Baptiste, 1984; Biever, Bobele, & North, 1998; Crohn, 1995, 1998;

211

Hsu, 2001; Ibrahim & Schroeder, 1990; Okun, 1996; Perel, 2000; Rubalcava & Waldman, 2004). Within the United States, the use of the word *interracial* has begun to decrease, and it is being replaced with *intercultural*. This paradigm shift moves beyond defining interracial relationships as being between only persons of European American and African American descent and includes intercultural unions between individuals of a wide range of racial, ethnic, or religious backgrounds from across the globe (Fu & Heaton, 2000; Ho, 1990; Ibrahim & Schroeder, 1990; Roy & Hamilton, 2000). For the purposes of this chapter, the term *intercultural* will be defined as relationships between immigrants from different countries of origin (Youakim, 2004). This chapter will provide an overview of challenges facing intercultural immigrant families as well as provide recommendations for providing counseling to this typically underserved population. Within the context of intercultural families, race, ethnicity, socioeconomic status, gender roles, and religion will be explored (McFadden, 2001). Intercultural families are not limited to unions between a male and a female. However, to date, the literature on immigrant families is largely based on heterosexual couples, thus this chapter will address only male–female relationships.

Challenges Facing Intercultural Immigrant Families

Immigration to a New Country

Intercultural immigrant families have a diverse multicultural background and heritage and perhaps a unique set of challenges associated with issues of acculturation, racial/ethnic identity, legal concerns, social system, and supports (Rosenblatt, 2009). One common factor that may affect intercultural couples is immigration status. The process of immigrating to a new country can come with several challenges (Sue & Sue, 2003). Families often experience isolation from their social support networks and host country, not to mention they experience culture shock and try to understand and navigate through the cultural nuances of a new environment (Al-Issa, 1997). Additional stress may be associated with involuntary migration versus voluntary migration and the treatment of immigrants in the host culture. Immigrants, or refugees, who flee home countries because of political unrest, civil or religious wars, inferior treatment, or poverty may not have an opportunity to plan to leave, request the proper paperwork, or provide adequate documentation to apply to be a citizen in a new country (Chung, Bemak, Ortiz, & Sandoval-Perez, 2008). The process of traveling may be unsafe and uncertain because of anti-immigrant groups and the potential for armed military patrols to shoot at, imprison, or physically abuse individuals who are perceived to be illegal immigrants (Abraido-Lanza, Armbrister, White, &

Lanza, 2006). Family members may be displaced, killed, or abused, and financial resources in addition to food and clothing may become depleted in an effort to try to gain access and passage to a new country. Immigrants may also be detained in unsanitary holding facilities while waiting for transport to the new country (Bemak & Chung, 2008). After migrating, immigrants may struggle to gain employment; be faced with racism, discrimination, or possible deportation; or receive verbal and physical threats and/or abuse, which can all pose a significant strain on a family unit (Chung & Bemak, 2007). For families who may have recently immigrated, securing housing, employment, day care, and insurance benefits may place an increasing financial burden on families depending on the level of education of the partners and proficiency in speaking the native tongue of the country in which the couple resides (Coltrane, Gutierrez, & Parke, 2008; McLoyd, Cauce, Takeuchi, & Wilson, 2000).

Culture, Family of Origin, and Gender Roles

There are several unique challenges associated with merging two or more families of origin (Bray, 2005). A therapist should try to understand not only the cultural complexities of the intercultural union but also how the couple came to be joined together (Rosenblatt, 2009). When working with partners from intercultural unions, therapists cannot afford to ignore cultural beliefs and how worldviews inform complex interactions. These cultural values provide a context for the meaning of events in the family (Perel, 2000). A major role of a therapist working with intercultural unions is to move beyond a superficial acknowledgment that a couple has differences and be able to access, on a deeper level, how individuals in a couple conceptualize and process information (Livingston et al., 2008).

A further examination of intercultural couples has to include an understanding of value systems and address how partners can integrate these systems. A partner's family of origin and cultural backgrounds often influence how a household is managed (Ganong & Coleman, 2004), which may pose a challenge for cross-cultural unions in which the children and/or spouses may need to adjust to a new familial structure (Cauce & Rodriguez, 2002). Another factor to consider is a couple's views about marriage (Rosenblatt, 2009). One partner may envision a marriage as a merging of two families, whereas another partner may see the union as the formation of a separate family unit with little interaction from parents and other relatives (Breger & Hill, 1998). Intercultural immigrant unions can cause distress between family members. Whereas some family members may be supportive of intercultural marriage, other family members may be just as opposed to it (McFadden, 2001). Couples may be ostracized within their own cultures, and their union may not be recognized by family members or in certain religious contexts. This may be a significant issue of concern for couples who emigrate from countries in which polygamy or arranged marriage is a part of their cultural heritage, but those practices may be viewed with disdain by a new partner's family or the new country in which the couple resides (Grearson & Smith, 2009).

Issues of social class and how the couple is perceived are of importance in how the couple may fit within a sociocultural system (Kashima, 2000). A female spouse, for instance, may enter a union to gain financial stability for herself and her family. Family members may desire for the children to marry someone who is more affluent as a way to help the family move into a higher socioeconomic group. Furthermore, there might also be an expectation of an obligation for a new partner to help take care of parents, children, or siblings (Rosenblatt, 2009). Another factor to consider is if the marriage was arranged either by family members or through a service that can help an individual locate a potential spouse through a financial exchange. One of the criticisms of such agencies is that women are marginalized and treated more as servants or prostitutes than spouses (Piper & Roces, 2003).

Other factors that could result in conflict are the couple's views about love, expectations about autonomy versus time together as a couple, and communication (Ting-Toomey, 2009). It may be easy to assume that couples fall in love and then get married, but this may not always be the case (Bray, 2005). Views of love can vary not only across gender but also across ethnicity (Piller, 2009). One member of the couple may see love as something that develops through the marriage once a partner has been identified. Another member of the couple may value individualism in the relationship and struggle with investing in a romantic love relationship (Dion & Dion, 1996). Partners may have difficulty being able to negotiate time apart and forming a relationship based on romantic love. Different communication styles may prove to complicate having a conversation about these differences. Effective communication, on some level, requires an understanding of and sensitivity toward cultural values that inform how information is communicated verbally and nonverbally. Cross-cultural communication is influenced by gender, personality, tone, context clues, and other factors that may not be clear to a partner (Oetzel & Ting-Toomey, 2003). Helping a couple understand patterns of dominance, introversion, competition, assertiveness, passive-aggressiveness, and avoidance is important in decoding communication patterns and helping a couple address conflict in a healthy way.

Specifically, gender roles, perceptions, and values may influence the division of labor in the home, how finances are managed, and how responsibilities are delegated (Hurwitz, 1997). Some issues of concern may be related to caregiving for children and/or aging parents, financial management such as paying the bills, joint bank accounts versus separate bank accounts, and housework tasks of cooking, cleaning, taking out the trash, and manicuring the yard. For families that come from the same cultural background or differing cultural backgrounds, gender roles may be consistent. Men may take on more of the traditional roles of yard work and financial management, whereas women may take on more responsibility for cooking, cleaning, and caregiving (Behnke, Taylor, & Parra-Cardona, 2008). In addition to assuming the man's last name, women may also be expected to convert to the religion of the male, assume a parenting role over preexisting children, and conform to cultural traditions and gender norms present in the male's culture (Morrison & James, 2009). On the other hand, more acculturated partners may be able to discuss each others' strengths and delegate responsibilities based on preexisting skills a partner may have (Gaines & Agnew, 2003). A woman may take on the role as head of the household, manage the finances, and take on the roles of disciplinarian because she feels more comfortable and competent in these areas. And the man in that couple may provide meals, take care of housework both in and outside of the house, and be the primary caregiver for the children.

Cultural Brokering, Raising Children, and Religion and Spirituality

Children in immigrant families may often experience extreme pressure to perform well academically, take on jobs to help support the family, or even feel like they fit in with a particular social group (Steel & Valentine, 1995). For immigrants to the United States, who may speak very little English, children often take on roles as interpreters who have to negotiate with physicians, schools, and employers and handle financial and other business matters. Often the boundaries between parent and child can become skewed with a child knowing a lot about a parent's health and financial status. Refugees may experience severe medical concerns and post-traumatic stress during their travel to the place of resettlement (Prendes-Lintel, 2001). Children may be placed in the role of caregiver for the family or be treated as the head of household because they are multilingual and can communicate information as needed. Older siblings may also be placed in roles to take care of younger siblings because both parents need to work. Young children may take on roles as disciplinarian, teacher or tutor, and housekeeper in the home to make sure younger siblings complete homework, are fed, and are ready for bed at the appropriate time, which may be very overwhelming for a child. Children may also adopt different value systems as they become more immersed in the culture of the new country and may feel disconnected from parents (Sue & Sue, 2003). Immigrant families may also struggle with negotiating between two cultures and trying to fit within the environment to which they have recently moved (Merz, Oort, Özeke-Kocabas, & Schuengel, 2009).

Another issue of concern for immigrants is parenting practices, particularly around discipline (Bray, 2005). If a couple migrates to a new country, the parents may have to be mindful of the types of punishment used, rites of passage ceremonies, medicinal practices, and other aspects of their cultures that might be different from those practiced in the new country. Couples may also struggle with negotiating these boundaries within the family if the cultures of origin have different value systems around child rearing. One parent may believe in more physical types of punishment such as spankings and manual labor, whereas another parent may believe in using time-out or having a points system where privileges are earned for good behavior.

Another area of conflict may be religious and spiritual practices. Extended family members may also put pressure on a couple to keep certain family traditions that may conflict with personal beliefs of a member of the couple (Mignot, 2008). Grandparents and other relatives may threaten to cut off the new couple or not attend religious ceremonies and other events if the intercultural couple refuses to follow certain traditions (Bray, 2005). Children may feel trapped between parents' views of religious practices and the activities in which they would like to participate. Anderson (1994) discussed the need for sensitivity with grandparents, uncles, aunts, and other extended family members who may be mourning the loss of family traditions as an intercultural family begins to develop new traditions. There can be significant stigma within a religion regarding marrying someone who has a different faith background (Lara & Onedera, 2008). There is pressure to marry people to which we are equally yoked, and some denominations and churches may openly denounce intercultural marriage (Sherkat, 2004). Though the research suggests that couples who attend religious services together frequently have increased marital satisfaction (Shehan, Bck, & Lee, 1990), it is important for clinicians to encourage and support a strong religious affiliation as well as agnostic or atheist value systems.

Acculturation Issues Within Intercultural Immigrant Families

Acculturation may become a divisive factor in homes as some family members become more immersed in the culture of the country of which they are residing and subsequently begin to practice fewer of the traditions of the country of origin. Children in intercultural immigrant families may struggle with how they should identify (McFadden, 2001). They may often feel forced to choose who they are for the purposes of filling out paperwork for school or jobs. They may often be encouraged to adopt the views of the country in which they reside to fit in and be accepted, as a mechanism to manage feeling marginalized and to handle the effects of racism (Sullivan, 1998). Children may resent their parents' culture or the fact that they feel like they have to navigate between so many cultures daily. One parent may be less acculturated and dictate that children follow traditional values and customs at home such as traditional attire, language of country of origin, dating and marital practices, and food, whereas another parent may be more acculturated and less strict about traditional cultural practices. Tension between parents and their children may also exist because the children of intercultural immigrant families may feel pressured by their peers to be more Americanized, whereas families may insist that they retain their original cultural identities (Fuligni, 1998).

Perhaps the most widely known model of acculturation was developed by Berry (1990). Berry's model suggests that individuals from immigrant families are faced with two distinct tasks: (a) managing their desire and ability to maintain their culture of origin and (b) managing their desire and ability to engage in the mainstream and dominant culture. This model asserts that one's acculturation position is dependent on how he or she manages these tasks. These positions include (a) assimilation, which involves high engagement and participation in dominant culture; (b) integration or participation and engagement in both culture of origin and dominant culture; (c) separation, which is high engagement and participation in culture of origin; and (d) marginalization or low participation and engagement in either culture. How individuals from an immigrant family navigate the acculturation process contributes significantly to the development and maintenance of their identity.

Identity Development

The issue of identity is an important factor to consider in intercultural relationships. Within the United States, immigrants may feel that there are narrow choices for identity and that individuals are often forced into categories that do not capture how they view themselves as a cultural being (Karis, 2009). Use of the terms *interracial* and *cross-cultural* may be rejected by African American and Caucasian individuals, as it may feel like a categorization and limit how they would define their cultural union (Karis, 2003).

Factors such as a desire to raise bilingual children who feel a strong sense of ethnic identity and affiliation may be important to family members (Piller, 2009). One of the most challenging aspects of identity development for an individual from a blended immigrant family is feeling a sense of fit in a cultural or social group. Children from blended immigrant families have a particularly difficult time with this, because they often receive many contradictory messages about their identity from parents, school, and peers (Poston, 1990). These individuals often have to manage their bicultural identities in ways that will allow them to maintain relationships with all of these groups.

Benet-Martinez, Leu, Lee, and Morris (2002) proposed a model capturing the process by which individuals who are bicultural integrate their identities. The Bicultural Identity Integration (BII) model suggests that bicultural individuals view their cultures of origin and the mainstream dominant culture as either integrated and compatible or oppositional and difficult to integrate. Individuals with a high degree of BII find it easier to integrate multiple cultures, whereas individuals with a low degree of BII find it more difficult to integrate multiple cultures and often feel like these cultures are incompatible. As previously mentioned, children of intercultural immigrant families have a difficult time with this process, as peers may be engaging in styles of dress and dating practices that are very different from those subscribed to by their parents and cultures of origin.

Prejudice and Discrimination

Families with intercultural backgrounds often experience prejudice and discrimination at the hands of others. Xenophobia, specifically, refers to attitudes and behaviors that are prejudicial toward immigrants (Yakushko, 2009). Yakushko (2009) also discussed how immigrants as a group are often associated with increased violence and overpopulation and are often seen as uneducated, criminal, and poor. These types of beliefs in turn lead to difficult circumstances for individuals from blended immigrant families. Children often report being taunted and teased by peers (Fuligni, 1998; Sullivan, 1998), whereas adult family members often experience difficulties related to housing and employment (Dalmage, 2000). Perceptions by Americans that immigrants are depleting resources and taking jobs lead to these individuals having difficulty securing employment or community resources, which in turn significantly affects the quality of life they can provide for their family (Yakushko, 2009). In addition, the level of discrimination individuals from an intercultural immigrant family perceive affects their acculturation process. Individuals who believe they are being discriminated against because of their immigrant status may feel more pressured to assimilate to mainstream culture as opposed to finding a way to integrate both cultures. This can then lead to increased levels of stress and anxiety and decreased psychological health and adjustment (Horenczyk, 1996; Hovey, 2000).

Views of Help Seeking and Counseling Within Intercultural Families

The stigma of seeking mental health and medical services, disparities in access to care (poorer quality care, insurance, transportation), and discrimination continue to be barriers for ethnic and racially diverse families to seek support services

(Richman, Kohn-wood, & Williams, 2007; U.S. Department of Health and Human Services, 2001). On average, nonmandated therapy services are most often utilized by Caucasian females even when the cost of care and insurance coverage is similar across ethnic groups (Snowden & Thomas, 2000). Males and ethnically and racially diverse groups often feel that coming to therapy is a reflection of weakness and that individuals should be able to solve problems on their own or at most within existing familial or friendship support networks, and the effectiveness of therapy is questioned (Wells, Klap, Koike, & Sherbourne, 2001; Whaley, 2001). Families often do not want strangers being privy to intimate and personal matters that occur within the family. "What happens in this house stays in this house" is a mentality that many culturally diverse families develop. Mistrust of psychological services is warranted given negative experiences with heath care providers, a lack of culturally relevant support services available (particularly because of financial and geographical restraints), and negative views of blended, single, and diverse families that have existed in the history of psychology (Whaley, 2001). Intercultural families may face challenges when cultural and family values are at odds with views of therapy and its utility. According to Tsui (1985), immigrants may be unaware of mental health resources or feel shame in utilizing such services. For those who do follow through with the referral and make an appointment, therapy may be terminated prematurely. Ponizovsky and Grinshpoon (2009) found that whereas immigrants diagnosed with mood or anxiety disorders were likely to utilize both informal and formal support networks, immigrants who did not meet the criteria for a mental health disorder were more likely to use psychotropic medications as opposed to therapy. Thus, intercultural families may be less likely to seek therapy as an option to discuss relationships, parenting, or identity concerns.

Providing Therapy to Immigrant Families

Given the complexities that occur within intercultural families and those challenges that may affect immigrant blended families, several factors should be considered when working with immigrant populations. Rubalcava and Waldman (2004) suggested that mental health providers move beyond merely affirming diversity to really exploring the influence of the cultural heritage of each member of the family and how value systems affect family interactions. Clinicians should be engaged in an ongoing process of self-awareness that examines a therapist's biases, perceptions, stereotypes, and past experiences that may affect working with immigrant families (Ganong & Coleman, 2004). Therapists should also be aware of the wide range of concerns that may face an immigrant family, including issues of acceptance from ethnic groups and individual identity development (Mann, 2006). Other areas to explore include, but are not limited to, the experience of migration to a new country, the potential effects of racism and discrimination, social class, value systems around marriage, gender roles, spiritual and religious beliefs, parenting, and education level (Chung et al., 2008; Fu & Heaton, 2000; Ho, 1990; Ibrahim & Schroeder, 1990; Roy & Hamilton, 2000).

McFadden (2001) made several suggestions for encouraging healthy relationships between intercultural couples, including (a) respecting the qualities that make us all human; (b) communicating openly and honestly; (c) understanding and appreciating all cultures of origin; (d) providing an environment for multiracial children to develop healthy identities and be able to understand and confront racism; (e) adopting a broad worldview that encompasses all members of the family; (f), encouraging a strong sense of self, cultural identity, and security within the family; (g) addressing issues such as culture, race, ethnicity, spirituality, and religion that arise in the family and encouraging interaction with a variety of cultures; (h) encouraging collaboration between spouses and children; (i) being aware of issues of class, politics, gender, and other aspects of culture that may be specific to individuals in the family; and (j) placing value on one's purpose in the greater society and how each family member is going to contribute something positive to the world we live in (p. 41). It is strongly suggested that clinicians fully understand the unique contributions of each member of the family and how the family system works together. Clinicians should gain a thorough understanding of acculturation level, identity, worldview, family values, gender roles, cultural heritage, religion and spirituality, and role of extended family members (Merz et al., 2009). Family genograms may be useful in understanding the family system. Allow partners to share stories of growing up to provide a cultural lens through which to view how each partner functions within the relationship. Youakim (2004) stressed the value of understanding the dynamics of a marriage. He recommended exploring if a union is arranged or voluntarily entered. The condition under which a couple begins a marriage affects partner expectations, marital satisfaction, communication, and other relationship components (Piper & Roces, 2003).

Therapists may also have to act as advocates on behalf of families who may need medical care, assistance with employment, help enrolling children in school, assistance becoming citizens, or support with other concerns that may be of priority to the family. Once basic needs are met, then a therapist can begin to address restoring healthy interaction patterns and communication in the family. Families should receive a needs assessment so that they can receive the best care possible. Therapists also have to recognize limitations in providing care to survivors of torture or trauma who may be beyond their scope of services and training. Create a list of good community referrals for medical care, transportation, employment, day cares, and other needs that immigrants or blended families may have. Mental health providers are often front-line service providers to help families access other social, medical, career, and educational resources. In addition, a therapist should have a model of working with families that is culturally affirming and culturally relevant to the individuals being served (Tsui, 1985).

To help clinicians gain a thorough history of relationship dynamics and assist with treatment planning, we offer the following questions:

1. Tell me how your relationship started.
2. How is dating viewed within your cultures?
3. What led to your decision to enter into marriage?
4. Was the marriage arranged? If so, by whom?
5. What are your views about the roles of men and women in the marriage?
6. Who is the head of the household?
7. Does your family structure reflect more of a matriarchal system or patriarchal system?
8. How are household chores completed?
9. How are religious holidays and observances celebrated?
10. What languages do your family members speak?
11. Tell me about your migration experience.
12. Tell me about your family members' levels of education.
13. How do other family members view your union?
14. Did they express concerns about the family lineage?
15. What are your views about having and raising children together?
16. How do your families feel about you having multiracial children?
17. How are concerns addressed in your family?
18. How do your family members identify individually? As members of an ethnic group?
19. What are your relationships like with extended families?
20. How do your cultural backgrounds influence the family unit?
21. How do you view and treat your children?
22. What are the communication patterns in the family?
23. How do you discuss and utilize discipline in the family?
24. What are your roles in the family, and how do gender roles influence how you engage in the family?
25. How do you address conflict between you and your spouse and with the children? Identify dysfunctional patterns in the family.
26. How will family members and friends from each culture view you and your spouse?

27. How will family members' and friends' ability to speak your spouse's language and understand his or her culture affect the union?
28. How might previous marital history or past relationships affect this union when past partners might have been of a different ethnic background?
29. Tell me about your countries of origin.
30. What are the political climates of these countries?
31. How are intercultural relationships viewed?
32. Tell me about your religious and spiritual views.
33. How are those views similar and different from those of your families of origin?
34. How will religious and spiritual views be shared with children in the family?

This list is not exhaustive and is intended to guide a clinician in exploring potential areas of concern in immigrant intercultural relationships. Each couple is unique, and clinicians are discouraged from using the same approach with every family. Instead clinicians are encouraged to use the questions and information presented in this chapter to raise awareness of potential challenges couples may face and to guide interventions based on presenting concerns.

Tsui (1985) recommended utilizing behavioral strategies that provide direction and feedback to couples about ways to manage concerns and explore issues of shame within the relationship. Therapists should provide resources for improving communication, identifying and addressing familial concerns in a healthy way, identifying conflicts based on cultural or gender differences, and solving other problems. Falicov (2007) suggested that providers integrate the value systems of the couple as well as the extended family and community. An integral part of the intervention would be to understand sociocultural and political contexts. Therapists will be working to help families navigate between multiple identities to construct a collaborative set of familial values. The role of the mental health provider is not to criticize existing family values but to help the family members create a cultural worldview that makes sense in the context of their individual union (Biever et al., 1998). Clinicians can help identify goals for daily living and help individual family members make sense of their ethnic identity and group memberships (Falicov, 2007). Most important, therapists need to assist couples in identifying what needs they may have in the relationship. It is important that couples have a safe space to process their concerns and be able to articulate their specific needs as a family.

Counseling professionals should familiarize themselves with new legislation being passed related to immigrants in the United States to more fully understand some of the difficulties these clients may be encountering. Therapists can begin working with health care and insurance companies related to the provision of counseling services to immigrants. As language is often a barrier to seeking and receiving services, an interpreter is often needed. However, insurance companies rarely cover this service. Clinicians can facilitate discussions among counseling professionals about the ethics of working with immigrants, as unique legal and ethical challenges may arise when working with undocumented citizens. Training programs should include more curricula about the skills necessary to effectively work with intercultural families and in particular blended immigrant families. Counseling professionals working in areas with large numbers of immigrant families may want to work with local community agencies and the school systems to conduct needs assessments with the families to address some of the concerns outlined earlier in the chapter.

Future Recommendations

As noted earlier, this chapter focused on heterosexual relationships. The literature is sparse regarding same-sex intercultural couples and is an area that needs further attention. Blended intercultural unions are another area that could be further developed. What are the specific concerns of couples in which one partner has one or more children from a previous relationship? Qualitative studies that provide for a deeper understanding of the phenomena of interest would also add significantly to the literature on both immigrant intercultural families and blended families. Another area of growing interest is interreligious marriages. More research is needed in that area specifically in terms of providing both premarital therapy and marital therapy to immigrant couples.

References

Abraido-Lanza, A., Armbrister, A., White, K., & Lanza, R. (2006). Immigrants. In Y. Jackson (Ed.), *Encyclopedia of multicultural psychology* (pp. 237–243). Thousand Oaks, CA: Sage.

Al-Issa, I. (1997). Ethnicity, immigration, and psychopathology. In I. Al-Issa & M. Tousignant (Eds.), *Ethnicity, immigration, and psychopathology*. New York: Plenum.

Anderson, S. (1994). *And the two became one plus—An upfront look at today's blended family*. Easton, MA: Bridges of Hope.

Baptiste, D. (1984). Marital and family therapy with racially/culturally intermarried stepfamilies: Issues and guidelines. *Family Relations: Journal of Applied Family and Child Studies*, *33*, 373–380.

Behnke, A. O., Taylor, B. A., & Parra-Cardona, J. R. (2008). "I hardly understand English, but …": Mexican origin fathers describe their commitment as fathers despite the challenges of immigration. *Journal of Comparative Family Studies*, *39*, 187–205.

Bemak, F., & Chung, R. C.-Y. (2008). Counseling and psychotherapy with refugees. In P. B. Pedersen, J. G. Draguns, W. J. Lonner, & J. E. Trimble (Eds.), *Counseling across cultures* (6th ed., pp. 307–324). Thousand Oaks, CA: Sage.

Benet-Martinez, V., Leu, J., Lee, F., & Morris, M. W. (2002). Negotiating biculturalism: Cultural frame switching in biculturals with oppositional versus compatible cultural identities. *Journal of Cross-Cultural Psychology, 33*, 492–516.

Berry, J. W. (1990). Psychology of acculturation. In N. R. Goldberger & J. B. Veroff (Eds.), *The culture and psychology reader* (pp. 457–488). New York: New York University Press.

Biever, J. L., Bobele, M., & North, M. W. (1998). Therapy with intercultural couples: A postmodern approach. *Counseling Psychology Quarterly, 11*, 181–188.

Bray, J. H. (2005). Family therapy with stepfamilies. In J. L. Lebow (Ed.), *Handbook of clinical family therapy* (pp. 497–515). Hoboken, NJ: John Wiley.

Breger, R., & Hill, R. (1998). Introducing mixed marriages. In R. Breger & R. Hill (Eds.), *Cross-cultural marriage: Identity and choice* (pp. 1–31). New York: Berg.

Cauce, A. M., & Rodriguez, M. D. (2002). Latino families: Myths and realities. In J. Conteras, K. A. Kerns, & A. M. Neal-Barnett (Eds.), *Latino children and families in the United States* (pp. 3–26). Westport, CT: Praeger.

Chung, R. C.-Y., & Bemak, F. (2007). Immigrants and refugee populations. In M. G. Constantine (Ed.), *Clinical practice with people of color: A guide to becoming culturally competent* (pp. 125–142). New York: Columbia University, Teachers College Press.

Chung, R. C.-Y., Bemak, F., Ortiz, D. P., & Sandoval-Perez, P. A. (2008). Promoting the mental health of immigrants: A multicultural/social justice perspective. *Journal of Counseling and Development, 86*, 310–317.

Coltrane, S., Gutierrez, E., & Parke, R. D. (2008). Stepfathers in cultural context: Mexican American families. In J. Pryor (Ed.), *The international handbook of stepfamilies: Policy and practice in legal, research, and clinical environments* (pp. 100–121). Hoboken, NJ: Wiley.

Crohn, J. (1995). *Mixed matches: How to create successful interracial, interethnic, and interfaith relationships*. New York: Fawcett Columbine.

Crohn, J. (1998). Intercultural couples. In M. McGoldrick (Ed.), *Re-visioning family therapy: Race, culture, and gender in clinical practice* (pp. 295–308). New York: Guilford.

Dalmage, H. M. (2000). *Tripping on the color line: Black–White multiracial families in a racially divided world*. New Brunswick, NJ: Rutgers University Press.

Dion, K. K., & Dion, K. L. (1996). Cultural perspectives on romantic love. *Personal Relationships, 3*, 5–17.

Falicov, C. J. (2007). Working with transnational immigrants: Expanding meanings of family, community, and culture. *Family Process, 46*, 157–171.

Fu, X., & Heaton, T. B. (2000). Status exchange in intermarriage among Hawaiians, Japanese, Filipinos and Caucasians in Hawaii: 1983–1994. *Journal of Comparative Family Studies, 31*, 45–61.

Fuligni, A. J. (1998). The adjustment of children from immigrant families. *Current Directions in Psychological Science, 7*, 99–103.

Gaines, S. O., Jr., & Agnew, C. R. (2003). Relationship maintenance in intercultural couples: An interdependence analysis. In D. J. Canary & M. Dainton (Eds.), *Maintaining relationships through communication: Relational, contextual, and cultural variations* (pp. 231–253). Mahwah, NJ: Lawrence Erlbaum.

Ganong, L. H., & Coleman, M. (2004). *Stepfamily relationships: Development, dynamics, and interventions*. New York: Kluwer Academic/Plenum.

Grearson, J., & Smith, L. (2009). The luckiest girls in the world. In T. A. Karis & K. D. Killian (Eds.), *Intercultural couples: Exploring diversity in intimate relationships* (pp. 3–20). New York: Routledge Taylor & Francis Group.

Ho, M. K. (1990). *Intermarried couples in therapy*. Springfield, IL: Charles Thomas.

Horenczyk, G. (1996). Immigrants' perceptions of host attitudes and their reconstruction of cultural groups. *Applied Psychology: An International Review, 46*, 34–38.

Hovey, J. D. (2000). Acculturative stress, depression, and suicidal ideation in Mexican immigrants. *Cultural Diversity and Ethnic Minority Psychology, 6*, 134–151.

Hsu, J. (2001). Marital therapy for intercultural couples. In W. S. Tseng & J. Stresetzer (Eds.), *Culture and psychotherapy: A guide to clinical practice* (pp. 225–242). Washington, DC: American Psychiatric Press.

Hurwitz, J. (1997). *Coping in a blended family*. New York: Rosen.

Ibrahim, F., & Schroeder, D. G. (1990). Cross-cultural couples counseling: A developmental, psychoeducational intervention. *Journal of Comparative Family Studies, 21*, 193–205.

Karis, T. A. (2003). How race matters and does not matter for White women in relationships with Black men. In V. Thomas, T. Karis, & J. Wetchler (Eds.), *Clinical issues with interracial couples: Theories and research* (pp. 23–40). New York: Hawthorne.

Karis, T. A. (2009). "We're just a couple of people": An exploration of why some Black–White couples reject the terms *cross-cultural* and *interracial*. In T. A. Karis & K. D. Killian (Eds.), *Intercultural couples: Exploring diversity in intimate relationships* (pp. 89–110). New York: Routledge Taylor & Francis Group.

Kashima, Y. (2000). Conception of culture and person for psychology. *Journal of Cross-Cultural Psychology, 31*, 15–32.

Lara, T. M., & Onedera, J. D. (2008). Inter-religion marriages. In J. D. Onedera (Ed.), *The role of religion in marriage and family counseling* (pp. 213–226). New York: Routledge.

Livingston, J., Holley, J., Eaton, S., Cliette, G., Savoy, M., & Smith, N. (2008). Cultural competence in mental health practice. *Best Practices in Mental Health, 4*, 1–14.

Mann, M. A. (2006). The formation and development of individual and ethnic identity: Insights from psychiatry and psychoanalytic theory. *American Journal of Psychoanalysis, 66*, 211–224.

McFadden, J. (2001). Intercultural marriage and family: Beyond the racial divide. *The Family Journal: Counseling and Therapy for Couples and Families, 9*, 39–42.

McLoyd, V. C., Cauce, A. M., Takeuchi, D., & Wilson, L. (2000). Marital processes and parental socialization in families of color: A decade review of research. *Journal of Marriage and the Family, 62*, 1070–1093.

Merz, E.-M., Oort, F. J., Özeke-Kocabas, E., & Schuengel, C. (2009). Intergenerational family solidarity: Value differences between immigrant groups and generations. *Journal of Family Psychology, 23*, 291–300.

Mignot, J.-F. (2008). Stepfamilies in France since the 1990s: An interdisciplinary overview. In J. Pryor (Ed.), *The international handbook of stepfamilies: Policy and practice in legal, research, and clinical environments* (pp. 53–78). Hoboken, NJ: Wiley.

Morrison, M., & James, S. (2009). Portuguese immigrant families: The impact of acculturation. *Family Process, 48*, 151–166.

Oetzel, J., & Ting-Toomey, S. (2003). Face concerns in interpersonal conflict: A cross-cultural empirical test of the face-negotiation theory. *Communication Research, 30*, 599–624.

Okun, B. F. (1996). *Understanding diverse families.* New York: Guilford.

Perel, E. (2000). A tourist view of marriage: Cross-cultural couples—Challenges, choices, and implications for therapy. In P. Papp (Ed.), *Couples on the fault line: New directors for therapists* (pp. 178–204). New York: Guilford.

Piller, I. (2009). I always wanted to marry a cowboy. In T. A. Karis & K. D. Killian (Eds.), *Intercultural couples: Exploring diversity in intimate relationships* (pp. 53–70). New York: Routledge Taylor & Francis Group.

Piper, N., & Roces, M. (2003). Introduction: Marriage and migration in an age of globalization. In N. Piper & M. Roces (Eds.), *Wife or worker? Asian women and migration* (pp. 181–201). Lanham, MD: Rowman and Littlefield.

Ponizovsky, A. M., & Grinshpoon, A. (2009). Mood and anxiety disorders and the use of services and psychotropic medication in an immigrant population: Findings from the Israel national health survey. *The Canadian Journal of Psychiatry, 54*, 409–419.

Poston, W. S. C. (1990). The biracial identity development model: A needed addition. *Journal of Counseling and Development, 69*, 152–155.

Prendes-Lintel, M. (2001). A working model in counseling recent refugees. In J. G. Ponterotto, J. M. Casas, L. A. Suzuki, & C. M. Alexander (Eds.), *Handbook of multicultural counseling* (2nd ed., pp. 729–752). Thousand Oaks, CA: Sage.

Richman, L. S., Kohn-wood, L. P., & Williams, D. R. (2007). The role of discrimination and racial identity for mental health service utilization. *Journal of Social and Clinical Psychology, 26*, 960–981.

Rosenblatt, P. C. (2009). Theoretical frameworks for understanding intercultural couples. In T. A. Karis & K. D. Killian (Eds.), *Intercultural couples: Exploring diversity in intimate relationships* (pp. 3–20). New York: Routledge Taylor & Francis Group.

Roy, P., & Hamilton, I. (2000). Intermarriage among Italians: Some regional variations in Australia. *Journal of Comparative Family Studies, 31*, 63–78.

Rubalcava, L. A., & Waldman, K. (2004). Working with intercultural couples: An intersubjective-constructivist perspective. In W. J. Coburn (Ed.), *Transformations in self psychology* (pp. 127–149). Hillsdale, NJ: Analytic Press.

Shehan, C. L., Bck, E. W., & Lee, G. R. (1990). Religious heterogamy, religiosity, and marital happiness: The case of Catholics. *Journal of Marriage and the Family, 52*, 73–79.

Sherkat, D. E. (2004). Religious intermarriage in the United States: Trends, patterns, and predictors. *Social Science Research, 33*, 606–625.

Snowden, L. R., & Thomas, K. (2000). Medicaid and African American outpatient mental health treatment. *School of Social Welfare, 2*, 115–120.

Steel, M., & Valentine, G. (1995). New colors: Mixed race families still find a mixed reception. *Teaching Tolerance, 4*, 44–49.

Sue, D. W., & Sue, D. (2003). Counseling Asian Americans. In D. W. Sue & D. Sue (Eds.), *Counseling the culturally diverse: Theory and practice* (4th ed., pp. 327–342). New York: John Wiley & Sons.

Sullivan, P. (1998). "What are you?" Multiracial families in America. *Our Children, 23,* 34–35.

Ting-Toomey, S. (2009). A mindful approach to managing conflict in intercultural intimate couples. In T. A. Karis & K. D. Killian (Eds.), *Intercultural couples: Exploring diversity in intimate relationships* (pp. 31–49). New York: Routledge Taylor & Francis Group.

Tsui, A. M. (1985). Psychotherapeutic considerations in sexual counseling for Asian immigrants. *Psychotherapy, 22,* 357–362.

U.S. Bureau of the Census. (2004). *Interracial married couples: 1980–present.* Retrieved July 6, 2009, from www.census.gov/population/socdemo/hh-fam/tabMS-3.xls - 2004–09–15

U.S. Department of Health and Human Services. (2001). *Mental health: Culture, race, and ethnicity—A supplement to mental health: A report of the surgeon general* (Inventory No. SMA-01–3613). Rockville, MD: U.S. Department of Health and Human Services, Substance Abuse and Mental Health Services Administration, and Center for Mental Health Services.

Wells, K., Klap, R., Koike, A., & Sherbourne, C. (2001). Ethnic disparities in unmet needs for alcoholism, drug abuse, and mental health care. *The American Journal of Psychiatry, 158,* 2027–2032.

Whaley, A. L. (2001). Cultural mistrust and mental health services for African Americans: A review and meta-analysis. *Counseling Psychologist, 29,* 513–531.

Yakushko, O. (2009). Xenophobia: Understanding the roots and consequences of negative attitudes toward immigrants. *The Counseling Psychologist, 37,* 36–66.

Youakim, J. M. (2004). Marriage in the context of immigration. *The American Journal of Psychoanalysis, 64,* 155–165.

Chapter 13

The Future of Counseling Immigrants and Their Families

Evelyn Rivera-Mosquera, Marsha Mitchell-Blanks, Eréndira López-García, and Omar Fattal

Contents

The Changing Face of the United States

The face of the United States has and will continue to change rapidly and as a result will change the role of the mental health professional in the future. The U.S. Census predicts that the population is expected to rise from today's 305 million people to 439 million by 2050. However, the population will undoubtedly be quite different in terms of race and ethnicity in the future. According to the U.S. Census Bureau's (2008) *2008 National Population Projections*, the Hispanic/Latino and Asian populations are expected to double in the next two to four decades. In fact, Hispanics/Latinos are expected to be 30% of the population. Current projections indicate that people who regard themselves as Hispanic/Latino, Black, Asian, American Indian, Native Hawaiian, and Pacific Islander will become the majority by 2042 in the United States and will account for 54% of the population (Pew Research Center, 2008; U.S. Census Bureau, 2008). These dramatic cultural changes will not only shift who we will be seeing in our mental health offices and agencies but ultimately change the way that mental health providers perform many aspects of their jobs. We are talking about a paradigm shift that will move us toward serving diverse populations in a culturally and linguistically appropriate manner. Mental health providers will need to develop new competencies that will enable them to work more effectively and respectfully with immigrant and refugee populations (Chung, Bemak, Ortiz, & Sandoval-Perez, 2008).

In 2008, there were a record number of naturalizations, with 1,107,126 persons becoming American citizens. This is the highest number of naturalizations recorded since 1907 (Lee & Rytina, 2009). In addition, there were over 1.1 million persons given legal permanent residency. The leading countries of birth of persons who became citizens were Mexico (22.2%), India (6.3%), Philippines (5.6%), People's Republic of China (3.8%), and Cuba (3.8%). The leading countries of birth of persons who became permanent residents were Mexico (17.2%),

China (7.3%), India (5.7%), Philippines (4.9%), and Cuba (4.5%) (Monger & Rytina, 2009). The number of refugees or asylum seekers is also increasing in the United States.

In addition to experiencing the exponential growth of authorized immigrants and refugees, the United States has also experienced a tremendous growth in the number of unauthorized immigrants. The Pew Hispanic Center estimated that in 2008, there were 11.9 million unauthorized immigrants residing in the United States (Passel & Cohn, 2008; U.S. Census Bureau, 2008). The report indicated that the undocumented immigrant population grew rapidly from 1990 to 2006 but has since stabilized. More than three quarters (76%) of the nation's unauthorized immigrants are Hispanic/Latino, with the majority being from Mexico (59%). Other significant regional sources of unauthorized immigrants include Asia (11%), Central America (11%), South America (7%), the Caribbean (4%), and the Middle East (less than 2%). The center estimates that unauthorized immigrants compose 4% of the nation's population and account for 5.4% of its workforce. It is estimated that there were approximately 8.3 million undocumented immigrants in the U.S. labor force in 2008. Unauthorized immigrants differ from naturalized citizens and permanent residents in that they are more likely to live in a household with a spouse and children. Seventy-three percent of these families have children that were born in the United States and thus are American citizens.

Undoubtedly, immigrant families are changing the face of the United States of America. As of 2005, one fourth of young children (25%) in the United States lived in immigrant families. Nearly one third (32%) of young immigrant children live in linguistically isolated households, in which either no one over the age of 13 speaks English fluently or the only English speaker is a child under the age of 13, which can lead to serious access barriers for these families. In addition, more than one in five young immigrant children (22%) live below the poverty level. Furthermore, a significant number of immigrant families lack health insurance, ranging from 16% to 27% depending on their country of origin (Hernandez, Denton, & McCartney, 2008). These children will be the future labor force of America. Therefore, it is imperative that we begin to address the health and mental heath needs of these burgeoning communities.

Changing Domestic Migration Patterns

In general, most new immigrants tend to make their homes in states where a large number of immigrants already reside (i.e., California, Florida, New York, Texas, New Jersey, and Illinois). However, there appears to be a trend indicating that immigrants are more geographically dispersed than in the past. They are spreading more broadly into states where relatively few had settled decades ago

(Passel & Cohn, 2008). As a result of this new domestic migratory pattern of immigrants in the United States, states such as Ohio, Pennsylvania, Arkansas, South Dakota, Delaware, Missouri, Colorado, New Hampshire, North Carolina, Virginia, Georgia, Indiana, and others are beginning to experience considerable increases in immigrant populations in both the urban areas and the rural areas (Chung et al., 2008). Unfortunately, this new domestic migratory pattern has begun and will continue to create serious problems for the already precarious and fragile public mental health system, which is ill equipped to handle the language and cultural needs of these growing populations. This is particularly of great concern for geographic regions that are homogenous in terms of diversity and where the system has had very little experience with working with ethnically and racially diverse groups of people (Layton & Keating, 2006). Overall, research suggests that there is a significant gap between the need for and availability of mental health services for immigrants with limited English-language proficiency (Alegria et al., 2007; Derose & Baker, 2000; Ku & Mutani, 2001). There is a shortage of bilingual, culturally competent mental health providers in the United States, which can lead to less accurate diagnoses and mistakes between treatment needs and resources (Alegria et al., 2008). For example, it is estimated that there are only 29 Hispanic mental health providers per 100,000 Hispanics in the population. For Caucasians, the rate is about 173 mental health providers per 100,000 (U.S. Department of Health and Human Services, 2001).

Further compounding these disparity issues is the fact that many of these states have lower per capita mental health providers and expenditures on mental health services. This generally translates in to fewer dollars available and spent on the development and delivery of culturally and linguistically competent services for at-risk minority and immigrant populations now residing in those states (Mark, Shern, Bagalman, & Cao, 2007).

The Future Mental Health Needs of Immigrants

Mental Health Disparity in Immigrants

As is evident, this new wave of immigration is coming from countries where the immigrant may possibly be classified as an ethnic minority once he or she arrives in America. Therefore, it is highly likely that many of these new immigrants will be subjected to the same stressors and barriers that U.S.-born ethnic minorities face such as racism, anti-immigrant sentiment, discrimination, and poverty (Chung et al., 2008; Gurchiek, 2005; Wu, 2002). Unfortunately, ethnic minorities suffer serious health and mental health disparities in the United States. These disparity issues have been well documented by a number of national reports, including the U.S. surgeon general reports (U.S. Department of Health and Human Services, 1999, 2001), New Freedom Commission Report (U.S. Department of Health and Human Services, 2003), and the National Academy of Sciences Institute of Medicine (2006). Disparity is defined as a chain of events signified by an inequity that is unjust, unfair, and unequal (Carter-Pokras & Baquet, 2002). Ethnic minorities struggle with both access issues (entering the system) and poorer treatment outcomes when they enter the mental health system for services. In addition, ethnic minorities have a greater burden of disability in coping with the mental illness (U.S. Department of Health and Human Services, 2001).

There are a number of reasons why immigrants in the United States face these disparity issues. Language and cultural barriers, poverty, lack of health insurance, and lack of transportation and child care are just a few of those obstacles (Bemak & Chung, 2008; Bemak, Chung, & Pedersen, 2003). Stigma is another serious barrier that immigrants face. Nadeem et al. (2007) found that stigma was a significant barrier identified by immigrant women and that stigma concerns were associated with lower rates of wanting mental health care. The authors recommended that effective stigma-reducing educational campaigns targeting immigrant populations be implemented to combat this serious barrier.

Unauthorized immigrants and refugees may also be at risk of suffering from mental health issues even before arriving in the United States. Refugees generally are fleeing war or persecution in their native countries and thus may have witnessed extreme violence and trauma, which may lead to the development of post-traumatic stress, anxiety, and other disorders. Unauthorized immigrants may also be at risk of trauma as a result of the dangerousness of crossing the border. Many immigrants are sexually abused, assaulted, robbed, or at times left to die on their journey to the United States. They may also be subjected to anti-immigrant sentiment or rejection, deportation proceedings that separate families, incarceration, and public humiliation once they arrive in the United States (Perez, 2006). These experiences can clearly impact their mental health and can lead to the development of post-traumatic stress disorder, panic disorder, separation anxiety, and other related disorders (Abraido-Lanza, Armbrister, White, & Lanza, 2006; Chung et al., 2008; Paget-Clarke, 1997). For example, Miranda, Siddique, Der-Martirosian, and Belin (2005) found that separation from family and children increases an immigrant women's risk for depression.

Mental Health Prevalence Rates in Immigrants

In a landmark study on the prevalence rates of psychiatric disorders in Asian and Latino populations, the National Latino and Asian American Study (NLAAS) found that overall, foreign-born Latinos and Asians appeared to have lower rates of psychiatric disorders compared to U.S.-born Asian and Latino Americans (Alegria et al., 2008; Takeuchi et al., 2007). This suggests that immigrants appear to be more resilient when they arrive in the United States, supporting the Immigrant Paradox theory, which suggests that foreign nativity protects against psychiatric disorders. The investigators cautioned, however, against generalizing these findings to all subgroups. For example, although the theory held up for Mexican participants for mood, anxiety, and substance disorders, it did not for Puerto Ricans, who actually were found to have higher prevalence rates that were comparable to rates for Caucasians (Alegria et al., 2008). In addition, Takeuchi et al. (2007) found that Asian women did appear to follow the Immigrant Paradox theory, with foreign-born Asian women having lower rates of psychiatric disorders than their U.S.-born counterparts. On the other hand, Asian men who spoke English proficiently were found to have lower rates of lifetime psychiatric disorders, which is counter to the Immigrant Paradox theory. Nevertheless, a key finding of the NLAAS is that the longer an immigrant lives in the United States, the more likely he or she will suffer from a mental health problem.

Acculturation and Mental Health in Immigrants

As the NLAAS findings point out, acculturation plays a key role in the development of mental health problems for immigrants (Berry, 2002; Casas & Pytluk, 1995; Chung & Bemak, 2007). Social scientists coined the term *acculturative stress* to describe the impact of acculturation on the well-being of immigrants. Acculturation is the process in which individuals adjust to and/or redefine their beliefs, values, norms, and customs to the dominant culture's values, norms, beliefs, and customs as a result of having continuous contact with that group (Mainous, 1989; Moyerman & Forman, 1992; Padilla, 2006; Smart & Smart, 1997). Acculturation has been viewed from unidimensional (Szapocnik, Scopetta, Kurtines, & Arnalde, 1978), bidimensional (Huynh, Howell, & Benet-Martinez, 2009; Marin & Gamba, 1996), and multidimensional (Zea, Asner-Self, Birman, & Buki, 2003) perspectives. Multidimensional perspectives theorize that a person while acculturating can become monocultural or bicultural. Bicultural individuals may adopt values from the host culture while retaining certain values from their own culture (Moyerman & Forman, 1992). Research suggests that those who successfully reach biculturalism are most likely to be successful in coping with a multicultural setting like the United States, compared to monocultural individuals who simply retain their own culture.

Generally, children acculturate faster than their parents, thus creating an "acculturation gap" between generations that is thought to foster parent–child conflict. These parent–child acculturation conflicts are thought to precipitate stress in immigrant families, which in turn can lead to increased risk of mental health problems in both the children and the parents (Hernandez & McGoldrick, 1999; Szapocznik & Kurtines, 1980; Szapocznik et al., 1986). Therefore, mental health professionals must consider the effects of acculturation when working with immigrant families.

The U.S. Mental Health System: Is It Ready to Meet the Challenge?

Undoubtedly, immigrants suffer from language, cultural, and economic barriers and disparities in the United States that clearly impede their access to basic human services. Because many immigrants lack insurance coverage and/or have low incomes, the public mental health system is probably the only option they may have should they require mental health services. The president's New Freedom Commission reported that the mental health delivery system was fragmented and in need of transformation (U.S. Department of Health and Human Services, 2003). The National Academy of Sciences Institute of Medicine (2006) followed with another major report proposing a major overhaul of our behavioral health care system. In 2006 and 2009, the National Alliance for the Mentally Ill (NAMI) released its reports *Grading the States: A Report on America's Health Care System for Serious Mental Illness*. The reports measure each state's progress in providing evidence-based, cost-effective, recovery-oriented services for adults living with serious mental illness (NAMI, 2006, 2009). The states were graded in four areas, including Health Promotion and Management, Financing and Core Treatment/Recovery Services, Consumer and Family Empowerment, and Community Inclusion and Social Inclusion. In both 2006 and 2009, the overall national grade for the public mental health system was a D. States where significant numbers of immigrants are choosing to live such as Texas, Florida, Illinois, North Carolina, and Georgia received Ds. Other states such as California, Arizona, New Jersey, Virginia, and Ohio received Cs. New York was the only major state that received a B. The reports also indicated that, overall, states were not ensuring that their service delivery was culturally and linguistically competent. Most of the states with the largest ethnic minority populations scored low on the cultural competence indicator. As research indicates, the public mental health system is in need of transformation and may not be in any shape to handle the growing mental health disparity needs of ethnic minority and immigrant populations now or in the near future. This is of great concern, because the United States is facing its greatest economic challenge since the Great Depression (NAMI, 2009). Therefore, we as a society and mental health providers need to begin to think progressively about how to prevent this impending collision. We must look at developing cost-effective, culturally competent, community-based approaches that focus on increasing prevention and access and reducing stigma as well as developing evidence-based approaches targeting these vulnerable immigrant populations.

Effectiveness of the Western Model of Treatment With Immigrants

Psychology and counseling in America is based on Western principles and primarily follows the medical model of assessment, diagnosis, and treatment. The universal assumptions inherent in Western psychology have led to the belief that the same clinical interventions can be applied and are effective with all clients, regardless of racial/ethnic background. Unfortunately, this ethnocentric bias may negatively affect ethnically diverse groups of people (Nikelly, 1997). For instance, the high value set on self-disclosure that is embedded in Western counseling interventions may be incompatible with immigrant native coping styles (Asai & Barnlud, 1998; Barry, 2003; Shechtman, Goldberg, & Cariani, 2008). Sue and Sue argued, "Economically and educationally marginalized clients may not be oriented toward talk therapy" (2008, p. 45). As a result, numerous scholars have challenged traditional models of psychological theory and practice and have voiced a great need for change (Bingham, Porché-Burke, James, Sue, & Vasquez, 2002; Nagayama Hall & Maramba, 2001; Sue & Sue, 2008). Breaking through the numerous layers generally defined by immigrants regarding sharing their emotions with strangers and talking about their problems outside their community and family can be particularly challenging (Hsu & Alden, 2008; Panganamala & Plummer, 1998). For immigrants, psychotherapy may be an intimidating, threatening, unusual, and/or scary experience (Chen & Mak, 2008; Power, Eiraldi, Clarke, Mazzuca, & Krain, 2005). On the other hand, immigrants may have their own healing traditions ignored by Western practitioners; these healing practices may be equally legitimate methods of treatment and may be more welcomed by immigrant clients than those used in Western countries (i.e., use of *curanderos*, *espiritistas*, shamans, acupuncture, homeopathy, verses from the Koran and Bible, herbal remedies, etc.). Use of these alternative healing practices could be quite powerful if integrated in treatment to assist immigrants (Sue & Sue, 2008). Unfortunately, the Western model rarely acknowledges or integrates these practices into treatment.

In an effort to address multicultural and diversity issues in research and practice, the American Psychological Association published "Guidelines on Multicultural Education, Training, Research, Practice, and Organizational Change for Psychologists" in 2002. The guidelines set forth the parameters under which psychologists are to assess, diagnose, and treat ethnically diverse populations in a culturally competent manner. Despite these guidelines, clinicians still face the real challenge of diverging from their ethnocentric Western training and applying new and innovative approaches to diverse immigrant groups. Future clinicians will need to be cognizant of the inherent issues in assessing, diagnosing, and treating ethnic minority and immigrant populations.

Assessment Issues

One of the major assessment issues in working with immigrants is the use of standardized psychometric measures. The use of instruments that were constructed and standardized with primarily White, middle-class norms (Sue & Sue, 2008) is erroneous and can elicit detrimental results that can negatively affect the immigrant client. Because certain instruments are used as tools for job employment and promotions, diagnosis determination, treatment outcomes, educational accommodation services, and other vital life-enhancing reasons, administering tools that are not reliable and valid with the immigrant population will fail to produce an accurate assessment of the problem. Therefore, it is imperative that culturally and linguistically competent assessment tools and processes be utilized in working with immigrant clients that assess such variables as acculturation level, impact of discrimination and racism, immigration experience, comfort with ethnic identity, length of time in the United States, and/or social experiences with other groups (Miranda, Nakamura, & Bernal, 2003).

Diagnosis Issues

Since the inception of the *Diagnostic and Statistical Manual of Mental Disorders* (*DSM*) in 1952, criticisms have arisen on its ethnocentric approach to develop categories to classify disorders (Hays, 2001). Over the years, various editions emerged, and the *DSM-IV* (American Psychiatric Association, 1994) marked an important acknowledgment of the role of culture in symptom expression and presentation.

A glossary of culture-bound syndromes, some common idioms of distress, brief descriptions of specific cultural features that may be present in various disorders, a broader definition of Axis IV, and the inclusion of new culturally sensitive "V" codes were introduced in an attempt to address issues and controversies that the *DSM-IV* predecessors aroused (Francis et al., 1991; Smart & Smart, 1997; U.S. Department of Health and Human Services, 1999; Wilson & Skodol, 1994). Although the most recent *DSM* edition included culturally relevant information designed to enhance the cultural validity of the manual, work remains to be done to facilitate culturally diagnostic practices. Some authors believe that the *DSM-IV* lacks depth and has a narrow scope in reflecting the dynamic role of culture in mental health problems and disorders (Hays, 2008; U.S. Department of Health and Human Services, 1999). In addition, the "Outline for Cultural Formulation," instead of being integrated into the multiaxial system, is buried in an appendix at the back of the manual, deemphasizing its importance and making it less likely to be used or seen by practitioners (Hays, 2001; Lopez & Guarnaccia, 2000). In addition, some scholars note that the presence of idioms of distress is limited and fails to distinguish the nuances between everyday common cultural symptoms, hiding the real symptoms that cause distress (Kirmayer & Young, 1998).

Certainly, the *DSM-IV*'s additions of cross-cultural elements in establishing diagnostic reliability need to be recognized; however, the inconsistent attention to cultural influences is an area that clearly needs to be addressed in the future revision of the *DSM*. It has been said that the *DSM-V* that is planned to be published by 2012 is giving more attention to cross-cultural issues and goes from the categorical to a dimensional assessment that is believed to be less rigorous (Kamphuis & Noordhof, 2009).

Treatment Issues in Working With Immigrant Populations

Evidence-Based Therapies for Minorities and Cultural Adaptation of Therapy

There appears to be no consensus regarding the definition of evidence-based therapies in the literature. More important, there is no consensus on the definitions of the terms *treatment efficacy* and *treatment effectiveness*. The term *efficacy* is generally used to refer to studies that have been demonstrated to be effective in a controlled setting. Studies demonstrating efficacy usually test a specific treatment for a specific condition in a very well-defined population. Chambless et al. (1996) published a widely used classification system that divides treatment studies into the following three categories: (a) well-established treatments, (b) probably efficacious treatments, and (c) possibly efficacious treatments. A well-established treatment has at least two independent studies demonstrating efficacy, includes a treatment manual, has well-defined study populations, utilizes reliable outcome measures and appropriate data analysis, and treats a specific problem. A probably efficacious treatment has at least two experiments showing that treatment is effective. The possibly efficacious treatment has at least one treatment demonstrating efficacy without conflicting evidence. Obviously, well-established treatments are considered to have the highest evidence for efficacy. On the other hand, the term *effective* is used to refer to treatments that have been demonstrated to be effective in real-world settings. Effectiveness studies usually include larger sample sizes and more diverse populations with comorbid conditions.

Researchers have noted that the implementation of evidence-based treatments in practice provides guidance to practitioners to better serve mental health consumers. It also offers the opportunity to evaluate treatment practice, meeting the ethical obligation of providers in ensuring the delivery of the best treatment option (Whaley & Davis, 2007). In 1992, when the Task Force on Promotion and Dissemination of Psychological Procedures was conceived, treatment effectiveness was assessed in the managed care system. Counseling services were found to be in danger of not being covered by the potential implementation of a national health policy (Beutler, 1998). Thus, the Society of Clinical Psychology (Division 12) of the American Psychological Association assembled a group of science practitioners, chaired by Dianne Chambless, to identify treatments with proven treatment efficacy (Barlow, Levitt, & Bufka, 1999). Since then, the emergence of empirically supported treatments has grown significantly since the early 1990s (Blom, 2009; Whaley & Davis, 2007) and continues to expand today (Drake & Goldman, 2003).

In an attempt to disseminate this information, the surgeon general's report (U.S. Department of Health and Human Services, 1999) provided a range of empirically validated treatments that have proved their efficacy in treating several mental health conditions. This publication aims to make information available to providers, consumers, and other stakeholders. Despite this effort, evidence-based treatments are not being implemented routinely in mental health settings because it has been perceived that there is a lack of connection between research and practice (Drake et al., 2001). Some scholars have indicated that the gap between research and practice is due to the disconnection between clinical trials and population (Kazdin, 2009). This detachment is more pronounced in minority groups where empirical research has ignored them by omitting and/or limiting their participation. For instance, most studies on mental health treatment fail to address sample representatives, or the ethnicity of the participants is not clearly identified. In the surgeon general's report (U.S. Department of Health and Human Services. 1999), it was found that of 9,266 participants involved in the efficacy studies forming the major treatment guidelines for bipolar disorder, schizophrenia, depression, and attention deficit/hyperactivity disorder (ADHD), only 561 Blacks, 99 Latinos, and 11 Asian American or Pacific Islanders were included. No Native Americans were included in these studies. Few of these studies had the power necessary to examine the impact of care on specific minority populations (U.S. Department of Health and Human Services, 2001).

Despite the requirement of National Institutes of Health (NIH) Revitalization Act of 1993 that all NIH-funded human subject research include women and persons from racial or ethnic minority groups (NIH, 1994), subsequent research has found that few of these studies actually complied with the act. Braslow et al. (2005) reviewed four leading psychiatric and psychological journals published between the years of 1981 and 1996 to measure the generalizability of studies on mental health treatment and outcomes to ethnic minorities. The results indicated that ethnic minorities were documented in only about 25% of the studies. Seventy-five percent of the studies did not explicitly address sample representativeness. Braslow et al. did find that studies that utilized National Institute of Mental Health (NIMH) funding were more likely to include minorities than studies with no NIMH funding. The authors concluded that over the 16-year period, the generalizability of treatment and outcome to ethnic minorities remains low.

The Division 12 Task Force of the American Psychological Association charged with defining and identifying empirically supported therapies (ESTs) was not able to identify any psychotherapy treatment research that meets basic criteria important for demonstrating treatment efficacy for ethnic minority populations. More specifically, this task force was not able to identify studies that met the following criteria: (a) pre- and posttreatment status is assessed for clients from one or more ethnic minority group; (b) clients are blocked according to their particular ethnic group membership and randomly assigned to different treatments or to treatment and control groups; (c) multiple, culturally cross-validated assessment instruments are employed; and (d) findings are replicated (Chambless et al., 1996).

Given these findings, a large body of literature argues that ESTs that have been developed on nonminority populations cannot be automatically applied to minorities. As discussed in previous sections, minorities—particularly immigrants—come from unique backgrounds and have different concepts of illness and treatment than the majority Caucasian American population. Furthermore, immigrants face a multitude of stressors when relocating to the United States and have to deal with barriers unique to them. Therefore, several experts on culture and ethnicity have vocalized that ESTs might not be appropriate when used with minorities (Bernal & Scharrón-del-Río, 2001; Hall, 2001). These advocates strongly believe that ESTs should be culturally adapted to become more appropriate to minority populations.

In the case of immigrants, the need for cultural adaptation of therapy becomes even more apparent and necessary in situations where traditional therapy is simply not feasible because of language barriers and other social economic factors. Over the years, there have been several theoretical models that have been suggested for cultural adaptation of psychotherapy. In 2006, Hwang developed the psychotherapy adaptation and modification framework (PAMF). According to this model, the cultural adaptations are grouped into dynamic issues and cultural complexities, educating clients about mental health and psychotherapy, understanding cultural beliefs about mental illness, improving client–therapist relationship, being familiar with cultural differences in communicating distress, and addressing specific cultural issues that are unique to each population (Hwang, 2006). Bernal, Bonilla, and Bellido (1995) proposed a framework that consists of eight dimensions (language, persons, metaphors, content, concepts, goals, methods, and context) to serve as a guide for developing culturally sensitive treatments and adapting existing psychosocial treatments to specific ethnic minority groups.

In 2001, Hall reviewed the theoretical models of cultural adaptation of various therapies and was able to identify three main constructs (interdependence, spirituality, and discrimination) that were common to all of these models (Hall, 2001). Hall found that ethnic minorities value interpersonal relationships and group identity as opposed to individualistic values. Therefore, the utilization of interpersonal and family approaches when working with these populations should be considered in treatment. Hall also concluded that spirituality, which encompasses social and political dimensions as well as religion and spirituality, should be incorporated in culturally adapted therapies. Finally, Hall pointed out that the impact of racism and discrimination has serious implications for treatment and must be considered in working with ethnic minorities (Hall, 2001).

Obviously, these concepts can be applied to immigrants coming to the United States. Whaley and Davis (2007) also concluded that all processes of cultural adaptation fall under one of three major categories: (a) changes in the approach to service delivery, (b) changes to the nature of the therapeutic relationship, and (c) changes in the components of the treatment itself to accommodate the cultural beliefs, attitudes, and behaviors of the target population (Whaley & Davis, 2007). Griner and Smith (2006) conducted a meta-analysis of 76 studies describing culturally adapted interventions in minorities, primarily targeting youth. The most frequently used cultural adaptation involved explicitly integrating cultural values into the intervention. Other interventions included matching clients with therapists of the same ethnicity and who spoke the same language. The meta-analysis showed that interventions targeted to a specific cultural group were four times more effective than interventions provided to groups consisting of clients from a variety of cultural backgrounds. It also showed that interventions conducted in a client's native language were twice as effective compared to interventions conducted in English.

On the other hand, some advocates of the universal theory of illness have recommended applying ESTs to minorities and immigrants. Chambless et al. (1996), the authors of the original EST project, argued that given the absence of ESTs for minority populations, the published ESTs should be used with minorities. Furthermore, Weisz, Jenson-Doss, and Hawley (2006) conducted a meta-analysis on 32 trials that compared evidence-based psychotherapy treatments (EBTs) with usual treatment. They found that EBTs were superior to usual care and that this superiority was not reduced by including minority youths in the studies. They concluded that EBTs were equally efficacious in minorities. Please note that the study did not specify which minority groups were included in these studies.

Huey and Polo (2008) conducted a recent review of the literature on the psychosocial treatments for minority youth. In their review, they attempted to answer the question of whether culturally responsive EBTs lead to better outcomes. They divided the interventions into those that included cultural modifications and those that did not include cultural modifications and found that cultural responsiveness did not lead to better outcomes in the treatment of minorities. They cited several examples such as studies showing that individual treatment for depression in Puerto Rican youth was as effective as group therapy in this same population, which goes against the assumption that group therapy would be more effective in Latino youth given the importance of the extended family and community in this culture. These conclusions should be taken with a grain of salt, however, given that these authors reviewed studies conducted mostly in Latino and African American youth and suffered from many methodological limitations such as small sample sizes. In addition, it appears that acculturation levels were not evaluated in these youths. Therefore, the youths may have been more Americanized and therefore would probably respond more positively to Americanized treatment modalities.

Examples of Efficacious and Effective Treatments in Ethnic Minorities and Immigrants

One way of classifying these modalities and interventions is to group them into two major groups: "structural" adaptations and "substantive" adaptations. Structural adaptations include the physical location of the services, the delivery of the services (by using staff that is linguistically competent), and the integration of mental health services with primary care services. On the other hand, substantive adaptations include adjusting current treatment modalities (psychotherapy and medications) to make them appropriate for the population being treated. We have to keep in mind that certain adaptations use a mix of structural and substantive adaptations.

Examples of Structural Adaptations

Cultural Consultation Model. This model was tested among mental health practitioners and primary care clinicians. Clinicians in this model use translators and cultural brokers as consultants to provide cultural formulations and recommendations. This model resulted in good outcomes such as reaching a more accurate diagnosis, more appropriate treatments, and a better doctor–patient relationship. This model had several limitations such as the need for a lot of human resources. It also raises issues of privacy and confidentiality and does not provide long-term follow up that is usually needed in these settings (Kirmayer, Groleau, Guzder, Blake, & Jarvis, 2003).

Ethnospecific Mental Health Services and Clinics. Kinzie, Tran, Breckenridge, and Bloom (1980) described one of the earliest culturally competent mental health clinics in 1980. The report described a psychiatric clinic that caters to Indochinese (Vietnamese, Cambodians, and Laotians) refugees using an Indochinese psychiatrist and counselors. The clinic adopted therapies that are acceptable to the Indochinese patients (emphasizing the medical approach of the physician and focusing on symptoms). This clinic demonstrated success as evident by increased referrals and reduced symptomatology. A more recent study looked at "matching" Asian American, African American, Mexican American, and White clients with therapists according to ethnicity and gender. Except for African Americans, ethnic match resulted in lower dropout rates. Ethnic match was related to greater number of sessions in all groups and resulted in better treatment outcomes for Mexican Americans. Among clients who did not speak English as a primary language, ethnic and language match was a predictor of length and outcome of treatment (Sue, Fujino, Hu, David, & Zane, 1991).

Cultural Competence Training. The American Psychological Association has required the inclusion of programs that explore multicultural issues in psychology training programs. Over the past 10 years, the field of psychology training has witnessed an increase in emphasis on training psychologists in cultural competency (Giannet, 2003). The question remains on how best to train psychologists in cultural competency and how to measure it or define it.

One solution to minimize ethnic disparities in access to mental health services is to integrate mental health services into primary care. A study in 2007 tested this model by integrating mental health and substance abuse treatment for older Caucasian and Black patients in primary care clinics. The integrated model of care was effective in improving access to and participation in mental health and substance abuse treatment among Black primary care patients (Ayalon, Areán, Linkins, Lynch, & Estes, 2007).

Delivering mental health services within the communities where ethnic clients reside increases access to these services. For example, Asian Americans who attended mental health clinics located in Asian neighborhoods in Los Angeles had better outcomes than Asian American patients who attended mainstream mental health clinics (Yeh, Takeuchi, & Sue, 1994). There are a lot of studies describing the efficacy of school-based therapies mostly for refugee children (Kataoka et al., 2003; Rousseau & Guzder, 2008).

The "WE Care" project followed minority women with depression for one year. The study found that short-term medications (selective serotonin reuptake inhibitors or Wellbutrin) and cognitive behavioral therapy (CBT), which are considered EBTs for treatment of depression, in addition to some cultural adaptations such as offering extensive outreach, providing child care for patients, facilitating transportation, and providing flexible scheduling, was effective in lowering depression and increasing social functioning in these low-income minority women (Miranda et al., 2006).

Examples of Substantive Adaptations

Wood, Angela, Wei-Chin, Jeffrey, and Muriel (2008) described a step-by-step process on how to adapt CBT for Mexican American students with anxiety disorders using the PAMF model. In their article they introduced 10 principles that should be considered when adapting CBT to Mexican American students to achieve good results: spend time learning about the family's cultural practices, migration history, and acculturation status including languages proficiencies; actively collaborate with school staff to reduce parental anxiety about the process; provide early orientation and education to the family; respect the family's understanding of mental illness and its treatment; establish CBT goals that are valuable to the family to improve the working relationship; learn about the cultural practices and beliefs that influence parenting; engage the extended family in the treatment; align CBT techniques with cultural beliefs and traditions of the family such as collectivism and *simpatía*; consider that culturally based communication styles are masking poor adherence to treatment; and be aware of the acculturation gap between children and parents.

Another example of culturally adapted therapy is the Chinese Taoist cognitive therapy (CTCP), which is a cultural adaptation of CBT. CTCP combines elements of cognitive therapy and Taoist philosophy (conforming to natural laws, letting go of excessive control, and flexibly developing personality). Their model was labeled "ABCDE," and it has been found to be effective in treating generalized anxiety disorder in Chinese patients (Zhang et al., 2002).

The GANA (Guiando a Ninos Activos, which is Spanish for "guiding active children") program is a version of parent–child interaction therapy (PCIT) that has been adapted to Mexican Americans. McCabe et al. described the process of creating this program in a report published in 2005. The authors developed this culturally adapted treatment using information from the clinical and empirical literature on Mexican American families on barriers to treatment and effectiveness of treatment, expert opinion, and qualitative data collected from Mexican American parents and therapists (McCabe, Yeh, Garland, Lau, & Chavez, 2005). The GANA program adopts a basic philosophy that it is the provider's responsibility to reach out to families who are in need of treatment. It incorporates multiple components such as an initial comprehensive assessment of various cultural concepts that might play a role in the response to treatment such as the families' perception of presence of illness; expectations from treatment; guilt over the presence of the illness; presenting the program as an educational intervention rather than actual treatment to minimize stigma; engaging both parents and extended family; early orientation regarding the treatment to manage expectations; increased focus on rapport building between the therapist and the family; encouraging the family to verbalize complaints; and translation and simplification of written handouts (McCabe et al., 2005).

Rosselló and Bernal (1999) conducted a study to evaluate the efficacy of CBT and interpersonal therapy (IPT) in the treatment of depression in Puerto Rican adolescents. They randomized 71 Puerto Rican adolescents with depression into three groups: CBT, IPT, and waiting list. Both CBT and IPT significantly reduced depression compared to waiting list and differed little from one another. Furthermore, IPT was superior to waiting list in improving self-esteem and social adaptation. In this study, culturally adapted CBT and IPT were used, the treatment manuals were translated into Spanish, and words, phrases, concepts, and illustrations were modified to make them culturally appropriate. Concepts such as familism (strong identification with the family) and *respeto* (respect for others, especially older people) were included in these interventions (Rosselló & Bernal, 1999).

Matos, Bauermeister, and Bernal (2009) published a study evaluating the efficacy of a culturally modified version of the PCIT in the treatment of ADHD in Puerto Rican preschool children. At 3.5 months following treatment, the group that received PCIT showed significant reduction in hyperactivity, inattention, and aggressive and oppositional behaviors in the kids and reduced stress and improved use of adequate parenting skills in the mothers. The process of cultural adaptation of the PCIT included translating the PCIT manual and handouts into Spanish, modifying examples used in the treatment to make them more consistent with the daily experience and idiomatic expressions of Puerto Rican families, increasing time at the beginning of the sessions to foster better therapeutic relationships, and including extended family members in the treatment in a constructive way (Matos et al., 2009).

In 1986, Costantino, Malgady, and Rogler used *cuentos* or folktales to treat maladaptive behavior in around 200 Hispanic (mostly Puerto Rican) kids in kindergarten through third grade in New York who have showed maladaptive behavior using the Costantino's Behavior Rating Scale. The study identified 40 stories that represented thoughts, feelings, values, and behavior of Puerto Rican culture. They divided the kids into four groups: One group received the original folktales, another group received folktales that were adapted to make them more consistent with the modern times and the geographical location of the United States (e.g., mango trees were changed to apple trees; a rural plantation was changed to an urban playground), one group received art and play therapy, and one group received no intervention. In the groups that received the folktales intervention, the therapists and mothers read these stories to the kids over 20 weekly 90-minute sessions followed by a discussion of the stories and specifically discussions of adaptive and maladaptive consequences of actions. The adapted *cuento* therapy was most effective, followed by the original *cuento* therapy in reducing trait anxiety using the Trait Anxiety Scale of the State-Trait Anxiety Inventory in these kids (Costantino et al., 1986).

For a more complete list of these interventions in minorities, we refer the reader to the three major reviews that have been written about this topic by Miranda et al. (2005) and Huey and Polo (2008). Miranda et al. divided the studies in their review into efficacy studies of children and youth (Caucasians, African Americans, Latinos, and very few Asians) in the areas of depression, anxiety disorders, ADHD, and disruptive behavior disorders; prevention studies with minority children and youth (Latinos, African Americans, and Chinese); efficacy studies for minority adults in the areas of depression, anxiety, and schizophrenia; and effectiveness studies in minority adults. Huey and Polo listed the studies by condition: anxiety-related disorders, depression, conduct problems, substance use problems, trauma-related problems, mixed behavioral and emotional problems, and other psychosocial problems. They also summarized all these studies in a gigantic table. Huey and Polo identified 30 studies that met criteria for being probably efficacious and possibly efficacious, using Chambless's criteria. These studies covered different psychotherapies such as CBT, group CBT, interpersonal therapy, anger management, multidimension family therapy, and resilient peer training for a wide variety of psychiatric conditions such as anxiety disorders, depression, disruptive behavior, conduct disorder, and ADHD. However, these studies included only African American and Latino youth. No studies included Native American, Asian or Pacific Islander, or immigrant youth. The authors concluded a meta-analysis on these 30 studies and concluded that overall these interventions produced treatment effects of "medium" magnitude. In other terms, overall, 67% of the treated participants were better off than control participants (Huey & Polo, 2008).

There is a large overlap in the studies and interventions covered in the reviews published by Miranda et al. (2005) and Huey and Polo (2008). Miranda et al.'s report has the advantage of covering preventive interventions and includes interventions with adults. Huey and Polo's review includes interventions primarily targeting youth.

Ethnopsychopharmacology

Similar to psychotherapy, ethnicity and culture seem to play a big role in the response to medications. As in the case of psychotherapy, the literature is divided between those who believe in the universality of psychopharmacology (the use of medications for treatment of psychiatric conditions) and those who believe that psychopharmacology should be adapted to the ethnicity and culture. Those opposed to this growing field believe that variations within individuals of the same ethnic group or culture are the same as variations between individuals from different ethnic groups or cultures. Furthermore, they question the method of defining what constitutes an ethnic group or a culture (Chaudhry, Neelam, Duddu, & Husain, 2009).

Although there is a large body of studies that have shown that ethnicity and culture play a significant role in the response to medications (whether in terms of clinical effectiveness of the medications or in terms of side effects and metabolism rates), research suggests that ethnic minorities and immigrants are generally not recruited into psychotropic medication studies in sufficient numbers that would allow for this type of analysis to be conducted on the data, which in turn skews the results. Researchers must work harder to recruit a representative sample into their studies for their results to be applicable to ethnic minorities and immigrants. A variety of genetic factors and cultural dimensions such as diet and social attitudes have been found to contribute to these issues (Chaudhry et al., 2009). Therefore, it is critical that both the genetic factors, such as metabolism rates and proper dosages for ethnic minority and immigrant clients, and the social factors, such as fear of medications and mistrust of the system, be included as variables and investigated in all psychopharmacological studies conducted in the United States.

The Future Role of the Counselor
Cultural Competence Paradigm Shift

As mentioned earlier in this chapter, the primary roles of the counselor in the Western model are assessment, diagnosis, and treatment, all of which are changing and will continue to change because of the immigration influx. The United States is in the midst of a paradigm shift in service delivery that is heading toward true cultural competence. As a result, mental health professionals not only will need to become culturally and linguistically competent but may also have to take on new roles in serving these at-risk and hard to reach emerging majority immigrant populations.

Given the expected shift in the population composition of our society, there has been a great deal of interest in the concept of cultural competence. As a result, numerous definitions have evolved. In 2001, the U.S. surgeon general defined cultural competence as the delivery of services responsive to the cultural concerns of racial and ethnic minority populations, including their languages, histories, traditions, beliefs, and values. The National Center for Cultural Competence (2009) at Georgetown University defined cultural competence as a developmental process that evolves over an extended period of time for which both individuals and organizations are at various levels of awareness, knowledge, and skills along the cultural competence continuum. The Substance Abuse and Mental Health Services Administration (n.d.) defined cultural competence as an approach to service delivery where mental health services are provided in the most relevant and meaningful cultural, gender-sensitive, and age-appropriate context for the people being served. Tervalon and Murray-García (1998) introduced another interesting concept that they called "cultural humility." They described "humility" as a lifelong process of self-reflection and self-critique. Cultural humility acknowledges that we can never truly understand the cultural and environmental experiences of another cultural group of which we are not members; thus it differs from the concept of cultural competence in that it does not believe that we can actually master or become competent in someone's culture. Cultural humility calls for the practitioner to have a respectful attitude and approach toward diverse points of view and have a willingness for self-awareness that leads to cross-cultural exploration. This is not to say that we no longer need to gain knowledge in the cultural practices, norms, beliefs, and values of other ethnic groups, but we must go beyond basic knowledge to build respectful partnerships based on our client's worldview and not our own.

As more and more definitions emerge on the scene, the concept of cultural competence continues to evolve. More recently, cultural competence has evolved to include all aspects of a system. The notion is that all levels of employees of the mental health system, including upper management (i.e., board members, CEOs, department chairs, top administrators), middle management (i.e., supervisors, managers), and line or client-level employees (i.e., counselors, caseworkers, administrative support staff), have a role and responsibility within the agency to serve persons in a culturally competent manner and, thus, must all possess cultural competence skills (Betancourt, Green, Carrillo, & Ananeh-Firempong, 2003; Whaley & Longoria, 2008). Unfortunately, most of the training in cultural competence is geared toward line staff and overlooks the role that top and middle management play on policy development as well as the overall funding and implementation of systemic cultural competence initiatives. This has led to floundering cultural competence programs that have not permeated the system (Whaley & Longoria, 2008).

Unfortunately, without the buy in of the leadership and managers of the organization, cultural competence cannot and will not take root as a part of the organization's overall culture, which not only is a necessary ingredient for the cultural competence paradigm shift to occur but is imperative for effective culturally competent programs to be developed and implemented for at-risk immigrant populations. As a result, ethnic minority populations will continue to experience disparities within the mental health system. Therefore, it is imperative that individual, organizational, and system cultural competence go beyond the superficial appearance of being culturally competent, which unfortunately is often the case, toward a true holistic phenomenological acceptance and incorporation of ethnic minority experiences. Without this level of understanding and acceptance of the experiences of immigrant and ethnic minority populations, the assessment, diagnosis, and treatment they receive may continue to be ineffectual in its outcomes. A list of cultural competence resources is included in Appendix A at the end of this book to assist practitioners in furthering their professional development.

Social Justice, Advocacy, and Prevention Work

There are three premises that will underlie this cultural competence paradigm shift—social justice, advocacy, and prevention work. These are basic elements needed in the field of mental health to truly begin to address mental health disparities in ethnic minority populations. Hage et al. (2007) argued that prevention work needs to be at the forefront of a comprehensive mental health agenda. They called for psychologists, and we extend the invitation to all mental health professionals, to actively engage in prevention practice that is culturally relevant and inclusive and addresses both individual and social contextual factors to prevent human suffering. In addition, they called for focusing on the reduction of risk factors contributing to mental health problems and the promotion of a strengths-based approach in the targeted population to enhance emotional well-being. Preventing human suffering may require mental health professionals to go the extra step of actively advocating for social change so that disenfranchised groups have fair access to societal resources. Therefore, issues like human rights, exposure to violence, discrimination, racism, immigration status, and other societal injustices must become an integral part of mental health providers' work agenda. Kenny and Hage (2009) saw this as the next frontier in primary prevention, which seeks to reduce the onset of some psychological conditions that are rooted in social injustice. Given the vast number of experiences within immigrant, refugee, and asylum-seeking populations, this type of prevention approach is essential, especially in community-based mental health settings to overcome the stigma, fear, and distrust in the system, as well as the cultural and linguistic barriers that are inherent in serving at-risk ethnic minority and immigrant populations. Prevention programs can be used as a tool to address stigma and disparities by providing culturally relevant community education that promotes emotional wellness and demystifies mental health and illness.

This bold step toward prevention and social justice in a field that is entrenched in psychotherapy and counseling represents a true paradigm shift. For counselors to be properly prepared for this work, they must be educated early in their training on how and why they should engage in prevention and social justice issues. Prevention theory, research, and practice needs to be embedded into counseling curriculums at all levels (BA, MA, PhD, PsyD) to prepare future mental health professionals to work effectively in the prevention field. In addition, counselors should seek opportunities to expand their repertoire of skills to include cross-disciplinary training in advocacy, grant writing, and program development and to immerse themselves in grassroots community initiatives that build trust and facilitate treatment outcomes (Blustein, Goodyear, Perry, & Cypers, 2005; Rivera-Mosquera, Dowd, & Mitchell-Blanks, 2007).

Recommended Approaches for Engaging Immigrants

The development of effective approaches for reaching and serving immigrants is crucial. Effective approaches targeting immigrants must help reduce stigma and facilitate access to the mental health system. They should utilize a holistic perspective (body, mind, spirit), incorporate family-centered approaches if warranted, and include psychoeducation in the role of acculturation and its impact on mental health in clients and their family. These interventions should also be done in the immigrant's community or in places where the immigrant feels safe and comfortable. One example of such a program is the work being done by the first and second authors at the National Alliance on Mental Illness of Greater Cleveland, Ohio (NAMI GC), Multicultural Outreach Program. The purpose of the NAMI GC Multicultural Outreach Program is to promote mental wellness among minority populations by providing outreach, information and referral, education, and support that is culturally and linguistically specific and empowers minorities to access services and seek mutual support. Currently the program targets the two largest ethnic minority populations in Ohio and the Greater Cleveland area: Latinos and African Americans. The program has adopted a prevention approach that utilizes community engagement techniques and culturally and linguistically specific psychoeducational sessions that address the stigma associated with mental illness and educate on mental health conditions, signs and culturally specific symptoms, and available treatment modalities. Psychoeducational sessions are delivered by culturally and linguistically competent psychologists and/or mental health professionals who introduce the concepts of "emotional wellness" from a holistic (mind, body, spirit) perspective in nonthreatening community sites (i.e., churches, libraries, community centers, senior center, and schools) that are well respected by the ethnic minority population being served. Culturally and linguistically appropriate literature is available on mental health conditions, as well as community-based mental health services, in an effort to link participants to existing resources. Food and child care are available at sessions to further reduce barriers to participation, and sessions are held in the evening and on weekends to facilitate ease of access. Mental health professionals working for the Multicultural Outreach Program are encouraged to actively engage in the immigrant community by attending church and religious services and events, community health fairs and events, and other outreach efforts to build trust between the targeted population, mental health professionals, and the mental health system. The effectiveness of the program has not been fully evaluated as of this publication date; however, the approach appears to be successfully reaching both Latino and African American communities, as community groups are actively seeking out and requesting program services.

A second example of how practitioners can engage ethnic minorities and immigrant populations is through collaborations with grassroots organizations like Tova's N.E.S.T. Inc. in Columbus, Ohio. This grassroots organization grew out of two profound personal experiences of its African American founder with the mental health system: (a) being the mother of a teenager daughter who has bipolar disorder and (b) reclaiming her own life after suffering a brain aneurysm. Tova's N.E.S.T. puts forth the model of a nest that includes nutrition, education, sleep, and therapy that can be adapted to meet the needs of individuals and families coping with the stigma associated with mental illness and encourages and empowers them to seek help from culturally competent mental health professionals. The powerful personal experiences of the founder's struggles with stigma, the lack of knowledge of mental health conditions, and the systemic indifference toward cultural humility have led to the organization's collaboration with mental health systems and professionals to heighten their awareness of these conditions through workshop presentations. In addition, Tova's N.E.S.T. outreaches to faith-based communities and immigrant and other at-risk populations and supports individuals challenged with mental health issues and co-occurring disorders through joint psychoeducational sessions with culturally humble practitioners and individual presentations on stigma. These kinds of collaborative program models can be very powerful resources for mental health professionals seeking to access immigrant and ethnic minority populations, build trust in that community, and help empower immigrant populations to seek mental health services before conditions become severe.

Ethical Dilemmas in Working With Immigrants

Working with immigrant populations will inherently be wrought with some ethical dilemmas. One of the first issues that must be grappled with is the counselor's or therapist's role in working with undocumented individuals (persons who may not have legal status) living in the United States and seeking services. The American Psychological Association (2002) and the National Association of Social Workers (2008) clearly stated in their ethic codes to "do no harm" to clients. However, in our current environment of anti-immigrant sentiment and policies that are negatively affecting undocumented persons, counselors may find themselves caught in the current political battle raging on immigration in the United States. What should counselors do if they find undocumented clients in need of mental health services? Should counselors be obligated to serve them? In addition, many undocumented persons have children who were born in the United States and are American citizens. Current policies in terms of deportation of undocumented persons separate children from their parents and place them in the already overtaxed foster care system. How would a counselor or a mental health system serve this type of mixed family? In addition, some immigrant cultural norms, traditions, and values may be vastly different from those of the mental health professional and may lead to interpersonal value conflicts that need to be addressed through supervision. Such mental health professionals may be reluctant to bring these conflicts to supervision and continue to provide service while in this conflicted state. This may have the direct consequence of therapists imposing their own worldview on their clients. These are just a few of the issues that the mental health system will be grappling with and will need to resolve in the near future. Clearly, these ethical and moral dilemmas that mental health professionals will face in serving immigrants must be analyzed from both an individual framework and an organizational framework.

Summary

Undoubtedly, the face of the United States and the clients that counselors will be seeing in their offices will change drastically in the next two to four decades. The Western model of assessment, diagnosis, and treatment may not be sufficient or may need some serious tweaking to fight stigma and to increase access of mental health services to immigrant populations. A concerted effort will need to be made to gain the trust of immigrant populations to ensure their participation in psychotherapy and pharmacological studies so that additional treatment modalities can be developed that improve their outcomes. Furthermore, the incorporation of native immigrant healing practices may be helpful in attracting and retaining these populations in treatment.

It is imperative that mental health providers and systems develop culturally competent programs and services to reach at-risk ethnic minority and immigrant populations. Because acculturation plays a key role in the lives of immigrants, it is imperative that it be assessed and integrated in effective treatment approaches. Social justice models and prevention interventions need to underlie this paradigm shift so that we can truly begin to eliminate mental health disparities in ethnic minority and immigrant populations in the United States. Mental health providers will be called on to take on new roles such as advocate and community psychoeducational prevention specialist. These roles will take providers out of their comfortable offices and put them right in the heart of the immigrant community. To prepare mental health providers for this journey, we included a list of questions at the end of this chapter that mental health professionals should ask themselves before working with immigrant populations. In addition, Appendix B provides a list of helpful practical guidelines for counselors serving immigration populations to further enhance their professional development.

Discussion Questions

Below are questions that all mental health professionals should explore when serving or planning to serve immigrant clients:

1. How do I personally feel about immigrants and immigration policies in the United States?
2. Do I hold any biases or prejudices against immigrants?
3. Do I believe immigrants should be allowed to receive medical and mental health services in the United States?
4. If I do hold certain biases, should I refrain from seeing immigrants or seek out supervision to work through any issues?
5. What does the code of ethics for my profession state about working with immigrants or vulnerable populations?
6. At the organizational level, professionals should ask what the policies are at their agency for seeing immigrants.
7. Does the agency require that undocumented immigrants be reported to authorities?
8. Can immigrants be seen without documents at my agency?
9. How can I become an advocate for immigrants in the United States?
10. What skills and training do I need to obtain to effectively serve an immigrant?

References

Abraido-Lanza, A., Armbrister, A., White, K., & Lanza, R. (2006). Immigrants. In Y. Jackson (Ed.), *Encyclopedia of multicultural psychology* (pp. 237–243). Thousand Oaks, CA: Sage.

Alegria, M., Canino, G., Shrout, P. E., Woo, M., Duan, N., Vila, D., Torres, M., Chen, C., & Meng, X. (2008). Prevalence of mental illness in immigrant and non-immigrant U.S. Latino groups. *American Journal of Psychiatry, 165*(3), 359–369.

Alegria, M., Mulvaney-Day, N., Torres, M., Polo, A., Cao, Z., & Canino, G. (2007). Prevalence of psychiatric disorders across Latino subgroups in the United States. *American Journal of Public Health, 97*(1), 68–75.

American Psychiatric Association. (1994). *Diagnostic and statistical manual of mental disorders* (4th ed.). Washington, DC: Author.

American Psychological Association. (2002). *Ethical principles of psychologist and code of conduct.* Retrieved from http://www.apa.org/ethhics/code2002.pdf

Asai, A., & Barnlud, D. C. (1998). Boundaries of the unconscious private and public self in Japanese and Americans: A cross-cultural comparison. *International Journal of Intercultural Relations, 22*(4), 431–452.

Ayalon, L., Areán, P. A., Linkins, K., Lynch, M., & Estes, C. L. (2007). Integration of mental health services into primary care overcomes ethnic disparities in access to mental health services between Black and White elderly. *American Journal of Geriatric Psychiatry, 15*(10), 906–912.

Barlow, D. H., Levitt, J. T., & Bufka, L. F. (1999). The dissemination of empirically supported treatments: A view to the future. *Behavior Research and Therapy, 37,* S147–S162.

Barry, D. T. (2003). Cultural and demographic correlates of self-reported guardedness among East Asian immigrants in the US. *International Journal of Psychology, 38*(3), 150–159.

Bemak, F., Chung, R. C.-Y., & Pedersen, P. B. (2003). *Counseling refugees: A psychosocial approach to innovative multicultural interventions.* Westport, CT: Greenwood.

Bemak, F. & Chung, R. C.-Y. (2008). Counseling disaster survivors: Implications for cross-cultural mental health. In P. B. Pedersen, J.G. Draguns, W. J. Lonner, & J.E. Trimble, (Eds.), *Counseling across cultures* (pp. 325–340). Thousand Oaks, CA : Sage.

Bernal, G., Bonilla, J., & Bellido, C. (1995). Ecological validity and cultural sensitivity for outcome research: Issues for the cultural adaptation and development of psychosocial treatments with Hispanics. *Journal of Abnormal Child Psychology, 23,* 67–82.

Bernal, G., & Scharrón-del-Río, M. (2001). Are empirically supported treatments valid for ethnic minorities? Toward an alternative approach for treatment research. *Cultural Diversity and Ethnic Minority Psychology, 7,* 328–342.

Berry, J. W. (2002). Conceptual approaches to acculturation. In K. M. Chun, P. B. Organista, & G. Marin (Eds.), *Acculturation: Advances in theory, measurement and applied research* (pp. 17–38). Washington, DC: American Psychological Association.

Betancourt, J., Green, A., Carrillo, J., & Ananeh-Firempong, O. (2003). Defining cultural competence: A practical framework for addressing racial/ethnic disparities in health and health care. *Public Health Report, 118,* 293–302.

Beutler, L. E. (1998). Identifying empirically supported treatments: What if we didn't? *Journal of Consulting and Clinical Psychology, 66*(1), 113–120.

Bingham, R. P., Porché-Burke, L., James, S., Sue, W. D., & Vazquez, M. J. T. (2002). Introduction: A report on the national multicultural conference and summit II. *Cultural Diversity and Ethnic Minority Psychology, 8*(2), 75–87. doi:10.1037//1099–9809.8.2.75

Blom, B. (2009). Knowing or un-knowing? That is the question in the era of evidence-based social work practice. *Journal of Social Work, 2*, 158–177.

Blustein, D. L., Goodyear, R. K., Perry, J. C., & Cypers, S. (2005). The shifting sands of counseling psychology programs' institutional contexts: An environmental scan and revitalizing strategies. *The Counseling Psychologist, 33*, 610–634.

Braslow, J. T., Duan, N., Starks, S. L., Polo, A., Bromley, E., & Wells, K. B. (2005). Generalizability of studies on mental health treatment and outcomes, 1981 to 1996. *Psychiatric Services, 56*, 1261–1268.

Carter-Pokras, O., & Baquet, C. (2002). What is a "health disparity"? *Public Reports, 117*(5), 426–434.

Casas, J. M., & Pytluk, S. D. (1995). Hispanic identity development: Implications for research and practice. In J. G. Ponterotto, J. M. Casas, L. A. Suzuki, & C. M. Alexander (Eds.), *Handbook of multicultural counseling* (pp. 155–180). Thousand Oaks, CA: Sage.

Chambless, D. L., Sanderson, W. C., Sholam, V., Bennett Johnson, S., Pope, K. S., Crits-Cristoph, P., et al. (1996). An update on empirically validated therapies. *The Clinical Psychologist, 49*, 5–18.

Chaudhry, I. B., Neelam, K., Duddu, V., & Husain, N. (2009). Ethnicity and psychopharmacology. *Journal of Psychopharmacology, 22*(6), 673–680.

Chen, S. X., & Mak, W. S. (2008). Seeking professional help: Etiology beliefs about mental illness across cultures. *Journal of Counseling Psychology, 55*(4), 442–450.

Chung, R. C.-Y., & Bemak, F. (2007). Asian immigrants and refugees. In F. T. L. Leong, A. G. Inman, A. Ebreo, L. H. Yang, L. Kinoshita, & M. Fu (Eds.), *Handbook of Asian American psychology* (2nd ed., pp. 227–244). Thousand Oaks, CA: Sage.

Chung, R. C.-Y., Bemak, F., Ortiz, D. P., & Sandoval-Perez, P. A. (2008, Summer). Promoting the mental health of immigrants: A multicultural/social justice perspective. *Journal of Counseling and Development, 76*, 310–317.

Costantino, G., Malgady, R., & Rogler, L. (1986). Cuento therapy: A culturally sensitive modality for Puerto Rican children. *Journal of Consulting and Clinical Psychology, 54*(5), 639–645.

Derose, K. P., & Baker, D. W. (2000). Limited English proficiency and Latino's use of physician services. *Medical Care Research and Review, 57*, 76–91.

Drake, R. E., & Goldman, H. H. (2003). The future of evidence-based practices in mental health care. *Psychiatric Clinics of North America, 26*, 1011–1016.

Drake, R. E., Goldman, H. H., Leff, H. S., Lehman, A. F., Dixon, L., Mueser, K. T., & Torrey, W. C. (2001). Implementing evidence-based practice in routine mental health service setting. *Psychiatric Services, 52*(2), 179–182.

Francis, A., Widiger, T. A., First, M. B., Pincus, H. A., Tilly, S. M., Miele, G. M., & Davis, W. W. (1991). *DSM-IV*: Toward a more empirical diagnostic system. *Canadian Psychology, 32*(2), 171–173.

Giannet, S. (2003). Cultural competence and professional psychology training: Creating the architecture for change. *Journal of Evolutionary Psychology, 24*, 117.

Griner, D., & Smith, T. B. (2006). Culturally adapted mental health interventions: A meta-analytic review. *Psychotherapy: Theory, Research, Practice, Training, 43*(4), 531–548.

Gurchiek, K. (2005). Public view of immigration improves, but negative attitudes persist in the U.S. *HR Magazine, 50*, 32–33.

Hage, S. M., Romano, J. L., Conyne, R. K., Maureen, K., Matthews, C., Schwartz, J. P., & Waldo, M. (2007). Best practice guidelines on prevention practice, research, training, and social advocacy for psychologists. *The Counseling Psychologist, 35*(4), 493–566. doi:10.1177/001100000629441

Hall, G. (2001). Psychotherapy research with ethnic minorities: Empirical, ethical, and conceptual issues. *Journal of Consulting and Clinical Psychology, 69*(3), 502–510.

Hays, P. (2001). *Addressing cultural complexities in practice: A framework for clinicians and counselors.* Washington, DC: American Psychological Association.

Hays, P. (2008). *Addressing cultural complexities in practice: Assessment, diagnosis, and therapy.* Washington, DC: American Psychological Association.

Hernandez, D. J., Denton, N. A., & McCartney, S. E. (2008, November). The lives of America's youngest children in immigrant families. *Zero to Three*, 5–12.

Hernandez, M., & McGoldrick, M. (1999). Migration and the life cycle. In B. Carter & M. McGoldrick (Eds.), *The expanded family life cycle: Individual, family, and social perspectives.* Needham Heights, MA: Allyn & Bacon.

Hsu, L., & Alden, L. E. (2008). Cultural influences on willingness to seek treatment for social anxiety in Chinese- and European-heritage students. *Cultural Diversity and Ethnic Minority Psychology, 14*(3), 215–223.

Huey, S., & Polo, A. (2008). Evidence-based psychosocial treatments for ethnic minority youth. *Journal of Clinical Child and Adolescent Psychology, 37*(1), 262–301.

Huynh, Q. L., Howell, R. T., & Benet-Martinez, V. (2009). Reliability of bidimensional acculturation scores. *Journal of Cross-Cultural Psychology, 40*(2), 256–274.

Hwang, W. (2006). The psychotherapy adaptation and modification framework: Application to Asian Americans. *American Psychologist, 61*, 702–715.

Kamphuis, J. H., & Noordhof, A. (2009). On categorical diagnoses in *DSM-V*: Cutting dimensions at useful points. *Psychological Assessment, 21*(3), 294–301.

Kataoka, S., Stein, B., Jaycox, L., Wong, M., Escudero, P., Tu, W., Zaragoza, C., & Fink, A. (2003). A school-based mental health program for traumatized Latino immigrant children. *Journal of American Academic Child Adolescent Psychiatry, 42*(3), 311–318.

Kazdin, A. E. (2009). Bridging science and practice to improve patient care. *American Psychologist, 64*(4), 276–279.

Kenny, M., & Hage, S. (2009). The next frontier: Prevention as an instrument of social justice. *Journal of Primary Prevention, 30*, 1–10.

Kinzie, J. D., Tran, K. A., Breckenridge, A., & Bloom, J. D. (1980). An Indochinese refugee psychiatric clinic: Culturally accepted treatment approaches. *American Journal of Psychiatry, 137*(11), 1429–1432.

Kirmayer, L. J., Groleau, D., Guzder, J., Blake, J., & Jarvis, E. (2003). Cultural consultation: A model of mental health services for multicultural societies. *Canadian Journal of Psychiatry, 48*(3), 145–153.

Kirmayer, L. J., & Young, A. (1998). Culture and somatization: Clinical, epidemiological, and ethnographic perspectives. *Psychosomatic Medicine, 60*, 420–430.

Ku, L., & Mutani, S. (2001). Left out: Immigrant's access to health care and insurance. *Health Affairs, 20*, 247–256.

Layton, L., & Keating, D. (2006, August 15). Area immigrants top 1 million. *Washington Post*, pp. A1, A16.

Lee, J., & Rytina, N. (2009). *Naturalizations in the United States: 2008* (Annual Flow Report, Office Of Immigration Statistics Policy Directorate). Retrieved from http://www.dhs.gov/ximgtn/statistics/publications/LPR08.shtm. doi:09032766

Lopez, S. R., & Guarnaccia, P. J. (2000). Cultural psychopathology: Uncovering the social world of mental illness. *Annual Review of Psychology, 51*, 571–598.

Mainous, A. G., III. (1989). Self-concept as an indicator of acculturation in Mexican-Americans. *Hispanic Journal of Behavioral Sciences, 11*, 178–189.

Marin, G., & Gamba, R. J. (1996). A new measurement of acculturation for Hispanics: The Bidimensional Acculturation Scale for Hispanics (BAS). *Hispanic Journal of Behavioral Sciences, 18*(3), 297–316.

Mark, T. L., Shern, D. L., Bagalman, J. E., & Cao, Z. (2007). Ranking America's mental health: An analysis of depression across states. *Mental Health America*. Retrieved from http://www.mentalhealthamerica.net/files/Ranking_Americas_Mental_Health.pdf

Matos, M., Bauermeister, J. J., & Bernal, G. (2009). Parent–child interaction therapy for Puerto Rican preschool children with ADHD and behavior problems: A pilot efficacy study. *Family Process, 48*(2), 232–252.

McCabe, K. M., Yeh, M., Garland, A. F., Lau, A. S., & Chavez, G. (2005). The GANA program: A tailoring approach to adapting parent–child interaction therapy for Mexican Americans. *Education and Treatment of Children, 28*(2), 111–129.

Miranda, J., Green, B. L., Krupnick, J. L., Chung, J., Siddique, J., Belin, T., & Revicki, D. (2006). One-year outcomes of a randomized clinical trial treating depression in low-income minority women. *Journal of Consulting and Clinical Psychology, 74*(1), 99–111.

Miranda, J., Nakamura, R., & Bernal, G. (2003). Including ethnic minorities in mental health intervention research: A practical approach to a long-standing problem. *Culture, Medicine, and Psychiatry, 27*(4), 467–486.

Miranda, J., Siddique, J., Der-Martirosian, C., & Belin, T. R. (2005). Depression among Latina immigrant mothers separated from their children. *Psychiatric Services, 5*(6), 717–720.

Monger, R., & Rytina, N. (2009). *U.S. legal permanent residents: 2008* (Annual Flow Report. Office of Immigration Statistics Policy Directorate). Retrieved from http://www.dhs.gov/ximgtn/statistics/publications/LPR08.shtm. doi: 09032765

Moyerman, D. R., & Forman, B. D. (1992). Acculturation and adjustment: A meta-analytic study. *Hispanic Journal of Behavioral Sciences, 14*(2), 163–200.

Nadeem, E., Lange, J. M., Edge, D., Fongwa, M., Belin, T., & Miranda, J. (2007). Does stigma keep poor young immigrant and U.S. born Black and Latina women from seeking mental health care? *Psychiatric Services, 58*(12), 1547–1554.

Nagayama Hall, G., & Maramba, G. G. (2001). In search of cultural diversity: Recent literature in cross-cultural and ethnic minority psychology. *Cultural Diversity and Ethnic Minority Psychology, 7*(1), 12–26. doi:10.1037//1099–9809.7.1.12

National Academy of Sciences Institute of Medicine. (2006). *Improving the quality of health care for mental and substance use conditions: Quality Chasm Series, Committee on Crossing the Quality Chasm: Adaptation to mental health and addictive disorders.* Washington, DC: National Academies Press.

National Alliance for the Mentally Ill. (2006). *Grading the States 2006: A report on America's health care system for adults with serious mental illness.* Retrieved from http://www.nami.org/gtsTemplate.cfm?Section=Grading_the_States&lstid=676

National Alliance for the Mentally Ill. (2009). *Grading the States 2009: A report on America's health care system for adults with serious mental illness.* Retrieved from http://www.nami.org/gtsTemplate09.cfm?Section=Grading_the_States_2009

National Association of Social Workers. (2008). *Code of ethics.* Retrieved from http://www.socialworkers.org/pubs/code/code.asp

National Center for Cultural Competence. (2009). Foundation for cultural and linguistic competence. Retrieved from http://www11.georgetown.edu/research/gucchd/nccc/foundations/frameworks.html#ccdefinition

National Institutes of Health. (1994). *Guidelines on the inclusion of women and minorities as subjects in clinical research.* Retrieved from http://grants.nih.gov/grants/guide/notice-files/not94–100.html

Nikelly, A. G. (1997). Cultural Babel: The challenge of immigrants to the helping professions. *Cultural Diversity and Mental Health, 3*(4), 221–233.

Padilla, A. M. (2006). Bicultural social development. *Hispanic Journal of Behavioral Science, 28*(4), 467–497.

Paget-Clarke, N. (1997, September). Interview with Roberto Martinez: Immigration and human rights on the U.S./Mexico border. *Motion Magazine.* Retrieved from http://www.inmotionmagazine.com/border.html

Panganamala, D. R., & Plummer, D. L. (1998). Attitudes toward counseling among Asian Indians in the United States. *Cultural Diversity and Mental Health, 4*(1), 55–63.

Passel, J. S., & Cohn, D. (2008). *Trends in unauthorized immigration: Undocumented inflow now trails legal inflow.* Retrieved from http://pewhispanic.org/reports/report.php?ReportID=107

Perez, L. (2006, December). En Cherokee los indocumentados viven escondidos [In Cherokee the undocumented people live hidden]. *El Mundo Hispanico*, 28.

Pew Research Center. (2008). *U.S. population projections: 2005–2050.* Retrieved from http://pewhispanic.org/reports/report.php?ReportID=85

Power, T.J., Eiraldi, R. B., Clarke, A. T., Mazzuca, L. B., & Krain, A. L. (2005). Improving mental health service utilization for children and adolescents. *School Psychology Quarterly, 24*(2), 187–205.

Rivera-Mosquera, E., Dowd, E. T., & Mitchell-Blanks, M. (2007). Prevention activities in professional psychology: A reaction to the prevention guidelines. *The Counseling Psychologist, 35*(4), 586–593. doi:10.1177/0011000006296160

Rosselló, J., & Bernal, G. (1999). The efficacy of cognitive-behavioral and interpersonal treatments for depression in Puerto Rican adolescents. *Journal of Consulting and Clinical Psychology, 67*(5), 734–745.

Rousseau, C., & Guzder, J. (2008). School-based prevention programs for refugee children. *Child and Adolescent Psychiatric Clinics of North America, 17*(3), 533–549.

Shechtman, Z., Goldberg, A., & Cariani, R. (2008). Arab and Israeli counseling trainees: A comparison of ethnically homogeneous and heterogeneous groups. *Group Dynamics: Theory, Research, and Practice, 12*(2), 85–95.

Smart, D. W., & Smart, J. F. (1997). *DSM-IV* and culturally sensitive diagnosis: Some observations for counselors. *Journal of Counseling and Development, 75*, 392–398.

Substance Abuse and Mental Health Services Administration. (n.d.). Evidence-based practices: Shaping mental health services toward recovery. Retrieved from http://mentalhealth.samhsa.gov/cmhs/communitysupport/toolkits/family/competence.asp

Sue, D. W., & Sue, D. (2008). *Counseling the culturally diverse: Theory and practice.* Hoboken, NJ: John Wiley & Sons.

Sue, S., Fujino, D. C., Hu, L., David, T. T., & Zane, N. W. S. (1991). Community mental health services for ethnic minority groups: A test of the cultural responsiveness hypothesis. *Journal of Consulting and Clinical Psychology, 59*(4), 533–540.

Szapocznik, J., & Kurtines, W. (1980). Acculturation, biculturalism and adjustment among Cuban Americans. In A. M. Padilla (Ed.), *Psychological dimensions on the acculturative process: Theory, models, and some new findings* (pp. 139–159). Boulder, CO: Westview.

Szapocznik, J., Santisteban, D., Rio, A., Perez-Vidal, A., Kurtines, W., & Hervis, O. E. (1986). Bicultural effectiveness training (BET): An intervention modality for families experiencing intergenerational/intercultural conflict. *Hispanic Journal of Behavioral Science, 6*, 303–330.

Szapocznik, J., Scopetta, M. A., Kurtines, W. M., & Arnalde, M. A. (1978). Theory and measurement of acculturation. *Interamerican Journal of Psychology, 12*, 113–130.

Takeuchi, D. T., Zane, N., Hong, S., Chae, D. H., Gong, F., Gee, G. C., Walton, E., Sue, S., & Alegria, M. (2007). Immigration related factors and mental disorders among Asian Americans. *American Journal of Public Health, 97*(1), 84–90.

Tervalon, M., & Murray-García, J. (1998). Cultural humility versus cultural competence: A critical distinction in defining physician training outcomes in multicultural education. *Journal of Health Care for the Poor and Underserved, 9*(2), 117–125.

U.S. Census Bureau. (2008). *2008 national population projections.* Retrieved from http://www.census.gov/population/www/projections/2008projections.html

U.S. Department of Health and Human Services. (1999). *Mental health: A report of the surgeon general* (CMHS SMA-01–3613). Retrieved from http://www.surgeongeneral.gov/library/mentalhealth/chapter2/sec8.html

U.S. Department of Health and Human Services. (2001). *Mental health: A supplement to "Mental Health: Report of the Surgeon General"* (SMA-01–3613). Retrieved from http://www.surgeongeneral.gov/library/mentalhealth/cre/

U.S. Department of Health and Human Services. (2003). *Achieving the promise: Transforming mental health care in America* (New Freedom Commission on Mental Health Final Report). Retrieved from http://www.mentalhealthcommission.gov/. doi: SMA-03–3832

Weisz, J. R., Jensen-Doss, A., & Hawley, K. M. (2006). Evidence-based youth psychotherapies verses usual clinical care: A meta-analysis of direct comparisons. *American Psychologist, 61*(7), 671–689.

Whaley, A. L., & Davis, K. E. (2007). Cultural competence and evidence-based practice in mental health services. *American Psychologists, 62*, 563–574.

Whaley, A., & Longoria, R. (2008). Assessing cultural competence readiness in community mental health centers: A multidimensional scaling analysis. *Psychological Services, 5*(2), 169–183.

Wilson, H. S., & Skodol, A. (1994). Special report: *DSM-IV*; Overview and examination of major changes. *Archives of Psychiatric Nursing, VIII*(6), 340–347.

Wood, J., Angela, C., Wei-Chin, H., Jeffrey, J., & Muriel, I. (2008). Adapting cognitive behavioral therapy for Mexican American students with anxiety disorders: Recommendations for school psychologists. *School Psychology Quarterly, 23*(4), 515–532.

Wu, F. H. (2002). *Yellow: Race in America beyond Black and White.* New York: Basic Books.

Yeh, M., Takeuchi, D. T., & Sue, S. (1994). Asian-American children treated in the mental health system: A comparison of parallel and mainstream outpatient service centers. *Journal of Clinical Child Psychology, 23*, 5–12.

Zea, M. C., Asner-Self, K. K., Birman, D., & Buki, L. P. (2003). The abbreviated Multidimensional Acculturation Scale: Empirical validation with two Latino/Latina samples. *Cultural Diversity and Ethnic Minority Psychology, 9*(2), 107–126.

Zhang, Y., Young, D., Lee, S., Zhang, H., Xiao, Z., Hao, W., Feng, Y., Zhou, H., & Chang, D. (2002). Chinese Taoist cognitive psychotherapy in the treatment of generalized anxiety disorder in contemporary China. *Transcultural Psychiatry, 39*(1), 115–129.

Appendix A: National Resources on Cultural Competence

National Resources on Cultural Competence

Cultural Competence Mental Health Web Sites
www.nyc.gov/html/doh/downloads/pdf/qi/qi-ccpriority-resources.pdf
National Institute of Mental Health (NIMH)
Office of Communications
6001 Executive Boulevard, Room 8184, MSC 9663
Bethesda, MD 20892-9663
Phone: (866) 615-6464 (NIMH)
Fax: (301) 443-4279
TTY: (301) 443-8431
www.nimh.nih.gov

Substance Abuse and Mental Health Services Administration (SAMHSA)
Center for Mental Health Services
1 Choke Cherry Road Room 6-1057
Rockville, MD 20850
Phone: (240) 276-1310 or (800) 789-2647
www.mentalhealth.samhsa.gov

U.S. Department of Health and Human Services, Office of Minority Health
Resource Center
P.O. Box 37337
Washington, DC 20013-7373
Phone: (800) 444-6472
http://minorityhealth.hhs.gov

National Center for Cultural Competence
Georgetown University Center for Child and Human Development
3307 M Street, NW Suite 401
Washington, DC 20007
Phone: (202) 687-5387
TTY: (202) 687-5503
E-mail: cultural@georgetown.edu
http://www11.georgetown.edu/research/gucchd/NCCC/foundations/frameworks

National Alliance of Multi-Ethnic Behavioral Health Associations
3 Bethesda Metro Center
Bethesda, MD 20814
Office Phone: (301) 941-1834
Fax: (301) 657-9776
http://www.nambha.org

Multiethnic Advocates for Cultural Competence
1335 Dublin Road, Suite 105 C
Columbus, OH 43215
Phone: (614) 221-7841
Fax: (614) 487-9320
www.maccinc.org

National Alliance on Mental Illness (NAMI)
3803 N. Fairfax Dr., Ste. 100
Arlington, VA 22203
Main: (703) 524-7600
Fax: (703) 524-9094
http://www.nami.org

Asian

Asian American Psychological Association
216 North Central Avenue, #198
Phoenix, AZ 85004
Phone: (602) 230-4257
www.aapaonline.org/

Asian Community Mental Health Services
318 8th Street, Suite 201
Oakland, CA 94607
Phone: (510) 451-6729

E-mail: info@acmhs.org
www.acmhs.org

National Asian American Pacific Islander Mental Health Association
1215 19th Street Suite A
Denver, CO 80202
Phone: (303) 298-7910
Fax: (303) 298-8081
www.naapimha.org/

African American

Black Psychiatrists of America
2020 Pennsylvania Ave., NW #725
Washington, DC 20006-1811 USA
Phone: (877) 272-1967
http://www.blackpsych.org

National Association of Black Social Workers, Inc.
2305 Martin Luther King Ave. S.E.
Washington, D.C. 20020
Phone: (202) 678-4570
Fax: (202) 678-4572
E-mail: nabsw.harambee@verizon.net
http://www.nabsw.org/mserver/

The Association of Black Psychologists
P.O. Box 55999
Washington, DC 20040-5599
Phone: (202) 722-0808
www.abpsi.org/

Latino

National Association of Puerto Rican and Hispanic Social Workers
P.O. Box 651
Brentwood, NJ 11717
Phone: (631) 864-1536
www.naprhsw.org/index.php
National Latina/o Psychological Association
www.nlpa.ws/

Latino Psychological Association of New Jersey
c/o Milton Fuentes
Montclair State University
1 Normal Avenue
Montclair, NJ 07043
Phone: (973) 655-7967
www.lpanj.org/

National Latino Behavioral Health Association
P.O. Box 387
Berthoud, CO 80513
Phone: (970) 532-7210
Fax: (970) 532-7209
www.nlbha.org/about.htm

Deaf and Hard of Hearing

National Deaf Academy
19650 U.S. Highway 441
Mount Dora, FL 32757
Phone: (352) 735-9500
http://www.nda.com

Lesbian/Gay/Bisexual/Transgender (LGBT)

Association for Lesbian, Gay, Bisexual & Transgender Issues in Counseling
(AGLBTIC)
www.aglbtic.org/

GLBT National Help Center
www.glnh.org/

Gay, Lesbian, Bisexual, Transgender Health
http://www.apha.org/about/Public+Health+Links/LinksGayandLesbianHealth.
htm

Gay Men of African Descent (GMAD)
www.gmad.org/

Healthy Lesbian, Gay, and Bisexual Students Project
http://www.apa.org/pi/lgbt/programs/hlgbsp/toolbox.aspx#

The Mautner Project
www.mautnerproject.org

YouthResource
www.amplifyyourvoice.org/youthresource

Amish

Melissa K. Thomas, Director
Project Hoffnung: The Amish and Mennonite Breast Health Project
P.O. Box 28103
Columbus, OH 43228
Phone: 1-877-HOFFNUNG (toll free) or 1-877-463-3686
E-mail: projecthoffnung@yahoo.com

Scales for Practitioners to Recognize Cultural Identity
Acculturation and Cultural Identity Scales

Acculturation Rating Scale for Mexican-Americans (ARSMA)
Cuellar, I., Harris, C., & Jasso, R. (1980). An acculturation scale for Mexican-American normal and clinical populations. *Hispanic Journal of Behavioral Sciences, 2*, 199–217.

Multidimensional Measure of Cultural Identity for Latino and Latina Adolescents
Feliz-Ortiz, M., Newcomb, M. D., & Meyers, H. (1994). A multidimensional measure of cultural identity for Latino and Latina adolescents. *Hispanic Journal of Behavioral Sciences, 16*, 99–115.

Short Acculturation Scale for Hispanics (SASH)
Marin, G., Sabogal, F., Van Oss Marin, B., Otero-Sabogl, R., & Perez-Stable, E. (1987). Development of a Short Acculturation Scale for Hispanics. *Hispanic Journal of Behavioral Sciences, 9*, 183–205.

Suinn-Lew Asian Self-Identity Acculturation Scale (SL-ASIA)
Suinn, R. M., Richard-Figueroa, K., Lew, S., & Vigil, P. (1987). The Suinn-Lew Asian Self-Identity Acculturation Scale: An initial report. *Educational and Psychological Assessment, 47*, 401–407.

Group Identification and Cultural Identity Scales

African Self-Consciousness Scale
Baldwin, J. A., & Bell, Y. (1985). The African Self-Consciousness Scale: An Afrocentric personality questionnaire. *The Western Journal of Black Studies, 9*, 61–68.

Black Racial Identity Attitude Scale-Form B (BRIAS-Form B)
Helms, J. E. (Ed.). (1990). *Black and White racial identity: Theory, research, and practice.* New York: Greenwood.

Multidimensional Racial Identity Scale (MRIS)–Revised
Thompson, V. L. (1995). The multidimensional structure of racial identification. *Journal of Research in Personality, 29,* 208–222.

Multigroup Ethnic Identity Measure (MEIM)
Phinney, J. (1992). The Multigroup Ethnic Identity Measure: A new scale for use with adolescents and young adults from diverse groups. *Journal of Adolescent Research, 7,* 156–176.

White Racial Identity Attitude Scale (WRIAS)
Helms, J. E., & Carter, R. T. (1990). Development of the White racial identity inventory. In J. E. Helms (Ed.), *Black and White racial identity: Theory, research, and practice* (pp. 67–80). New York: Greenwood.

Value Orientation Scales

Chinese Values Survey
Chinese Culture Connection. (1987). Chinese values and the search for culture-free dimensions of culture. *Journal of Cross-Cultural Psychology, 8,* 143–164.

Cultural Adaptation Pain Scale (CAPS)
Sandhu, D. S., Portes, P. R., & McPhee, S. A. (1996). Assessing cultural adaptation: Psychometric properties of the Cultural Adaptation Pain Scale. *Journal of Multicultural Counseling and Development, 24,* 15–25.

Cultural Information Scale (CIS)
Saldana, D. H. (1994). Acculturative stress: Minority status and distress. *Hispanic Journal of Behavioral Sciences, 16,* 116–128.

Appendix B: Practical Guidelines for Mental Health Professionals Working With Immigrants

Assessment and Diagnosis

- Continuously seek training in cultural competence, and adopt a culturally humble approach to reach and serve immigrant populations.
- Assess acculturation levels of the person and the family and the role they may be playing in the presenting problem.
- Use linguistically and culturally appropriate assessment tools.
- Assess the worldview of the client on wellness and the role of religion or faith in wellness. This can be a strong source of support for the immigrant.
- Assess the history of violence, trauma, and exposure to danger during the journey to the United States.
- Be aware of potential diagnoses biases. Consider culturally specific syndromes.

Treatment, Prevention, and Advocacy

- Deal with acculturation gap issues if present in treatment, and utilize appropriate models, that is, family therapy, if warranted.

267

- Provide psychoeducation on the acculturation process to educate the family on its impact on mental health and how it may impact wellness. This can be a powerful intervention in treatment.
- Develop and promote culturally competent prevention psychoeducation, to help immigrants understand mental health stigma and mental health issues and help them access mental health services.
- Help the client build a natural community-based support system that may be missing since he or she left the home country.
- Promote and run community-based support groups in the immigrant community, that is, churches, clinics, community centers, and so on.
- Become an advocate and help fight stereotypes about immigrants and discrimination in the United States.
- Attend church services, health fairs, and other community-based programs in an effort to break down barriers such as stigma, lack of trust, and fear of mental health providers.
- Consult with spiritual or religious leaders and cultural brokers in the community you are trying to work with. Ask for advice or work closely with them if needed. Remember to tread carefully, because you want to make sure religion is helping the client have a better quality of life and not oppressing the client.
- Utilize a holistic approach to assessment, diagnosis, and treatment that integrates the body, mind, and spirit.
- Respect alternative approaches (e.g., yoga, tai chi, homeopathy, acupuncture, massage, *espiritismo*) to healing, and integrate their use in psychotherapy if needed to deal with psychosomatic symptoms.
- Seek training if available in culturally competent evidence-based treatment for immigrants and ethnic minorities.
- Become knowledgeable about the populations that are in your geographic area. Outreach to those at-risk populations that are in your service area.
- Learn another language if at all possible, particularly one that a significant number of immigrants speak.

Index